PIPE
DREAMS

PIPE DREAMS

A SURFER'S JOURNEY

KELLY SLATER
with Jason Borte

10 ReganBooks
Celebrating Ten Bestselling Years
An Imprint of HarperCollins*Publishers*

HarperCollins books may be purchased for educational, business, or sales promotional use. For information please write: Special Markets Department, HarperCollins Publishers Inc., 10 East 53rd Street, New York, NY 10022.

First paperback edition published 2004.

Designed by Nancy Singer Olaguera

The Library of Congress has catalogued the hardcover edition as follows:

Slater, Kelly, 1972–
    Pipe dreams : a surfer's journey / Kelly Slater with Jason Borte.—1st ed.
      p. cm.
    ISBN 0-06-009629-2
    1. Slater, Kelly, 1972– 2. Surfers—United States—Biography. I. Borte, Jason. II. Title.
GV838.S53A3 2003
797.3'2'092—dc21
[B]
                        2003046645

ISBN 0-06-009631-4 (pbk.)
04 05 06 07 08   QN/RRD   10 9 8 7 6 5 4 3 2 1

This book is dedicated to more people than I can
possibly thank for their contributions to my life

Contents

Introduction

WHEN I AWOKE ON December 3, 1991, I already felt pretty good about myself. Nineteen years old and six months out of Cocoa Beach High School, I was in the quarterfinals of my very first Pipeline Masters. The surfing spot, known as Pipeline, has become surfing's winter nucleus and is the epicenter of the surfing world. It's the ultimate arena. Swells from Alaska's Aleutian storms march through the Pacific and meet the Hawaiian Islands with open-ocean speed. As they near the shore, they focus on the reefs, which amplify their size and energy. Plenty of surf spots are longer, many are bigger, and some are even gnarlier, but Pipe, which sits midway along Oahu's North Shore, offers the greatest ten seconds on Earth. It is the yardstick by which all other breaks are measured.

When I walked up to the beach at Pipe for the first time seven years earlier, I was blown away by how big the waves were and how close they break to the beach. Off to the right the waves are tiny, but the reef at Pipe has a way of funneling the brunt of the swell perfectly. About forty yards off the beach, waves that are two stories high explode over a few feet of water. There's so much energy in these swells that if they didn't stack up on the reef and dissipate quickly, they would wash over the homes along the shore. Prior to the 1960s, Pipeline was considered too dangerous to surf, so the fact that I was even in the Pipeline Masters was unbelievable.

Since I was twelve, I had been coming to the North Shore during every Christmas vacation and watching the tail end of the Pipeline Masters. It was *the* big event in surfing. Organized by former world champion Fred Hemmings in 1971, it received national attention when *ABC's Wide World of Sports* covered it. Suddenly even people who didn't surf found it to be one of the most exciting events in the world. As a kid, I'd watch the contest and think how glad I was not to be in the water. In Cocoa Beach, Florida, where I grew up and learned to surf, the waves near the shore were tiny ripples. I started just off the beach and dreamed of one day making it out far enough to catch the two-foot waves that my dad and my brother were riding. I thought anything beyond that was a pipe dream.

In Oahu on the final day of the 1991 Pipe Masters, I had the first heat of the morning. I had been hyped as a future world champion, so now that I was competing on the Association of Surfing Professionals World Tour, all eyes were on me. It was a perfect tropical day, and I was the only rookie remaining in the contest—so already I felt as if I had proven myself.

On the North Shore, the ocean needs some time in the morning to get organized. Before the trade winds kick in, the waves tend to have a kind of morning sickness. Pipe can be more perfect than anywhere, but in a bad mood, it's scary. Surfers were calling the waves eight to twelve feet that day, but that number is deceptive. In Hawaii, height is measured by the back of a wave— not the face—so the scale is notoriously conservative. But height isn't the major issue. At Pipe, waves are just as thick as they are tall. They are dangerous enough without having to deal with wobbles and backwash, but I didn't have a choice. My heat began at nine sharp.

I was up against three Australians—Damien Hardman, Simon Law, and Mike Rommelse—and only two of us would advance to the semifinals that took place later that day. Halfway through the heat, I didn't have any good rides. In competition, the surfer who executes the most radical controlled maneuvers, with speed and style throughout, in the most critical part of the wave for the longest functional distance is deemed the winner. Of course wave size is definitely a factor as well. As I waited for a good wave, the commentators were announcing the judges' scores from the beach. I was way behind.

A wave popped up, and the other guys were a little out of position. I didn't realize how heavy the wave would be; I only knew I had to catch it if I wanted to have any chance of advancing. I paddled into it, just as the backwash hit, and stood on my board as the wave jacked up. There isn't much time to think once you've committed to a wave like this; the slightest hesitation and all is lost. From the top of the wave, I dropped about fifteen feet straight down. I barely stayed upright through the drop but somehow managed to redirect my momentum back up the face under the thickest pitching lip that came through all day. It was every bit as thick as it was tall, and the lip barely missed taking off my head. Inside the tube was the only safe place to be. Anywhere else and I would have been obliterated. There was no time to sit back and enjoy the ride. Once inside the tube, the hardest part was over. But I wasn't in the clear yet. I still had to navigate through the barrel without getting swallowed whole by this beast. I held on for all I was worth, knowing in the back of my mind that if I fell, I'd only score a few points and the whole ride would be worthless. If I made it out, I'd not only be on my way to advancing through the heat but I'd prove to everyone that I belonged here. One second I was staring out of a massive cave swirling around me, and the next I came shooting out in a cloud of spray. I raised my arm in a victory salute for a split second before a cross chop separated me from my board. At that point, it didn't matter. I had made it! Up until that moment, I had spent my surfing career running from big waves, but making it through that one gave me the confidence to ride anything.

I still needed another decent score, so I started paddling back out to the lineup. I passed a water photographer on my way out, and I said, "Wow, that was kind of heavy, huh?" He laughed at my understatement and said, "You don't know how heavy that was." I knew the wave was intense, but it wasn't until years later, watching it on video, that I realized how close I had come to getting seriously hurt. Sometimes I wonder what would have happened if I hadn't made it. If the lip had landed on me, it could have broken my back or even killed me. At the least, it would have sent me to the hospital.

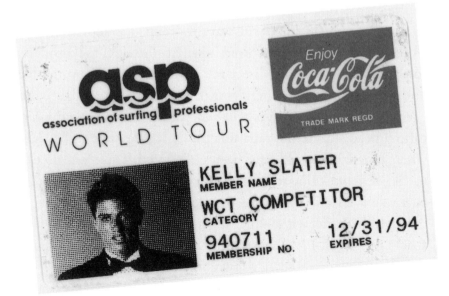

I didn't start surfing because I expected it to be my career. It was something I just had a good time doing. But once I started, I couldn't stop. Nothing compared to the thrill of riding waves, having the friendships and the lifestyle. I couldn't have imagined that the magazines I studied from cover to cover would become a scrapbook for my friends and me or that heroes I never thought I'd meet, let alone surf against, would eventually become my good friends. And I couldn't fathom that I would learn to thrive on the waves that scared me senseless.

1

Cocoa Beach

LEAVING ORLANDO INTERNATIONAL AIRPORT, the Beeline Expressway runs due east toward Brevard County. There's not much to see on the hourlong drive, except 3-D billboards covered with giant apes, extraterrestrials, and twisters, which lure tourists to Universal Studios and less expensive beachy versions of Ron-Jon's Surf Shop, the world's only twenty-four-hour stop for people who don't surf but want to take a T-shirt back home that says otherwise. Other than that, it's a straight road cut through the middle of dense clumps of palmetto and pine forests.

Entering Brevard County, also known as the Space Coast, the Beeline is nice enough to bypass the city of Cocoa, which in 1925 lent its name, originating from the native coconut palms, to Cocoa Beach, its new coastal neighbor. The Beeline also navigates around Cape Canaveral, the place that put Brevard on the map. Prior to 1961, the local economy was still juiced by the production of citrus products. The beach was nothing but a skinny twelve-mile strip of white sand, shoe box houses, and tiny rattrap motels sandwiched between the Atlantic Ocean and the Banana River. The Cape—flat, undeveloped, and close to water, with a climate that allows for year-round activity—was the perfect place to launch space shuttles. The sleepy scrubland was transformed into a major launch base, and because of the importance of beating Russia into orbit, astronauts were as valued in American culture as any movie stars. They brought a happening aura to a place that needed some life. For one glorious decade, when NASA embarked on the *Apollo* project, Cocoa Beach was a nonstop celebration, attracting young people from all over the nation.

Just past Canaveral, the road skirts south and morphs into Astronaut Boulevard, and eventually into the coastal highway known as A1A. Whenever I go home, I can't help but chuckle at the sign I see when I enter Cocoa Beach. "World Famous," it claims, but I can't figure out why. I guess it's because the 1960s sitcom *I Dream of Jeannie* was set there, although it wasn't filmed there. You can tell because there are mountains in the background on the show, when in reality the only mountain in Florida is the Space Mountain ride at Disney World. Ask any local what's so special about Cocoa Beach, and you're likely to hear that the most endearing customs are bikini contests, beer drinking, and stabbings at the pier.

Don't get me wrong. I love my hometown, but until now it certainly hadn't been a big surfing supporter. In all my years of flying the Cocoa Beach flag around the world, the city didn't so much as give me a phone call of congratulations until I started dating Pamela Anderson. Then they asked me to come to a town meeting. I did get a street named after me and a key to the city but that wasn't until November 2002, ten years after I won my first world title. Even though there have always been a lot of surfers around town, I guess the sport wasn't mainstream enough to warrant much attention.

A MATCH MADE IN PARTYVILLE

Steve Slater, my dad, was born in Ocala, Florida, but grew up in Daytona Beach, Florida. He claimed to be a descendant of Samuel Slater, a guy who became known as "the Father of the American Industrial Revolution" when he came over from England in 1789 and built a cloth factory in Rhode Island, but I haven't yet done the research to find out if it's true. In high school, my dad played football, basketball, and ran track, but his real interest was water sports. He loved to swim and fish, and by the end of the 1950s had become a lifeguard and surfer.

Surfing in the late 1950s was experiencing a population

explosion thanks to *Gidget* and other beachy Hollywood films, as well as the innovation from wood to lighter and easier-to-maneuver foam surfboards. Boards were still around ten feet in length, clunky compared to today's standards, and relatively dangerous. They had the potential to inflict a lot of damage on someone. (In the late 1960s, surfboards would undergo a revolution, shrinking to nearly half as long as the overriding philosophy went from stylishly walking up and down the board to making radical direction changes.) During a hurricane swell, my dad paddled out on his longboard and wiped out on a pretty big wave. The board came straight up and hit him between the legs, which caused them to turn black and blue from his waist to his knees. He claimed that if there hadn't been another guy in the water to drag him out, and a really cute girl on the beach to drive him home, he would have drowned.

After my dad finished high school, his parents moved two hours south to Cocoa Beach. My dad stayed in Daytona. When he was nineteen, his mother died from throat cancer. After her death, my grandfather decided to remain in Cocoa Beach and live on his own. A few years later he was in a pretty serious car accident, and my dad went down from Daytona to take care of him for a while. My grandfather recovered pretty quickly, but by that point, my dad had fallen in love with Cocoa Beach—the area had a way of sucking people in and keeping them there. He got a job as a construction worker, and once he got in the swing of the surf scene, he couldn't leave. Cocoa Beach was Partyville, U.S.A., and the waves were tailor-made for the boards of the day. (The local contingent, made up of Claude Codgen, Mike Tabeling, Gary Propper, and Dick Catri, was the best on the East Coast.) But since alcoholism ran in the family, Partyville was the last place my dad needed to be.

Judy Moriarity, my mom, was from a middle-class Irish family in Bethesda, Maryland. Her mom was a housewife, and her father was a car salesman who grew up during the Great Depression. Because he had lived without so much when he was younger, he made sure his family had everything they needed.

After high school, my mom decided to go to work as a secretary in Washington, D.C., for a huge development firm. A year later, in 1966, she and a friend took a well-deserved vacation in Cocoa Beach, supposedly just for a few weeks. It was so much fun that they got jobs and stayed. The schedule around town was strict: Monday was for nursing hangovers, Tuesday was for working, Wednesday was for struggling to get over the hump, Thursday set off talk of upcoming parties, and the next three days were a blur.

She was nineteen years old and already a regular at the bars where the most famous men in America, the *Apollo* astronauts, came to blow off steam. Other than their matching gold Corvettes, the astronauts tried to become part of the crowd and didn't want to warrant too much attention. Once when she ran into Alan Shepard, she pretended not to know who he was and asked him what line of work he was in. Always ready for such an occasion, he claimed to be a traveling salesman.

Later that year at a club called the Vanguard Lounge, a seedy but hip bar near the beach, Judy was on a date with a captain from Special Forces. He tried to get her to take a walk on the beach, and when she refused, he grabbed her. The bouncer stepped in and told the guy to get lost, and eventually offered to take her home himself. That bouncer was my dad.

Steve and Judy married on May 27, 1967, and decided to set up camp in Cocoa Beach. If you couldn't afford the lifestyles of the rich and famous in ritzy South Florida, this was the next best thing. The average age of the citizens was around thirty-four, and

the school system was considered among the best in Florida. It was a great place to start a family, so they did. (My brother Sean was born two years later.) In Cocoa Beach, the living was cheap, jobs were everywhere, there was always a party happening, and you could surf.

But by the 1970s, the town was already shriveling up. The *Apollo* project was close to splashing down, which would lead to a spike in unemployment and a blow to morale. Cocoa Beach became something of a ghost town and resorted to promoting itself as a beachy getaway from Orlando's newly built Walt Disney World. It lured retirees with low housing costs and drove the average age up to around fifty.

LITTLE BOBBY SLATER

When I drive through Cocoa Beach today, I strain to notice any signs of change other than it's continuing transformation into

Condominium Land, the ever growing wall of white high-rises that block out all signs of the ocean. The population is forever creeping upward of thirteen thousand. On the west side of A1A, more condos and small businesses back up to the Banana River, which is our link to the Intracoastal Waterway. At most, the town is a couple miles across, in some spots barely wider than a football field. As I continue south on A1A, I cross the only major intersection in town, Highway 520. This was, and still is, where you'd find our version of traffic, which is having to sit through two cycles at the stoplight during rush hour. It's still the hub of the city, but Ron-Jon's is the only remaining link to the past. Everything else, including the Vanguard Lounge, is gone. If you take Highway 520 inland a half mile, you come to Cape Canaveral Hospital, where, on February 11, 1972, I was born.

After seventeen hours of labor, the doctor's pulled me out with forceps, and I emerged with two black eyes and covered with hair. My mom said she looked at me and knew instantly that I was a Kelly, but my dad insisted I more closely resembled a monkey. Fortunately, the hair fell off within a few days.

In the event that I'd one day run for public office, my mom opted for the more professional sounding Robert Kelly Slater, after her little brother Bobby—although she failed to inform me of this until I was in kindergarten (at which time it was the best news I could have hoped for). In school, kids made fun of my name and said it was a girl's name. Sometimes they'd call after me with "Kelly Belly Jelly" or "Smelly," but what *really* pissed me off was when they'd say "Later Slater." As soon as I found out my real name was Robert, I started signing Bobby on all my school papers.

My uncle Bobby was my hero. He was big, and cool, and always ate my peas for me. He let me get away with murder. No matter what I'd do wrong, he'd tell my mom, "Shut up, Judy. He's just a kid." So I became a Bobby too, at least for a little while. Then in 1976, when *The Bad News Bears* came out, it did wonders for my image. The cool kid in the movie who could hit the ball the farthest was named Kelly, and suddenly that made my name cool. The Bobby thing wore off, and I went back to being Kelly.

I spent two years in kindergarten, since my mom thought it would be a good idea if I stayed back to be with my neighborhood friends. I got along with them better, and kindergarten was more fun the second time around—especially since I was finally bigger than everybody else. There was less teasing, and they had to do what I said—and I was a pretty tough kid.

Thanks to my mom, I spoke like a truck driver at an early age. I don't know if anyone remembers my first word, but they definitely remember me at two years old, when I walked into my grandmother's kitchen (where my entire family was standing), and said, "Oh, shit," because I'd dropped my bottle. You'd think it

would have changed the way my mom talked, but it didn't. My grandmother rode her about it for years, and even though my mom's language didn't clean up, she made sure that mine did.

Not much has stuck with me from the first few years of life, but it doesn't seem like a coincidence that my earliest memory is based around my brother and our competitive relationship.

When I was four, I knew what books were, but I didn't know how to read them. I remember watching Sean in amazement as he read out loud, "I ... am ... Sam. Sam ... I ... am." Suddenly I wanted to learn, so like any older sibling, he was proud to teach me. Little did he know that it would ignite a fire inside me that couldn't be stopped.

I remember the day I made sense of written words, and it seemed like the world was mine. I could open any of Sean's books, and the letters, when you put them together, made words. My chest swelled with pride. I wanted to tell everyone, "I can read." The feeling of comprehension was fascinating. A new world was opened, and my life had meaning. These symbols were alien no more. There they were, on a piece of paper, on a cereal box, on the television screen, everywhere I looked. They meant something. I put them together, and I understood the secret. I'd walk around the house and recite Dr. Seuss in each room. And then the feeling passed. I had to learn something else.

BROTHERLY LOVE

I've been called a lot of things, but perhaps the most common word to describe me is "competitive." Maybe I get it from my mom. She grew up trying to outdo her two brothers—actually, all boys in general. If she couldn't beat them at sports, she'd beat them up. She sat up at night planning how to win at everything—dodgeball, tennis, baseball, you name it. And even though she was as competitive as they come, her intentions were to teach us not to be bloodthirsty rivals. She never had a chance.

From the beginning, everything was a competition between Sean and me. It started with the deep end of the bathtub. It was easier for my mom to have us take baths at the same time, so we fought over who got to sit at the deep end, the end closest to the faucet. Sean was sneaky too. He'd pretend like he was going to let me have it, and as soon as I got in the tub (overjoyed by the fact that I won) he'd turn on the freezing cold shower or make it scalding hot. Then he'd just sit there laughing. Needless to say, he always got the deep end, but I never quit trying.

What we fought over most was calling shotgun. Sean would always claim the front seat before me and then antagonize me about it. He came up with different ways of calling it, like holding his arms as though he were aiming a rifle and saying, "chikt-chikt." Even when I called it first, he outran me to the car and took it. As a result, we'd fight the whole way to wherever we were going. With two kids yelling back and forth, it's a wonder my mom never wrecked the car. She flew off the handle a few times, just screaming her head off. When she finished, I'd looked at her with my most innocent face and asked things like, "Do eagles have babies?" Subconsciously, I was probably trying to lighten the situation, but mostly I really meant what I asked. I spent a lot of time in my own little world, wondering how things worked, and sometimes my questions didn't come at a time when my mom was most likely to answer them, so she didn't find it as amusing as we did.

Sean definitely did his brotherly duty of tormenting me. Sometimes it was painless, like leaving the bedroom light on when he went to sleep because he knew it bothered me. He'd stare at me from across the room just to piss me off. I'd whine, "Dad, he's looking at me again," and my dad would say, "Well, look at him back." Then there were other times when his teasing hurt, like when he purposely closed the toilet seat on my private parts while I was peeing because he thought it'd be funny. We didn't have the money to go to the doctor, so I was fortunate there was no disfigurement.

He never hesitated to show me who was boss, so I guess I felt inclined to take my aggressions out on other kids—primarily his friends. My mom used to take me with her when she would pick Sean up from kindergarten, and I quickly noticed that the good thing about being two years old was that I was just the right height to punch all his male classmates in the balls. So I did. Best of all, I was too small for them to hit me back. Karma came back to me, though. One day as I was running through a puddle to escape an angry victim, my feet went out from under me and I knocked myself unconscious when I hit the concrete. I never punched another kid again.

Sean helped toughen me up, so I didn't mind getting hurt when I was playing around outside. He and I would tear up the neighborhood and our bodies. And although the streets of Cocoa Beach weren't as rough as a lot of places, when you fell on them it hurt. And I fell a lot. People thought I was an abused child because I always had black eyes, cuts, and bruises from my childhood spills.

I was accident-prone. As soon as I learned to ride a bike, I had the brilliant idea to look behind me. Needless to say, I ate it. I was out cold, with two black eyes. As if that wasn't enough, when I was eight I rammed our minibike into a tree in our front yard. A bunch of my friends were watching when it happened, so my pride was hurt more than anything else. But my primary source of transportation and scrapes was my skateboard. It was a clunky metal board, but I thought the thing ruled. I used it for everything. Once, when I was five, Sean and I used it to transport rocks from the neighbor's house to our house to build rock piles and stuff. I was wearing my prized new cowboy boots and overalls, and was skating along the street, kneeling on the board, hunched over so I could hold onto the front of the board with both hands. My precious pile of rocks was beneath me, and I was using my right leg to push myself forward. I must have been about a foot and a half from the ground, so I couldn't have been too easy to see. The only car to come along belonged to a ninety-year-old woman who lived nearby. She may have seen me at the last minute, but her reactions weren't too quick. By the time she stopped, I was under the front of her car. I was too afraid to move. My neighbor came running out and said he had called an ambulance. I wasn't hurt other than a little scratch on my back, but I figured if an ambulance was coming, I must've been worse off than I thought. The guy pulled me out from under the car and carried me to my mom. I was still too scared to move, so the EMTs figured I should go to the hospital just to be safe. Getting to ride in the ambulance was pretty cool. They wanted to take off my cowboy boots to make sure my feet weren't injured, but I thought they wanted to steal them. No matter what, I wasn't going to let them take off my boots. I fought them until they gave up, figuring any kid with that much energy had to be fine.

A few days later, my whole family went to Gaithersburg, Maryland, to visit my mom's family. When we were kids, we spent every Christmas there and a couple weeks in the summer. Uncle Bobby and Aunt Sally had four kids, and we all played together in the woods behind their house. We'd catch fireflies, throw rocks at bats, play in a stream, and hike through the woods. After my "accident" Uncle Bobby asked me what happened to my back, and I told him, "I got wunned ova by a cawa."

About a year later, my little brother, Stephen, was born. Fortunately for Stephen, he was so much younger than Sean and I that he was outside our realm of competition. I remember how excited we were the day he was born. I was in the yard playing with Sean and our friends Johnny and Davey when the news broke. We were all holding hands and jumping up and down, saying, "Mom had a baby. Mom had a baby."

THE HOUSE OF SLATER

Minuteman Causeway marks the center of town, dividing the businesses and beachfront condos to the north from residential communities to the south. If you take the Causeway a mile inland, it ends at the Cocoa Beach Country Club. But before you get there, you pass several blocks of squat cinder-block tract homes, which were built to house the influx of NASA engineers around 1960. There, on the corner of Aucila Road, was the House of Slater.

The dingy three-bedroom box was where I lived from birth until age eleven. Out front, the carport housed everything from fishing poles to diving equipment, to tackle boxes, to shrimp traps, to bikes, to tools, to surfboards, to several of my dad's unfinished projects, like a glass-bottom boat that he abandoned halfway through construction.

There was nothing more than a stop sign and a few palm trees between the main road and the side of our house. It may not have been prime Florida real estate, but it did provide for a lot of family entertainment. One night, in a poor-white-trash scene straight out of *Cops,* a drunken lady smashed her car into the room next to mine. My mom was an EMT and went outside with my dad to help, only to run into a couple of the lady's equally drunk friends who were furious that we had the audacity to put our house next to a main thoroughfare. It escalated from there, so when the police eventually arrived it was to break up a brawl between this drunken woman, her friends, my parents, and the tow-truck driver. I was a heavy sleeper and missed the whole event, but my brother told me about it the next day. For a while, we were the talk of the town.

Inside, our home was just as fun. It was like the OK Corral. My dad's pellet gun was set up on a tripod in the living room, which was aimed directly at a mouse hole across from the couch. If you wanted to walk in or out of the room, you had to cross the line of fire—talk about child hazards. We all took turns watching the hole for twenty minutes or so, and as soon as the mice poked their heads out, *blam!* good night. It was so much fun that Sean and I hoped there would be some around so we could stay up late to shoot them. The mice in the living room I didn't mind, but the rats in the attic were a whole other story.

Most kids imagine they have monsters in their closet, but Sean and I actually did. We shared the master suite, which had a door to the attic set in the ceiling of our closet. Above the access door, rats constantly scurried at night. I was afraid they'd find their way down, so I was terrified to open the closet door. Every so often my parents took the pellet gun up there to shoot them, but the rats always came back.

One cold night I mustered the courage to go in the closet for a blanket, and just as I opened the door, somebody tapped on my window and said, "Hey, kid," nearly scaring me out of my skin. It was just some teenage thugs cutting through our yard, but I had a severe case of closet phobia after that.

Fortunately we had Hondo, our German shepherd, to protect us. He had been a part of the family longer than I, and constantly watched over us. My parents worked a lot, and the baby-sitter they left us with was not much older than Sean, so we pretty much took care of ourselves. If the baby-sitter wasn't around, there was always Hondo. He was smarter and cheaper than all the teenagers in town. Our house backed up to a canal, and whenever we got near the water, Hondo stood in front of us for protection. If we went swimming, he was right there with us. Living so close to the water put us in contact with all sorts of creatures, from fish to manatees, to alligators. The gators, which got as big as fourteen feet, sunned themselves in the grass behind our house, and Hondo did his part to try to scare them off. At night, he made the rounds to make sure everyone was safe. All our neighbors knew him. He'd run around town and eventually find his way back home, sometimes after a stop at the vet's office for a drink of water and a treat.

When I was seven, I was eating a bowl of cereal when my mom started screaming. Hondo was dead. It was my first experience with mortality, and to lose my lifelong guardian was traumatic. Coming home from school and not having him there was too much, so we got another German shepherd and called him Hondo II, which was a big mistake. Never name a dog after one that is gone; there's no way it'll ever live up to the real thing. He

was the dumbest dog in the world, so we changed his name to
Mo. He was too dopey to protect us, but he did once jump on an
innocent old lady and break her hip.

GOOD OLE BOY

Fishing was our first love, and we had all the gear you could
imagine. My dad really enjoyed it, and he taught us how to make
our own poles when we were very young. In addition to being a
construction worker, he owned a bait shop called Cocoa Beach
Bait and Tackle, which was a few blocks away from our house.
The big event of the week was when the shrimp man made his
delivery. I loved seeing the big truck pull up full of shrimp. We'd
scoop the shrimp out of the live wells for my dad and count
them. It was a huge deal, almost a holiday. Even after I started
surfing—I didn't care how good the waves were—we were waiting for the shrimp man.

I loved fishing so much as a kid that I slept with my fishing
pole occasionally. I was so eager to be the first one out there that
I'd get everything ready the night before and put it on the side of
my bed. I'd show up at the canal bright and early, but usually
some guy would already be there. He'd catch some trout and head
home as I arrived. Sean and I would fish all morning and hardly
ever get a bite. If I didn't catch anything, I'd go home bummed,
wishing I had spent the time doing something else.

The first picture ever published of me was for fishing. When
I was four years old the local paper ran a full-page sequence of me
going through my fishing routine. I guess they were pretty desperate for a story. My enunciation wasn't the best, and the photographer understood my name as Kevin Salter. That's how it
appeared in the caption, but I didn't care. I had a picture in the
paper and Sean didn't.

My dad liked shooting guns almost as much as fishing. He

bought guns for the whole family—all the kids and my mom. Thanks to my dad, by the time I was six, I knew how to take a gun apart, clean it, and make my own bullets.

On weekends we'd get in the van and go out to Merritt Island, across the river on Highway 520, to shoot. My dad shot skeet, and Sean and I would line up bottles to shoot or fire at the sand dunes. One day we went there with some friends of the family, the Townsends. We were armed to the hilt when another van—a big, dark creepy-looking thing—pulled up. Out stepped a bunch of rowdy bikers. They were drinking beer and shooting birds right out of the air. The place was a bird sanctuary, for heaven's sake. My dad got ticked off and went to tell them to cut it out. He had a beer in one hand and a gun in the other and demanded they stop shooting the birds. But these guys weren't taking orders from some family man. Mr. Townsend unloaded several rounds into the air to let them know he and my dad meant business. He reloaded the clip and told the biker, "Don't get within range, or I'm turning this thing on you."

My dad and Mr. Townsend moseyed back over and resumed shooting skeet. The rest of us were in the van manning our positions, each pointing a gun out the window. Finally the owner of the land showed up and made the bikers leave. Needless to say, we never went back there.

Then there was the incident at Patrick's Air Force Base, which was probably not the best place for a group of people to jump out of a van wielding guns. As soon as we got out, the military police were on us and asked, "What the hell are these kids doing?" We thought everything was cool, because we did that sort of thing all the time. The police thought differently and escorted us off the grounds. They must have said something to my dad, because we never went shooting as a family again.

I'm thankful for all the things my father taught me as a child, but I wonder if growing up around fishing poles, guns, and alligators make me a redneck. As far as I'm concerned, redneck is a state of mind, and I'm not there. Sean, on the other hand, is questionable. He lives and dies for fishin', chewin' tobaccy, and drinkin' beer.

2

Grommet

THE WAVES IN FLORIDA SUCK. I hate to put it so bluntly, but compared to most places around the world, it's true. Picture a perfect wave in your mind, and it's nothing like the waves I grew up riding.

There are so many different types of waves. Beach breaks are waves that break along a straight shoreline on a sandbar as opposed to on a reef or along a headland. Pointbreaks wrap around a headland and peel into a bay. Most surf destinations— California, Australia, Hawaii—offer some of each kind of break. In Florida, there's almost no variety in the coastline, so I was stuck with generic beach breaks. The waves don't vary. My friends and I would say, "I'm going to surf Thirteenth Street or Third Street or Twenty-seventh Street." But why did we bother going anywhere? It's all the same. On top of that, most swells heading toward Cocoa Beach are blocked by Cape Canaveral.

Along the whole East Coast, the width of the continental shelf, with the exception of Cape Hatteras, ruins any chances for powerful surf. Our swells drag along that shallow area of the ocean for miles and miles, depleting their strength.

I have a condo in Cocoa Beach; it's less than a mile past my childhood home. Whenever I go there I drive up to the Third Street beach for a mandatory surf check, knowing full well there is nothing to get excited about. Looking at it you'd never guess that in the 1970s and 1980s this was the place every Cocoa Beach surfer spent his formative years. Now it's just another condo filled with retirees, but at one time it was the site of a little burger shack called the Islander Hut that was my home away from home.

Throughout my career, people have asked how, coming from Florida, I became a top pro surfer. That's a silly question. As a young grommet, it was a great place to start. It gave my surfing a good foundation. The waves are slow and user-friendly. I could figure out my moves in slow motion before trying them at full speed. I've always thought it was easy to apply the moves I had learned there on bigger waves.

BEACH BABIES

The beach near my house was long and hard packed, and when we were kids, my mom drove our car straight onto the sand and set up camp. People used to drag race along it back in the 1960s, but apparently in the 1970s some girl had her legs run over by a car, and the city outlawed driving on the beach.

We weren't raised religious, but you could say the beach was our church. My mom worshiped the sun, and from the time we could crawl, we were already tanned dark brown—except for our stark-white butts. My mom could sit in the sun forever, so she did. After a few hours on the beach, Sean and I were ready to go skateboard-ing or fishing—anything but build another sand castle. We'd whine,

"Mom, can we go home now?" But she couldn't get enough, and we'd have to stay. Even now, whenever I smell coconut-scented tanning oil, it reminds me of piling out of our dune buggy and spending the entire day on the beach.

Since my mom wasn't budging from her beach chair, we had to find something to keep ourselves busy. We were pretty good swimmers because Mom signed us up for swim classes as babies, but really it was more like she just threw us in the water. I think it was out of boredom that Sean and I began riding waves.

When I was five, and Sean had already been surfing for two years, I followed him and my dad into the Atlantic. According to my mom, I would sit on the beach for hours studying the ocean. I rode a Styrofoam bellyboard, one of the cheap flimsy types you can find in tourist shops. It barely floated and the only thing it guaranteed was that sooner or later it would snap like a toothpick, but I weighed only forty pounds so that didn't matter to me.

THE ISLANDER HUT

The surfing lifestyle is centered on camaraderie. The Royal Hawaiian pastime, after nearly being wiped out by missionaries during the nineteenth century for promoting half-naked fun, was reborn at Waikiki around 1900. The local Hawaiian beach boys built their lives around the ocean, music, girls, and casual clothes. Californians caught on in the 1920s and 1930s, and added traveling to the mix as they went up and down the West Coast looking for more challenging waves. By the 1960s, Hollywood tapped into the scene, and surfing exploded onto the national radar. Everybody wanted to live on the beach, or at least hang out there and pretend like they surfed.

The beach behind the Islander Hut, even though essentially it was no different from any other beach in town, was the place everyone surfed. Dunes surrounded it on either side, and in the back sandbags ran down to the beach, protecting it from winter nor'easters and the occasional hurricane storm surge. The Hut was a little snack bar that served beer. There was a jukebox in the corner with the Doobie Brothers or Steely Dan always playing and a pinball machine right next to it where you'd usually find my dad, beer in hand. Hurricane, a local band, would play there, and I still see the guitarist around town every few years.

Sean and I were on the beach even in the winter, when the early morning temperature was usually around fifty degrees and the water temperature was just over sixty degrees. On the weekends, he and I got in our wetsuits as soon as we woke up and stayed in them all day. Between sessions, when the cold north wind blew, all the surfers huddled along the south wall of the restaurant where it was warm. We were lined up from one end to the other, checking out the scene and soaking up the sun. Next door was the Apollo Building, an abandoned office where at night, after the Islander Hut closed, the parking lot became a drive-up party. Bonfires burned, kegs were in people's trunks, and couples pulled up in their cars to make out.

Since the Hut was only a few blocks from our house, we seldom went anywhere else. All the best local surfers—Matt Kechele, Joe Doyle, Tom Black, Scott Robinson, George and Sam Drazich, Mark and Steve Sponsler, Allen Vulmer, Tommy Sharpe, Greg Taylor, Tony Graham, and Jim McClaren—hung out there. These were the guys who were winning local contests, getting sponsored, and traveling to faraway places to surf. They kept us in line and provided inspiration.

My mom eventually took a job at the Hut flipping burgers, mainly to pay off our hefty tab. But there were a lot of hot dogs and root beer going down, and at the end of each week, she'd get her paycheck and still owe forty bucks.

SOFT-CORE

I got the feeling that not many people surfed on Styrofoam bellyboards, since I often received odd stares followed by "How can you stand up on that thing?" It may have been a shapeless hunk of cheap foam, but as far as I was concerned, it was my surfboard. I was perfectly happy with it and didn't see a reason to ride anything else.

Since my dad also did construction work, he had lots of tools in the garage. One day, when I was bored and waiting for everyone to get ready to go to the beach, I went out and smashed little

circles into my board with a hammer. My dad was really bummed because it meant we had to stop at Ann-Lia's Gift Shop to pick up a new one. They always had three or four in stock, and since I went through one every couple weeks, I was their best customer.

Many times the waves weren't big enough to ride, so Sean and I improvised by making a surf swing in our backyard. We shaped a scrap piece of plywood into something that resembled a surfboard and used rope to tie it to a big tree branch. It felt like surfing, but with higher consequences. We bounced off the electrical wires and branches, and if we went the wrong way we smacked into the tree. Once, I went up as high as I could, which was around ten feet, and fell flat onto my back. It knocked the air out of me, but I had no serious injuries—it was like I was made of rubber.

Within a year, my parents were tired of turning over their paychecks to Ann-Lia's Gift Shop, but they weren't ready to foot the bill for a fiberglass board, so I graduated from Styrofoam to a real bodyboard. I had seen it in a surf magazine and had to have it. It was really chunky and had a W-shaped tail and two fins; I've never seen another one quite like it.

Bodyboarding has enabled a lot of people to become good waveriders in a short amount of time. A surfboard builder in Hawaii named Tom Morey invented it in 1971. He trademarked the name Morey Boogie in 1973, but that didn't stop a flood of knockoffs. Pretty soon, bodyboards were everywhere. The concept of bodyboarding is pretty simple: You lie on your belly the whole time with your feet hanging off the board as you scratch and kick into a wave. You can't fall off if you try. That style of riding wasn't for me. Bodyboarding was still something tourists did for fun; it was hardly considered a sport. I wanted to surf, so I rode it standing up, making balancing a little more difficult. Since I had already been standing on my Styrofoam plug, my bodyboard was a step up.

I rode my skateboard around the neighborhood every day, which helped improve my surfing skills. I practiced skate tricks, and

soon I was doing them in the water. I learned how to do little off-the-lips and 360s on my bodyboard. My mom saw how much I loved it, and since she would use any excuse to go to the beach, she sometimes let me skip school to go surfing. But since I was only in kindergarten, I still wasn't really that good at it.

I entered my first surfing competition in 1980, when I was eight years old, and I had to ride my bodyboard since I didn't have anything else. The contest was the Salick Brothers Surf Contest and was held in front of the Islander Hut. Phil and Rich Salick, two brothers who had a shop a block away, sponsored it. (It later grew into a huge event called the National Kidney Foundation Pro-Am, and is now held each Labor Day weekend in Cocoa Beach.) There were four kids in my division, and the waves were tiny—perfect for me. I won, and looking back, my opponents must have been shattered, losing to a kid on a bodyboard.

Matt Kechele, the teenage local hotshot who was on the verge of turning pro, remembers going surfing and seeing me riding my bodyboard. "There was this tiny kid, six or seven years old," he recalls, "who dropped in on this little wave and did three backside 360s in a row. Three-sixties were the thing back then, and to see someone do three of them backside blew me away. I couldn't believe how Kelly rode that thing. I was getting into shaping boards and thought to myself, 'I've got to make this kid a surfboard.'" But it would still be a few years before he got his chance.

THE REAL THING

Custom surfboard building is an art. It takes skill, patience, and attention to detail. The process hasn't changed much since the late 1950s. Before that, boards were shaped from wood, first as one solid plank, then as strips glued together. Once shapers found out about materials that were used during World War II, they quit using wood and started using foam cores covered with fiberglass cloth and polyester resin. A board shaper begins with a piece of dense foam. Using a plane, he mows the foam until he achieves the desired shape, sort of the way a sculptor works with a piece of stone. Once the shape is established, the board is covered with fiberglass cloth and resin. Fins are added on the bottom, and the board is sanded to get a smooth finish. Fiberglass boards are harder and more dangerous than bodyboards. When Sean was nine, he got a real surfboard because he was older and had been surfing longer. It was a single-fin with a dangerous pointy tail. It had a bungee cord leash, so whenever he fell, the leash stretched to its limit and the board came flying back at full speed. I borrowed the board whenever Sean took a break, and one time it was nearly fatal. I fell off, and the board snapped toward me, barely missing my head. Rather than scare me back to the safety of my sponge, riding it convinced me that I was ready to graduate to fiberglass.

Later that year, after plenty of begging, my dad gave in. We ordered new boards from Phil and Rich Salick. We would have bought boards right off the rack, but at the time nobody stocked boards for kids because there weren't many kids in the water.

It took them more than six months to finish our boards, which is a long time to wait, especially for an eight-year-old grommet. At the time it seemed like an eternity. That summer, any time we weren't in the water or eating at Islander Hut, we were hanging around the shop. We stopped by every day to see if they were finished, but the poor boards never seemed to be any further along. I desperately wanted a team logo on it—an instant tag of coolness—but after much debate, and considering I wasn't on a team, they decided to leave it off.

Rich Salick was a great airbrusher, so we put a lot of thought into our board designs. Sean's had a scene from *Star Wars* and mine had Jaws swimming after a naked lady, just like the movie poster. I could almost make out the girl's breasts, so I was ashamed to look at it when anyone was around. I didn't want people to think I was a pervert.

My new board was just over five feet long. I barely had time to pose for a picture with it before paddling out. It was a year before Simon Anderson came out with the last great innovation in surf-boards, the three-fin thruster concept, but my board already had three boxes. (The thruster proved to be the perfect trade-off, offer-ing much of the stability of single fin coupled with the twin fin's maneuverability.) I'm not saying my board was revolutionary; it was intended to be ridden as either a single or twin rather than with all three fins at once. Sometimes, I rode it with no fins at all so the board would spin freely and I could do 360s with ease.

Sean and I surfed a few contests around town over the next year, and when September came, we heard there were a couple empty slots in the 1981 Eastern Surfing Association (ESA) Championships in Cape Hatteras, North Carolina. The amateur organization ran contests all over the coast as well as the Great Lakes, and each year the best of the best gathered in Hatteras. Back then, it was difficult to find enough young kids to fill up a heat, but now the twelve-and-under Menehune (a name derived from a mythical tribe of Polynesian elves) Division has grown into one of the most popular and anticipated events.

My dad, Sean, and I made the twelve-hour drive to the Hatteras Lighthouse, a state landmark that marked one of the best surf spots on the East Coast. The waves were bigger than anything I'd ever surfed, or wanted to surf. Jaws and I took a good beating, and I decided to stick to the shore break, scrounging for leftover waves near the sand. Some of the other kids made it out farther, to where the waves were actually breaking, so my chances of winning were slim. I finished last in my first heat, landing me as the seventh ranked Menehune on the East Coast. Not bad, until you realize there were only seven competitors.

After traveling all over the world, driving up to Hatteras for the week now seems like running to the corner for some milk. But at the time, it was my first surf trip outside Brevard County, and the variety and intensity of the surf blew away anything I had seen. I realized there was far more to this sport than my nine-year-old mind imagined, and if I were to continue pursuing it, I'd have to find a way to deal with one tiny problem—I wanted my mommy.

TROUBLE BREWING

There may have been a time that my parents had a healthy relationship, but I don't remember it. By 1981 their marriage was in serious trouble. My dad constantly drank and my mom realized it wasn't a good idea for them to stay together. She threatened to leave several times, saying, "I just feel like getting in the car and never coming back." With three kids complaining and Dad drunk, it was too much for her to take. I was afraid to let her out of my sight for fear I'd never see her again. Whenever she tried to throw him out, I cried until she caved in. Reluctantly, she let him stay, and their problems persisted.

I wouldn't say I had a terrible childhood, but I remember nights where we would go outside or go in our rooms and put pillows over our heads to escape the noise. One night I slept outside on the concrete driveway. We had plans to go to the mall, so Sean and I went out to the car after dinner, no doubt battling for the front seat. The doors to the car were locked, but we decided we'd rather wait outside than go in. We heard my parents screaming, and my mom wasn't coming out. Sean might have gone in, but I decided to lie down on the concrete and go to sleep. At the time, I had plenty of friends whose parents were having similar marital problems, so it didn't seem like a big deal to me. My parents didn't physically abuse each other; there was just a lot of yelling. My mom would scream at my dad for hours until he'd finally pass out.

My dad drank a lot. He would be blind drunk and still say, "No, I only had two beers." Any time we asked him how many beers he had, it was always two. I can't tell you how many times I heard "two beers" come out of his mouth. It was a running joke in my family.

His drinking became such a problem that I was afraid to drive with him. Once a friend of mine had to get home from my house after surfing, but since my dad had been drinking my friend didn't want to drive with him. Unfortunately, there was no one else around and my dad refused to listen to reason—or anybody with reason—when he was drunk. So "two beers" later we pulled out of Third Street onto A1A heading directly into two lanes of traffic. Halfway across the street, my dad stopped and tried to reverse it to get out of the way. I thought we were dead. Cars were honking and swerving to avoid hitting us, and there we were in a little dune buggy with no seat belts. It's a wonder I lived to see my first sponsorship.

AT LAST, A TEAM STICKER

Dick Catri was a legendary local surfer and board builder who traveled the East Coast with his team of Brevard County

surfers, competing in, and winning, contests. He had grown tired of the older guys, whom he felt were jaded, and, in 1981, decided to put together a group of Menehunes to tour around Brevard County. He picked Todd Holland first, and then he picked Sean, David Speir, Sean O'Hare, Troy Propper, and Randy Sanders. They were the kids who were winning contests around town, and Dick was the first person to notice. I wasn't in the same league as they were, but they let me tag along since I was Sean's brother. So I became part of the team by default. They surfed anything the coast had to offer, while I stuck close to shore. Any wave bigger than I was, which was only four feet, was too big.

We were too young to do much traveling outside Brevard County, but the whole Dick Catri Surfboards team got together in Indialantic, a nearby town, every Sunday for practice. (Other than that, being a member of the team only meant that I got a deal on my boards and, more important, got all the team stickers I could handle.) All the kids judged one another in heats, allowing us to see things from a different perspective. Dick gave us all sorts of advice about surfing technique and competition, most of which I still use. Two things he told me that stood out were how to paddle faster by pulling my arms underneath my board on each stroke and to always keep my eyes open in the tube. The practices were friendly and fun, but I couldn't help feeling a strong desire to outdo my teammates. These were the best young surfers on the East Coast, and if I could hang with them, I was getting somewhere.

I guess I was a quick learner, because by 1982, I was winning most of the local Menehune contests. Dick took us to a trade show in Florida in hopes of finding us a clothing sponsor. A bunch of the top pros were there, so our main goal was to get autographs, and lots of them. It was there that I first met Tom Curren. A friend of mine knew Tom from competing with him as an amateur, and he introduced us. I was starstruck. I managed a shy hello and got Tom's autograph, but as I turned to leave, he laughed at how small I was. (He doesn't remember it, but I never forgot.)

That day we were also introduced to Jeff Hakman, the U.S. licensee of Quiksilver, and Danny Kwock, his team manager. They were judging a bikini contest, and Dick took us over to Danny and said, "I want you to meet the Slater brothers. These kids are gonna be the best surfers in the world one day." Danny was anxious to get back to his duties and said, "Sure kids, here's some shorts." Sean and

I got a free pair of Quiksilver trunks with stars all over them and thought that meant we were part of the team.

Dick also set up a deal for all of us with a company called Arena that made sweat suits for adults. I was the smallest, and they didn't make a suit in my size. For our team picture, Dick put me in a giant sweat suit and sent it to the company to show them they needed to make smaller sizes.

We eventually picked up a legitimate sponsor when Dick convinced Bill Yerkes, the owner of a Florida-based clothing line called Sundek, to provide clothing for the entire team. It was a great relationship; we became close with the Yerkes family and I remained a part of Sundek for the majority of my amateur career.

BIG-SCREEN INSPIRATION

Surf videos had yet to be invented, but every few months a new movie played for one night at the Surfside Playhouse in Cocoa Beach. It was a major event, bringing out all the best surfers in town. My dad, Sean, and I were the first group at the door, impatiently waiting to get inside. Surf-hungry, I stepped around the pitchers of beer and waded through the pot smoke, determined to find a spot where I could watch the movie without interruption.

Even before the reel was rolling, I was in heaven. I was in awe and poked Sean every time I saw one of the local rippers walk into the theater. "No way, there's Matt Kechele. There's Tommy Black." Around town, it was a major event.

The movies featured the world's best surfers—guys from Hawaii, Australia, South Africa, and California—doing unbelievable things on bigger waves than I ever imagined. As soon as the lights went dark and the movie started, I entered an untouchable world, totally mesmerized by the surfers, the waves, and the fact that they were surfing over reefs. I remember I found a piece of coral on the beach once, and it blew me away since there

weren't any reefs where I surfed in Florida. It was like a treasure from a faraway place. If you told me back then at the Surfside Playhouse that the places in those movies would one day seem like home to me, I would have died laughing.

The surfers in those movies were even better than the guys at home, and my favorite was Buttons Kaluhiokalani. He and fellow Hawaiian Larry Bertlemann could do anything on a wave—doing 360s in the barrel, sliding the tail, even hitting the lip and switching their stance—tricks that guys are still trying to do today. There was no limit to their imagination. I swore I saw Buttons go upside down and make a complete flip in one of the movies. (I saw the movie many years later and couldn't find the flip, but by then it didn't matter.)

I came out of that theater with a contact buzz, real and imagined, adrenaline pumping through my little body. Surfing filled my dreams, if I slept at all. The sun couldn't come up fast enough.

I started trying Buttons's moves, and my dad would say, "Why were you trying to go upside down out there? You were falling on every wave." I was thinking, "One day, I'm going to make one of those."

SEBASTIAN INLET

Brevard County has always been the hub of talent on Florida's eastern coast, and since the 1970s all of that has been centered on Sebastian Inlet, an hour's drive south from Cocoa Beach. It's a beautiful state park with lots of vegetation and very little development other than a long rock jetty. I'd been camping and fishing there with my dad and Sean, but surfing it was another thing. Even as a sheltered kid at Islander Hut, I heard people speak of Sebastian as hallowed ground. Guys got in fistfights over waves there. It was a world-famous surf spot, and Cocoa Beach was nothing.

Sebastian is the answer to a Florida surfer's prayers. The waves bounce off the jetty and jack up with good shape and power. It's a really short ride, but a lot steeper than anywhere else around. Of course it's where all the good surfers go when there are waves, so it isn't easy for a newcomer to make an impression. There's a definite pecking order, as opposed to the free-for-all around every other break in Florida. First Peak, an area in the lineup closest to the jetty, is where the best surfers get the best

waves. Guys who don't
know what they're doing
get dropped in on, yelled at,
beat up, and kicked out.

The first time I surfed Sebastian it was because the Catri team was
being filmed for the evening news. The waves were about two
feet and clean, not a drop of water was out of place. I wanted to
surf so badly, but the cameraman was determined to set up a shot
in which we would come walking over the dunes with our boards.
It was my first experience with the difficulties of stardom, and I
was still a ten-year-old no name. They finally let us surf, and
from my first wave, I was hooked.

Whenever I could scrounge a ride to Sebastian from my dad,
Matt Kechele, or anyone else, I was there. I was pretty shy and
always respectful of the older surfers, so the locals usually gave me a

few waves. My friend Alex Cox, on the other hand, didn't know when to shut up. He ran his mouth so much that he routinely took beatings and was thrown in trash cans. Some of his sarcasm wore off on me, but he was always a little brattier. As a result, he would suffer the consequences. I got my share of pink bellies and noogies, but I was lucky to have a friend like Alex, who always took the brunt of it. Grommet abuse can get pretty serious—in Australia, they strip kids naked and duct tape them to a pole, so I got off easy.

Although I never got too wise with the regulars, when a new face showed up in the lineup, it was open season. I knew the older guys had my back, so if a beginner got in my way, I had no problem calling him a "barney" or a "kook" and sending him down the beach, where the surf wasn't as good. It must have been traumatic for them, to get abused by some pimply little kid and not be able to do anything about it.

Nowadays, when I surf Sebastian, I see the same look in the kids' eyes when they see me as I once had when I watched guys like Jeff Crawford, Matt Kechele, Charlie Kuhn, and Pat Mulhern. Knowing they had competed against, and beaten, some of the top surfers in the world, I was content to watch and learn. It had a huge impact on my confidence, knowing that even though these guys were from Florida, they surfed well enough to compete on an international level.

ROLLER BOY

Growing up there was one place where kids ruled the roost—the Starlite Skating Rink in Merritt Island, which was the next town over. It was the only place a ten-year-old could cut loose on a Friday night. Going there became our weekend ritual. By the end of the night, we were dead tired but prayed our parents weren't waiting outside so that we could stand around and talk to the girls. I was too shy to talk, but at least I could look.

There were always fourteen- and fifteen-year-old girls at the Starlite who loved to mess with me. They came up and said, "Guess what? I think you're cute." It seemed like a conspiracy to embarrass me, so I came up with a plan. As soon as I heard "Guess what," I blurted, "I know, you think I'm cute, right?" They were speechless.

I was stylin'. Why wouldn't they be attracted to me? My attire usually included a pair of shiny bright red or yellow Sundek pants, which were tight, ankle-length surf trunks. Whenever I fell on the rink, the pants rubbed against my legs and gave me horrible rug burns, but I didn't care. I looked cool, and that was what mattered.

Like any group of prepubescent troublemakers, we found mischief anywhere. We zoomed around the rink at full speed and sometimes skated the wrong way and got kicked off for a few minutes. A guy named Tony, who got thrown out of Catholic school for hurling a chair out the window and throwing books at nuns, was the leader of the pack. Everyone skated around in clusters, and Tony loved to push us into big groups of people like a human bowling ball. Of course, the people we got thrown into thought we did it on purpose and wanted to beat us up, so they chased us around the rest of the night.

Sometimes the middle of the rink was sectioned off with cones for break-dancing competitions. Break-dancing was the thing to do (aside from surfing), and I was bummed I wasn't good enough to get into a break-off. Every now and then I'd find someone who wouldn't make me look too silly, but those nights were rare.

Skating backward, which was a necessity when it came to slow jams with the ladies, was another weaknesses of more. One night I was skating with my first girlfriend from school, Kelly, who was the sister of one of my friends from the Catri team, and I was too shy to even hold her hand, much less try for a kiss. We were a couple for several months, and I only put my arm around her once, on the back of her seat in the movie theater. I wanted to take the next step—first base—but I was too scared. I thought

she might break up with me if I tried. Anyway, we were slow skating one night, and I managed to trip over my skates while skating backward, which brought us both down. She landed on top of me, and it was almost as though we were hugging. Everyone laughed, and my face turned the color of my bright red Sundek pants. She got up and went straight off the floor and sat down. I was left sitting there in the middle of the rink, thinking, "Okay, I guess we're finished with that dance."

I WANT MY MOMMY

The 1982 ESA Championships came around in September. The competition was in Cape Hatteras again, and my dad volunteered to drive Sean and my friends from the Catri team in his pickup truck and trailer.

When it came time to leave Florida, I didn't want to let go of my mom. I was going to be gone for one week, maybe two, and for some reason I though she might use the opportunity to leave us while we were there. I finally managed to peel myself away from her and got in the truck. There were three people riding in the cab and five of us in the trailer. Fifteen minutes later, the truck broke down. I was tired and went to sleep in the back, and when I woke up the next morning, we were still in the same place—just a few miles from home. I couldn't believe it. I could have gone home, but instead I was sleeping on the side of the road. It wasn't a good way to start the trip. We drove for a while, broke down, and waited a little more. It took us forever to get there, and nobody ever figured out what was wrong with the truck.

Menehunes competed at the start of the week, which is a good thing considering I didn't have time to get homesick. I had come a long way since the year before and this time made the final. On my best wave, I didn't see that David Speir was behind me, and I accidentally cut him off. Not wanting me to risk disqualification for interfering with his ride, he bailed off his board and let me have the wave. Getting someone disqualified wasn't the way we thought back then; we were just having fun. David drove up in our truck, and to us the whole thing was like an exotic surf trip. The cutthroat competition came later.

Following the ESA contest was the United States Amateur Surfing Championships, and the top few finishers of the Eastern's got to move on. But by the end of the week, after watching my dad drink every night, I really missed my mom. It was scary being so far from home, and I decided that even if I earned a slot in the U.S. Championships, I wanted to get back to Cocoa Beach. On the twenty-minute drive from our campground to the ceremony near the Hatteras Lighthouse, the truck broke down again. My dad hitched us a ride and stayed behind with the truck, putting his first- and second-born sons in a car with a complete stranger, yet another example of the Slater safety factor. Luckily, we made it to the Lighthouse alive just as they were calling out fifth place in Menehunes. With each finisher called, I expected to hear my name, but in the end I was the last kid standing. I was only ten, and I couldn't believe I had beaten kids who were twelve-year-olds. When David Speir told me about his opportunity to disqualify me, it made me to want to win it again, just to show everyone that I could.

But at the time, all I wanted was to go home. I forfeited my slot in the U.S. Championships, and we packed up the truck. My dad had this great idea that the truck wouldn't conk out if we left the trailer behind. He figured he could drive back up and get it when the truck was fixed. Unfortunately, it was raining, and the five of us sitting in the back only had a canvas tarp for protection. I wanted to get home so bad that I didn't mind a little rain. We stopped at a party at the contest headquarters on the way out of town so my dad could have "two beers." The whole time we were whining, "Dad, c'mon, let's go." He was having fun, and we were pestering him to leave. Finally, he snapped and started yelling at us to quit complaining. It was the first and only time he ever became belligerent with me, and my life came to a screeching halt.

I sat there stunned, and eventually fell asleep. We made it home the next day, but things had changed for me. The next time my mom told me she wanted my dad to leave, I decided I would be right behind her.

3

Refugee

ANY OF THE GREATEST ATHLETES, artists, and overachievers of any kind come from imperfect families. It creates character. We can't choose what sort of home life we are given as a child, but it plays a big part in making us who we become. The more difficult things are, the more likely we are to latch on to something outside the home. My something was surfing, but unfortunately in many cases that something is negative.

As much as I fought to keep my family together, by 1982 the troubles were escalating. Alcoholism is a disease, and my father wouldn't admit he had a problem. At the time, I blamed him for our predicament, but it wasn't his fault. People tend to point the finger at the alcoholic, but it's a family problem and must be dealt with as a family. Besides, at that time, within the surfing community, if your dad drank or smoked weed it was nothing out of the ordinary given the lifestyles of the 1960s and 1970s.

We weren't a picture-perfect family, all playing together in the sand, but we found ways to get along. Sean and I would surf, my dad would drink beer or play pinball, Stephen would build sand castles in the dunes, and my mom would sit in her chair in the sun. It doesn't seem like much, but it was the last real bonding we had.

The ocean was my refuge. Surfing was the one thing that was always there for me; it made me smile. Rather than confront the issues at home, I closed up in my little shell and shut everyone out of my life. It seemed to me that Sean tended to side with my dad when it came to family disputes, the rivalry between us flared—even in the water, though we tried to pretend it didn't. Winning the East Coast title gave me confidence in my abilities and in myself. I wasn't cocky, but I knew what I wanted to do. As long as I continued to improve and win contests, our problems at home couldn't touch me.

GOOD MEDICINE

Surfing got me out of the house and kept me active and healthy. Like most children, we weren't conscious of what we ate. We only wanted the sweetest and most well-preserved food we could find.

The staples of the Slater household were chips and cookies. We had an Oreo jar filled with a variety of cookies and a huge Frito-Lay metal container loaded with Doritos, the snack of champions. The container was meant to hold individual snack-size bags, but my mom dumped a half a ton of chips in at a time. We had a skateboard ramp in the driveway and between runs we'd scarf down handfuls of chips. Wherever we went, the Frito-Lay can came with us.

Not surprisingly, I always had some form of ailment, from earaches to throat infections, to bronchitis. My wheezing wasn't severe enough to require a visit to the hospital but was usually bad enough to keep me up at night. The next morning I'd eat the same junk—we never guessed that my diet was part of the problem. My parents went to work before I left for school, so I'd make myself breakfast—a milk shake made with cupcakes, cookies, ice cream, and chocolate syrup. I loved sugary cereals like Fruity Pebbles, Boo Berry, and Count Chocula, and could eat them for breakfast, lunch, or dinner. If I ate something less sweet, like Rice Krispies, I first had to line the bowl with a coat of sugar so each spoonful would be half cereal, half sugar. Then later, when I was in class, I would double over from the pain in my stomach.

When we had a cold, rather than take us to the doctor, my mom sent us surfing. The salty air, she insisted, was the best medicine. We didn't argue.

JUST SAY NO

It's easy to get stuck in a rut in Cocoa Beach. There aren't too many business opportunities, so a lot of people just hang out, party, and don't go anywhere. It's like a whirlpool—they just keep getting sucked back in. It must be something in the water.

My parents unintentionally influenced me to stay away from drugs. My mom always told me if I wanted to smoke pot, or anything else, she would do it with me, even though she had never done it before. That thought alone was enough to keep me from experimenting. Watching my dad also kept me on track. I saw how he acted when he was drunk, and I felt embarrassed for him. I remember once in 1984, after winning a surfing contest, he went up to get his award at the ceremony and was so drunk that he stumbled in front everyone. Some people laughed at him, and my dad tried to make a joke of it by saying, "Who put that cable in the middle of the floor?" I was so embarrassed that I covered my face. I didn't want people to think that my whole family was a bunch of alcoholics, so I resolved to stay away from drinking.

As a teenager, I had every opportunity to experiment with drugs in my town. The bad influences around the beach greatly outnumbered the good ones, but I had seen the results of taking the wrong road. Many of the locals, whose surfing I admired, were total burnouts. I'd catch a ride with them to beach and find myself in a carload of guys who were all smoking pot. It's hard not to get caught up in it, but I never could see the good in getting stoned. Soon word spread that I was serious about not doing drugs. When I was sixteen, I was at a high school party and needed to write down somebody's phone number, so I turned around to ask one of the guys near me for some paper. He said, "Uh, yeah, just a minute," and returned with a few tabs of acid in his hand. I couldn't believe it and cussed him out. "Get that crap out of my face," I yelled. "If you ever offer that to me again I'm gonna get a baseball bat and break your head in!" The guy got the message. As I got older, I chose friends who felt the same way about drugs as I did.

Surfing is my high. Drugs might be fun for a night, but the long-term damage they do—and the dreams they steal—lasts much longer. I feel a sense of obligation to promote a clean image, but more important, I don't want to destroy my body and my family.

FORSAKING ALL OTHERS

When I got home from Hatteras, after winning the East Coast title, I signed my first autograph. Rita Granger, whose husband, Don, owned the Islander Hut, had me autograph a napkin for her because she insisted that I was going to be a famous surfer one day. If I hadn't thought it was so funny, it would've been embarrassing. Most of my good friends in Cocoa Beach didn't even surf, and not many people in my school knew anything about surfing, so winning the title wasn't a big deal.

A few months later I read an interview with Sean Mattison, a kid from Jacksonville, Florida, who was a few years older and finished runner-up in the U.S. Championships that year, the contest I missed due to homesickness. When asked if there was anything else he wanted to accomplish, he said, "I want to be World Champion." I thought, "Pfft, come on. People from Australia are world champions. You're from Florida." Jeff Crawford had won the Pipe Masters in 1974, and a few other guys were making an impression in Hawaii, but a world champion? From Florida? Fuhgeddaboudit.

I was still playing Little League baseball and football, mainly to fit in with my friends. Although I had been the biggest kid in kindergarten, everyone outgrew me in elementary school. I was born with a stocky, muscular build, but I was really short. If I wasn't the shortest kid in class, then I was pretty close. In football, I used my vertically challenged status to my advantage by playing noseguard and often dove between the center's legs to make a tackle. We would play against these huge kids from neighboring towns of Cocoa and Rockledge, whose demographics were the opposite of the mostly white populous of Cocoa Beach.

My dad coached my Little League football team when I was eight, and we didn't win a single game. He was a pretty lenient coach. We had no set schedule, and he never busted our balls or singled anyone out for not trying. My size ruled out a career beyond Mighty Mite League football, and by then I was already surfing every day. I'd skip practice to go to the beach, and he sometimes ended up coaching without me.

I stayed with baseball for a couple more years. In addition to my mom's many other jobs (which ranged from firefighter, waitress, bartender, and EMT, to working for Sundek, Ron-Jon's, a cruise line, a phone company, and an engineering firm), she was a Little League umpire for one year. And she was just as tough as any of the guys out there, maybe even more so. In one game, Sean got hit in the face with a fly ball and was knocked out. My mom called it a ground rule double and told the batter to stop at second base, but his mom was yelling at him to keep running. No one was going to disobey my mom, so she turned around to the lady and said, "Shut your goddamn mouth. It was a double." Needless to say, the woman said no more.

When I was in sixth grade, baseball started to get in the way. Saturdays were tough, trying to work around surf contests and baseball games. I played shortstop and pitched occasionally, but I didn't have much control. No one was safe with me on the mound. In the first game of the year, after I pitched the first throw, the other team protested that it was too fast. I don't blame them; with my wild throws, they were scared for their lives. After a forty-five-minute debate between the coaches, my mom asked me if I had had enough. When I said yes, she said, "Kelly, take off your uniform. We're going home." It was my last game.

Leaving team sports was okay with me; compared to surfing, everything else was boring. Perhaps it can be said of other sports, but surfing is more of a lifestyle and an attitude. And the best part was that I didn't have to depend on anyone. There are individuals like Michael Jordan who really shine on a team, but one person's performance—no matter how spectacular—isn't necessarily going to make the whole team win. Even something you do individually, like tennis, directly involves another person. With surfing, you don't have to worry about anything but the wave. You have no one but yourself to blame when you don't perform at your best.

Both my parents believed in letting kids do their own thing when it came to after-school activities. They were always supportive of our surfing, but they weren't screaming at us on the beach when we lost. They made sure we got to the contests and had boards and wetsuits, then stood back and let us go. My mom was too nervous to watch and had to walk away, and my dad was happy just to see us doing something we loved. It irks me to see parents living their dreams through their kids or putting extra pressure on them to succeed. I remember playing football and hearing a mom tell her son, "If you don't score a touchdown, you ain't getting no food tonight. You might as well not come home."

I've seen it happen in surfing as well. I had a friend in California whose dad was renowned for screaming at him in front of everyone at contests. When we'd go surfing just for fun, his dad would call him in and say, "These waves are too good. You need to go practice on some crappy waves." Since contests are planned far in advance and are typically held in crummy surf, his dad felt riding good waves wasn't the best preparation. His son resented him for it, and that took the fun out of surfing.

Parents ask me all the time, "How much money should my kid be making? How can I get little Johnny sponsored?" I tell them to back off. If the kid is good enough, he'll win the right contests and sponsors will come to him. When you're fourteen it's not about the dollars, it's more important to get experience and enjoy what you're doing. When you're eighteen or twenty and still not getting results, that's when it's time to look for a different career.

BROKEN HOME

In 1983, after three years of trying to keep our family together, we finally gave up. We knew my dad wasn't going to stop drinking, and it was creating an unhealthy environment. My brothers and I finally agreed that things would be better if he left. The day after my mom kicked him out, I felt a sense of relief. The air around the house seemed lighter.

Even though things were more difficult in some ways, we knew it was the best decision. My dad only lived a few blocks away, right on the beach next to the Islander Hut, so we still saw a lot of him. Until I turned sixteen, he drove us all over the state to surf contests. And although there was never a shortage of emotional support from my parents when it came to surfing, financially it was another story.

We were never rolling in money, but after my dad left things got tight. My mom made a lot of sacrifices to keep food on our table and a roof over our heads. She couldn't afford to pay the mortgage on the house, so we were soon forced from one low-rent condo to another. She went from job to job, never making enough to get ahead. On the outside it looked as if everything was fine, so people didn't know there were any problems. In fact, her friends came to her for support and advice, never knowing the stress she was under.

We weren't starving, but things like heat and hot showers were a crapshoot. Cocoa Beach doesn't fall in the polar region, but in winter it can still get pretty cold. We had an oil heater in the hall that came on for ten minutes and shut off for ten minutes. Sean and I took turns standing in front of it to stay warm. (Steven was too young to partake in this fun activity, he was probably with my mom.) When it shut off, we waited for it to cool just enough so as not to burn us, and we leaned against it for warmth. Each morning before school, we went through five or six cycles of this before working up the courage to get in the shower. My mom rigged the water heater to come on only during certain times to save money. Sometimes we had hot water; sometimes we didn't. (I soon figured out how to adjust it so it was always running.) If we could have worn our wetsuits and still gotten clean, we would have tried it.

MAKING THE MAG

For a kid from Cocoa Beach in the early 1980s, surfing was the most exciting thing imaginable. Reading surf magazines and dreaming of surf trips, riding different types of waves and meeting different people was such an adventure. I'd check the weather reports and when I knew the surf was going to be good the next day, I couldn't sleep. I was up all night waxing my board, getting ready to catch the waves at sunrise. The ocean was my liquid confidence. It provided a comfort zone that allowed me to come out of my shell, and people began to take notice.

In 1983, the *Sun News,* a small local paper, wrote a story about me after I won the East Coast Championships. I was eleven years old and still too shy to talk about surfing, so I wasn't the easiest interview. The reporter knew nothing about the sport, but in my mind, everybody surfed. I responded to some of his sillier questions by looking at him like he was crazy. It probably wasn't his best article. The photographer had me pose inside with my trophies and then again in my backyard with my surfboard. It felt creepy. I was proud of my accomplishments but shy whenever anyone drew attention to them. I mean, why would anyone want to read about *me?* My mom made sure I didn't get

a big head by telling me not to brag or act cocky.

Next, *US Surf,* a small Florida surf magazine, used me in an ad. It had nothing to do with my abilities; it was more to say, "Hey, subscribe to *US Surf,* we cover everything from cute little grommets to old hodads." I was the shortest surfer they could find, so they took a photo of me pointing up to a really tall older surfer named Wayne Coombs, who made a name for himself carving wooden tikis, which are little statues of Polynesian gods. I remember as my mom drove me to the magazine's office to have the picture taken I was really excited because I was going be in the magazine. They didn't pay me anything, but I guess I could say it was my first modeling assignment.

My first surfing photo was published in *Waverider* later that year. You'd have needed a magnifying glass to make out my photo. It was no bigger than a postage stamp, but I was stoked to get a picture of me surfing in a magazine devoted to the sport. In the same spread, there was a huge photo of Todd Holland, another kid from Cocoa Beach who ended up becoming a big rival for Sean and me.

Tom Dugan was the photographer who took my shot. Years later when I asked him why, he said it was because Matt Kechele walked up to him and said, "Hey, you should take pictures of that kid. He's gonna be the guy." Tom said he thought Matt was crazy. Now surfing is all about the kids, but then the twenty-year-olds were the hot guys. They didn't even have Menehune Divisions in most contests. He shot three pictures of me and gave one to a local magazine. I was more of a novelty at the time; they were more interested in my brother, Sean. He was fourteen years old and winning contests in the highly competitive Boys Division. I was just his little brother.

EAST COAST ALL-STAR

My only competitors in Central Florida were David Speir and Alex Cox, and they were both growing tired of losing to me.

In amateur events, several of us competed at one time, which means there are only so many waves to go around. And since we were usually the only three Menehunes in an event, we were always surfing against one another. Before one contest at Sebastian, they came up with a plan to double-team me (although David didn't tell me about it until later that day). They took turns blocking me from catching waves while the other one surfed, and since the waves at Sebastian usually break in the same spot every time, it was easy for them to keep me out of the loop. Their strategy paid off for the first fifteen minutes of the twenty-minute final; I couldn't catch a thing. In the last five minutes of the event, I finally figured out their little trick. I paddled over to Second Peak, just as the waves magically stopped breaking where they were. In Florida, where you're surfing along a straight beach and waves pop up in random places rather than peeling in an orderly fashion along a point or reef, you learn to hunt for your prey instead of waiting for it to come to you. I grabbed three quick waves, scored high on each, and foiled their plan. Thanks to the guidance I received from Dick Catri at our weekly practices, my competitive act was coming together.

The trip to Hatteras was still the highlight of my year. I looked forward to defending my ESA title. As an amateur, it was the highest goal one could attain on the East Coast, and the waves were still better than anything I had at home. Most kids dreaded the end of summer because it meant the end of fun. To me, September meant Hatteras.

It wasn't all great waves and competition at the ESA Championships. Aside from the man-eating mosquitoes, there was the infamous swirlie. Depending on where you stood in the food chain, there was always a bigger guy that would stick your head in the toilet and flush it. Somehow I managed to avoid this heinous act by resorting to my old standby, squealing like a baby. My old friend Alex Cox got his share of swirlies, and deservedly so, but I screamed and cried until they let me go. Another one of my friends from Cocoa Beach, David Glasser, once gave himself a swirlie, just so he wouldn't get one forced on him.

As more and more young kids were competing and joining the ESA, I had to stay ahead of the game. David Speir, Danny Melhado, and Alex were giving me a run for my money, and I certainly didn't win every heat. My dedication and determination, however, were enough to give me an edge, earning me top honors in Hatteras every year from 1982 through 1987.

Beginning in 1984, the ESA selected an All-Star team consisting of twenty-two of the year's top finishers in Hatteras. The ESA All-Stars traveled together and competed against the West Coast All-Stars and other teams from the Caribbean. A weird-looking guy from Connecticut named Colin "Doc" Couture was in charge of the United States Surfing Federation, of which the ESA was a branch. He was overweight, had stringy brown hair, and wore nerdy glasses, but he ran the ESA All-Star team anyway. As part of the team, I was skeptical of him. He wasn't like any of us; he probably couldn't even swim.

Doc was an extremely giving person, and he constantly helped amateur surfers without wanting any recognition for his deeds. I didn't realize the extent of his generosity until much later. If I couldn't afford to get to a contest, he said, "Let me work on it and see what I can do." He called my sponsors, Sundek clothing and O'Neill wetsuits, and scraped together enough funds to get me places, sometimes using his own money. Next thing I knew, I was on planes to surf competitions throughout the United States. One year right after the ESA Championships, he chartered a flight out of Hatteras for me so I could get back to Florida without missing any school.

Unfortunately, I wasn't able to thank Doc for all he did for me. In the summer of 1986, I was away in California when he had an aneurysm and passed away. He was my first manager and

did more for my early career than anyone else. The ESA erected the "Doc Rock" in his honor, a big boulder outside the Surf Motel in Hatteras, with a plaque explaining some of his many contributions to amateur surfing. If you're ever on the Outer Banks, stop and pay Doc Rock a visit.

4

Traveler

I LEARNED EARLY IN LIFE THAT a big fish in a small pond gets bored, stagnant, and bloated. It swims around in circles, never evolving, and smells really bad. I was the same way—except I didn't smell bad. The more I learned about different places, the more I wanted to travel. Movies and magazines had shown me what was out there. By 1984 we had a VCR, so Sean and I would pick up videos from local surf shops, and suddenly moving images of perfect waves and pro contests were in my living room. Because things had calmed down around the house, I felt safe venturing beyond the county line. Surfing was my chosen path, and I couldn't wait to see what the world had in store.

The entire U.S. surfing industry has always been based in southern California, and according to the surfing magazines of the 1980s, the successful surfers came from places near the Pacific Ocean or from faraway lands like Australia, anywhere but the eastern seaboard. East Coast surfers weren't supposed to succeed. We were outsiders, second-class citizens, and so the industry placed a glass ceiling over our end of the country. We had just as many surfers and surf shops on the East Coast, but in terms of waves, publicity, sponsors, and talent, it was as if the rest of the country thought we had nothing.

WELCOME TO THE JUNGLE

So this is pro surfing, I thought as I gripped my board, put my head down, and prepared to make my way through the mishmash of beer, bikers, drunks, frat boys, fights, policemen, and girls flash-

ing their boobs from hotel balconies. Spring break was in full effect at the Holiday Inn at Melbourne Beach, Florida, and the only route to the beach was right through the middle of a giant nonstop party. Welcome to the 1984 Sundek Classic, my first pro contest.

Spring break probably wasn't the best environment for a twelve-year-old, but the only thing I was focused on was the surf.

Sundek paid my entry fee in the pro contest, but I'd have to turn down any prize money to retain my amateur status. I wasn't ready to turn pro, but I figured a pro contest would be a good learning experience. It was: A lot of big-name pros showed up. Lucky for me, the surf was typical knee-high Florida mush. I surfed through the trials and came up against an Australian named Mike Newling in the first round of the main event. He was a big guy, around 220 pounds. I was used to amateur contests where four or six people compete at once, so being pitted man-on-man against one giant Australian was nerve-racking, to say the least. I was shocked when I beat him. If all pro contests were held in one-foot waves, I could have turned pro right there. I lost my next heat, but the fact that I beat a pro—and not just any pro, an Australian—told me I was making progress.

CALIFORNIA BAD DREAMIN'

That summer, on July 3, 1984, my dad, Sean, and I left Cocoa Beach and landed in Los Angeles, California, so that I and the other ESA All-Stars could try out for the U.S. team trials. We were hoping to represent our country in the World Amateur Championships, which would take place the following week.

The first World Contest took place in 1964. Since then, all the best surfers in the history of competition made their mark in the event, from Australian Nat Young in 1966 to Californians Rolf Aurness and Tom Curren in 1970 and 1980, respectively. When a world professional tour known as the IPS (International Professional Surfing) came into being in the mid-1970s, the World Contest became known as the World Amateur Championships. The thing to do as an amateur was to win this event before turning pro. It was every young surfer's dream, and since the event only took place every two years, it was a huge deal. The event has gradually become less important thanks to political struggles within the surf industry about who gets to select the team that represents the United States. Because the industry doesn't support the contest, nowadays the best surfers rarely attend. Hopefully, that will change.

The ESA covered our room for most of the trip, so we were able to afford to stay in California for a few weeks. I was stoked, because up until then, my biggest surf trip had been to North Carolina, so I felt like Balboa discovering the Pacific. California has countless surf spots—rock jetties, piers, pointbreaks, reefs, and beach breaks, everything you can imagine.

The ESA, WSA (Western Surfing Association), and NSSA (National Scholastic Surfing Association) were each allotted twenty spots for the team trials. There were twenty-two of us on the ESA All-Star team, and unfortunately that meant two of us wouldn't get the chance to compete. We had two days of surfing before the trials, and based on how we did, our coach, Bruce Walker, would pick who got to move on. Bruce is a legend in the skateboarding and surfing communities. His company, Ocean Avenue, has been building surfboards and skateboards in Florida for more than thirty years, and since the 1970s, he has sponsored and coached some of the best skaters and surfers—among them street skater Rodney Mullen and surfer Matt Kechele. He was a great coach, and we all respected his opinion.

On the first day, the waves were bigger than anything I'd ever seen. We surfed Salt Creek, a spot in Orange County that sits down the cliff from the Ritz-Carlton in Dana Point. All the other guys had traveled more and surfed bigger waves than I, so to them the conditions were perfect. But for me, it was terrifying. I overheard one of my teammates talking about how the waves were so much more powerful in California than in Florida, and that didn't help my confidence. For hours, I sat on the beach trying to work up the nerve to paddle out. When I finally did, I took the extra precaution of wearing two leashes to make sure I wouldn't lose my board.

I got to the lineup and kept paddling, about forty yards past everybody, so I wouldn't get cleaned up by a big wave. Gradually, I worked my way closer to shore so that I could catch a wave. I saw that one of my team members was riding a wave right behind me, but I didn't care. I dropped in on him and made a beeline for the beach. Normally, I wouldn't have cut someone off, especially not at a foreign beach, but all I cared about was getting out of there. The wave fizzled out, and I wasn't about to wait around for another. I scratched into a tiny whitewater wave, desperate to get to shore. Normally, catching only two waves would bum me out, but that day it was more than enough. I sat on the beach and didn't get up until we were ready to leave.

The next day we surfed about an hour south in Oceanside, and the surf was just as big. Oceanside has a long jetty that gives the waves good shape, but that was the last thing on my mind. I was in survival mode and scurried back to the beach again after two waves. Two days of surfing in California and all I had was a total of four waves to my credit.

That night, Bruce had to turn in his list of ESA surfers who would be competing in the trials. It was a no-brainer: Sean and I were out. Bruce didn't know if the waves would be big again. If they were, he couldn't take the chance on us since Sean and I were the least experienced in big waves. To make up for it, he offered us a consolation prize, a slot in the kneeboard trials. That's like sending a kid out to right field and hoping nobody hits the ball to him. As dejected as I was, I was that much more determined to improve.

Of course, on the day of the trials, the waves were three feet and glassy—perfect for me, but I was stuck on the beach. I didn't place in the kneeboarding competition, but I did my first barrel roll. I flipped over with the lip and kept riding. The only problem was, nobody saw it.

Around twenty surfers qualified for the U.S. team, including

Todd Holland and Bill Johnson from Cocoa Beach. Sean, my dad, and I went every day to watch the World Contest and support the Americans. We were amazed at the level of surfing. Gary Elkerton, a brash young Australian, was the favorite to win the world title. He went by the name Kong and wore one black glove like Michael Jackson. (This was when Michael Jackson was cool.) Everyone thought Elkerton was a bad-ass. On the first day of the contest, my dad and I were eating a bag of pretzel rods on the beach when I looked up and there was Kong. I nearly choked. He looked down at me and said, "Mate, you think I could have one of those pretzels?" I was so stoked. I was telling all my friends for days that Gary Elkerton asked *me* for a pretzel. It was the highlight of my trip.

During our last few days in California, we stayed in Ventura with a friend of my dad's. We surfed a place called C Street, which was our first time riding a pointbreak. Pointbreaks give you a much longer ride because the waves wrap into a cove and taper perfectly instead of shutting down all at once. The difference between that and most waves on the East Coast is night and day.

After spending two weeks in California, it was time to leave. Sean arranged to stay with my dad's friend for another week, so my dad and I set out for the airport together—only we underestimated the traffic and missed our flight. The next day, we did it again. We drove all the way down to LAX, missed our flight, and drove back up to Ventura. My dad didn't learn his lesson, because the third day, we hit traffic again. We were so late that my dad parked the rental car at the curb and dropped the keys off at the rental desk. We ran to the plane, but when we got to the gate, the door was closed. After three days of missed flights, my dad couldn't take it anymore. He had a full breakdown, like you'd expect your mom to have. He collapsed to the floor and sobbed like a baby. It was the first time I saw him cry, and I was terrified. There I was, twelve years old, and my dad was throwing a tantrum in the airport. It must have worked, because the ticket agent felt sorry for me and got us on the plane.

To make the trip complete, I arrived in Florida to find that my boards hadn't made the flight. I quickly learned that surf travel wasn't all fun and games, and I was thankful my first trip was finally behind me.

TICKET TO RIDE

A couple months later, my dad took Sean and me to a surfing contest in Jacksonville, Florida, called Hart's Birthday Bash. Dave Hart was the owner of a surf shop in Jacksonville, and he threw himself a big party every year. The winner of each division competed in a superheat, and the overall champion would earn a ticket to Hawaii. The waves were good—around three feet and clean. I won the Menehune Division, so I was the youngest surfer in the superheat, up against guys like Bill Johnson. He was nineteen years old and the top amateur on the East Coast. I was sure I couldn't win, but second prize was a new stereo, so I had something to shoot for.

Surfing against more accomplished competitors made me try much harder, and since I didn't really think I could win, I didn't feel any pressure. I surfed without a care in the world. I remember catching one wave that was a little bigger than what I was used to. As the wave broke, I rode up and off the lip. When I landed without falling, I felt like my surfing had advanced to another level. I won the heat and was ready to dance the hula on my way to Hawaii.

Bill was freaking out because he lost. My dad felt so sorry for him that he swore up and down he was going to raise the money to send Bill to Hawaii. My mom said, "What the hell's wrong with you, Steve?" We didn't have the money to send Sean to Hawaii, but my dad insisted that Bill deserved to go. He wanted to have parties and fund-raisers for Bill, but people looked at him like he was crazy. I stood there thinking, what about me? I couldn't believe my dad was so worried about Bill, and I was a little hurt that he didn't take my side.

Beating Bill and winning the ticket were too much for me to take, and I started bawling uncontrollably, "I'm going to Hawaii-ee-ee-ee." I knew the North Shore was the epicenter of surfing and was overwhelmed at the thought of being there. It was scary and exciting and gave me a feeling of heading into the unknown.

Every surf spot has a name. Some are labeled after the beach in front of where they break, but others, like Pipeline, are given titles that describe the waves themselves. Pipeline is on the North Shore of Oahu, and it's the focal point of Hawaiian surfing. Covered in dangerous underwater caves, the reef has killed more surfers than any other spot. Sean and I had a poster of Pipe on our wall, and I spent years just staring at it. The photo was taken on a perfect day with huge waves and only four guys out. In the foreground, one of them was swimming for his board. He didn't have a leash, and this big blue wave was getting ready to crush him. I'd think to myself, it couldn't be that big every day, could it? When a four-foot mushburger in Florida scares you, it's hard to think about riding Pipe. Going to Hawaii felt like stepping off the edge of the earth. But I knew that if I ever wanted to get really good, I had to go.

When Theodore Roosevelt Middle School let out for Christmas break, I had my 4'9" and my 5'1" boards packed and ready for two weeks on the Islands. Not only was I heading into the unknown, I was also leaving a girlfriend behind. The night before I left, a girl from school named Kathy called and said she was coming over to give me a Christmas present. I was crazy about her but tried to play it like it was no big deal in front of my family. I don't remember what the present was, but in the living room, right in front of my dad, she gave me my first kiss. I ran to Sean and bragged, "I kissed her right in front of Dad. How is *that*?" Since he was a few years older, he didn't think it was a big deal.

HAWAII

On the night of December 17, 1984, Sean and I arrived in Honolulu. Matt Kechele, who also rode for Sundek and had become our surfboard shaper and mentor, convinced the company to help cover Sean's expenses so I wouldn't have to go alone. Matt wasn't getting paid to help us, but he saw that we had potential and did everything he could to nurture it. He was already in Hawaii and picked us up at the airport. We drove to the North Shore to stay with him in his rented room at Mark Foo's Backpacker's Lodge. Mark was originally from the East Coast and a famous big-wave rider. He was establishing his bed-and-breakfast near Waimea Bay, where thousands of visiting surfers stayed over the years. (Unfortunately, in 1994 he drowned at a big-wave spot in northern California called Maverick's.)

Earlier that afternoon, Joey Buran, the California Kid, had become the first Californian to win the Pipe Masters. Up until that point, it had been held by Hawaiians, Australians, South Africans, and even a Floridian, Jeff Crawford. As soon as we woke the next morning, we went to look at Pipeline. Joey happened to be coming up the walkway and stopped to say hello to Matt. It was our first day in Hawaii, and here was the Pipe Master, talking to *us*. It was too good to be true.

For an hour or so, we just sat and watched the waves, which were two to three times overhead—way bigger than anything I would have ridden at the time. I saw a guy completely disappear in the tube at Backdoor, the wave on the other end of Pipeline. I thought, "Why is this guy going right at Pipeline?" (Waves are referred to as "rights" or "lefts" depending on the direction they break from a vantage point facing the beach from the lineup.) In magazines, everybody went left at Pipe because it was more photogenic. Little did I know the right would later become my favorite wave and provide the setting for many of my victories.

At the next spot down from Backdoor, a place called Off the Wall, we walked up the path and saw Tom Curren in the water. He was on his way to becoming the most popular American surfer ever, and breaking the era of Australian domination by winning three world titles. We watched in amazement as Tom took off and did an unbelievable turn off the top, slapping the water with his board as he landed at the bottom of the wave. There was a picture of it in *Surfer* magazine that winter, and I put it on our wall at home. Anyone who came in my room had to listen to how I saw that turn and heard it from the beach.

Luckily, there were places in Hawaii where I wasn't too scared to paddle out. At many spots, there are deep channels where you can make it to the lineup without getting hit by a single wave. There are huge waves breaking in one area, and right next to it the ocean is like a lake. It wasn't until I was in the lineup that I'd realize I was in over my head.

My first session was at a place called Chun's Reef, which is pretty tame by North Shore standards. Matt saw that I was afraid and advised me against paddling across the reef to get back to the beach. He told me to paddle around it, but I was too scared to hear what he said. I paddled straight toward the beach and got dragged across the coral by a wave. Other than scraped knuckles, I was physically okay. It was my first day in Hawaii, and the only thing I'd proved was that I was a chicken.

I didn't expect to charge out at Pipe, but I was hoping to surf it, even if it was tiny, just to be able to tell my friends, "Yeah, I surfed Pipe." One day Sean and I were at Ehukai Beach Park, the mellow sandbar just down the beach, and I decided to paddle over to Pipe. The waves were no taller than I was, and I got a few short rides with only one other guy out there. In Florida, we'd be freaking over these waves, but for Hawaii it was considered flat.

This was it, I thought. "I'm surfing Pipeline. This isn't so hard." Then, suddenly, I was staring up at what looked like a big blue mountain about to come crashing down on me. The wave was only a few feet over my head, but it looked every bit as big as the one on the poster on my wall. It exploded right in front of me and picked me up and slammed me like a rag doll. I hit the reef and it scared me back down to Ehukai, paddling as fast as my little arms would take me. I wasn't hurt, but I stayed away from Pipe for the rest of the trip.

After a week on the North Shore, Sean and I prepared to leave on Christmas Day for Oahu's west side. But first we had to settle our tab with Mark Foo. The rates were five bucks per person per night, so the bill for Sean and me was $70. We had assumed that Sundek was covering our accommodations, and it was $70 we didn't have. Matt was also on a tight budget and had nothing to spare, so we spent Christmas Eve listening to Mark and his girlfriend fight over how much to charge us. She wanted to let us off easy, but Mark was saying, "Screw that. This is a business." We were in the next room and heard everything. I felt so bad listening to how pissed Mark was. We ended up paying $2.50 per night for both of us, so the bill was $16.50 for the week. You won't find those rates on the North Shore anymore.

U.S. CHAMP

Our second week in Hawaii was spent at Makaha, competing in the U.S. Amateur Surfing Championships. All I knew about Makaha was that Greg Noll supposedly rode the biggest wave in history there in 1969. Every morning, I crossed my fingers as we came around the last turn and prayed the surf wouldn't be giant. Thankfully, somebody was listening.

Sean and I stayed with some friends of ours, Shawn and Tony Sutton, who had moved to Oahu from Florida with their family. They lived near the naval air station, Barbers Point, a few miles south of the contest.

Makaha was a scary place for a twelve-year-old kid from the mainland. There's a lot of poverty around there and a few locals who don't take kindly to visitors. One day during the contest, Sean and a friend went hiking in the nearby mountains. A local kid told me that there was a big marijuana field where Sean was hiking, and that if the owner caught him he'd be in big trouble. I was convinced my brother was going to get killed, so I wasn't exactly focused on the competition. Fortunately, nothing happened to Sean.

The waves at Makaha weren't scary, but the contest itself was intimidating. These were the best surfers from all over the country, and everyone was ripping. Matt Archbold, a kid from San Clemente, California, really stood out. He was going faster and getting more radical than anyone. Everyone else was hitting the lip and coming back down, but he was already starting to blast through the lip and into the air. Fortunately, he's a couple years older than I am and was competing in another division.

Surprisingly, I advanced through a few heats and found myself in the final. I didn't know who Shane Dorian was, or Keoni Watson, or any of the other Menehunes I was up against, but since they were from Hawaii I figured they must be good. After the final was over, I felt confident but didn't think I had enough waves to win. The judges counted our four best waves in early rounds but for the final it was the best five, which can be very hard to catch in twenty minutes. I only caught five waves total. I would have been happy with third place, but when they called out the results, it came down to a kid named Keone Gouveia and me. The announcer, trying to be funny, said, "In second place, his name starts with a 'K'," so I started walking up to get my trophy. When he called Keone's name, I stopped in my tracks. I was the U.S. Menehune Champion. I thought it was a mistake. Nobody knew who I was. I wasn't supposed to win.

The event organizers were going to run a superheat, in which the winners from each division would have to compete. I was praying they'd decide against it. I would have had to surf against Matt Archbold and a bunch of other great surfers, and they would have killed me. Fortunately, they called it off. I made a lot of friends in Makaha that I've had ever since—Shane Dorian, Keoni Watson, Matt Archbold, Sunny Garcia, Matty Liu, Brock Little, Todd Chesser, Ronald Hill and his family, and many others. I was pretty shy, but they all came up and talked to me. By the end of my stay, I actually felt comfortable around them.

After two weeks in paradise, it was time to get back to reality. School was starting, and I wanted to see Kathy and resume my new love life. By the time I got home, she decided she didn't want to be my girlfriend anymore. She had moved on, and in a way, so had I.

ESCAPE FROM FLATNESS

Winning the U.S. title deepened my resolve to keep improving, so I went back to Florida from Hawaii intent on doing nothing but surfing. Unfortunately, in Florida that isn't possible. We can go weeks on end without seeing a surfable wave, so we need to improvise. My best friend, Johnny Ross, had a boat, and we used to ride around on the Banana River and tow each other on our surfboards or on hydroslides, which were basically knee-boards. We'd bank off the boat wake as if it were a wave and even launch airs. Occasionally we'd nose-dive while going full speed and nearly break our necks, but it was fun. It was the next best thing to surfing.

We were so into it that we decided to make our own boards. I wanted to make one shorter and more maneuverable than the boards we already had, so I knelt down on a piece of paper and traced the outline around my legs. I used this as a blueprint for my new board and took it to school the next day to show everyone. Johnny, a couple other friends, and I bought a foam core like the ones surfboards are crafted from and grabbed all the tools we could find—nails, sandpaper, and saws. We used nails to chip away at the foam, splattered paint all over it, and took it to the Quiet Flight surfboard factory (where my surfboards were made) to get it glassed.

The first day we tried the board, I was towing Johnny around an island in the canal. I don't know if there's a legal driving age for boats, but I probably hadn't reached it. My idea was to whip him around so he could spray the trees with water, so I came in close to the island and turned super hard. I sprayed the trees with the wake from the boat and when I looked back to see how Johnny was doing, he was gone. There was nothing but a bunch of mangrove trees, and somewhere inside them was Johnny. I had turned too hard, and he lost control and went flying into the bushes near the shore. He emerged with cuts everywhere and didn't want to ride anymore. This meant it was my turn for the rest of the day, which was fine with me.

When our little brother, Stephen, was seven, Sean and I asked Matt Kechele to make him a tiny 4'7" surfboard. Sean and I took Stephen to Sebastian and pushed him into a perfect little wave at First Peak. He wiped out and didn't know which way was up. He came up crying, went to the beach, and wouldn't surf for years. We really wanted him to learn to surf, and I think that's why he didn't. I would sometimes offer him twenty bucks to paddle out with me for the day, but he refused. He was into fishing and camping. He'd go out in his friends' boats on the Banana River and explore the little islands along it. At the beach, he spent his time playing in the dunes.

And so the only Slaters competing in events were Sean and I.

During the 1985 Easter Surfing Festival in Cocoa Beach, which is a pro-am event, Matt came up to us and said, "Hey, Kelly and Sean, come to the car with me. I've got something for you guys." On the way to his car, he was raving about his secret weapon, how he had an advantage over the competition. Halfway there, I got suspicious and was afraid he'd try to push drugs on us. "Wait a minute," I said. "This stuff isn't bad for you, is it?" He assured us it was okay, and we got in his van to find out his secret. It was a little oxygen tank.

He explained that none of the other pros knew about it and that he could take it anywhere. The tank had a little tube attached to a mask, and we took turns breathing with it for a few minutes. Matt said it was the best investment he'd ever made, and that it was the key to being charged up in heats. He doesn't own one anymore, but he still swears by it. I won the contest, but I don't think it was due to the oxygen. I've never used it again, and I've done all right.

That year Sundek used Sean and me in ads in the major surf magazines, giving us our first exposure outside the East Coast. To provide us with some sort of income, since it was illegal to pay a salary to amateurs, Sundek introduced the Sean and Kelly Slater signature model surfboards, which were shaped in California by Tony Channin. I didn't like the way the boards looked and never rode them, but that didn't stop other kids from wanting the Kelly Slater model. Regardless of the number of boards sold, I made $105 cash per week. Sean was making $120, so I still had something to strive for. As much as I appreciated having money, the whole idea turned me off. Before we knew it, we were getting hundreds of letters from fans around the world. I was shocked when one came from a boy in Indonesia, addressed only to Kelly Slater, Cocoa Beach, USA. I didn't read all of them. I tried to pick out the ones with the pictures inside, hoping they came from cute girls.

Sundek set up autograph signings for us at malls all over Florida and Sean, who just turned sixteen, would drive us there. Sometimes we were so far inland doing promos that we were in the hills, hundreds of miles from the nearest coast. It was beyond our reasoning why someone would want to meet us. A few people recognized us from magazines, but to most of them we were just two kids giving away free surf posters at the mall.

The company also sent Sean and me on road trips in Matt's van up the East Coast from Florida to New York during that summer in 1986. We got to escape the flatness of Florida for a couple weeks, stopping at various towns to go surfing and hand out stickers. Along the way, Matt coached us on heat strategy, board design, and health. He was a great motivator. Whenever I rode a wave, he was yelling, "Let's see it" or "Big air." Since he competed on the world tour every year, he told us what all the pros were doing and how to improve our surfing. Whenever we needed him, we could call him for advice. He was there for us all the time, watching over our careers like a big brother.

Thanks to our trips up the East Coast, we learned a lot about traveling and dealing with fans, and, like anyone cooped up in a van for weeks, we occasionally clashed. I don't know if it was because Sundek wasn't giving Matt much of a travel budget, but we spent almost every night in his van. We hardly took showers—just the occasional rinse with a hose at a beachfront cottage—and we were always searching for ninety-nine-cent breakfast specials. The fact that we only had one tape to listen to during the entire trip made things even worse. We must have heard Thomas Dolby's "She Blinded Me with Science" a thousand times. Sean had a shorter fuse than I, and he and Matt were always getting into it. Sean would scream, "Drop me off at the airport. I'm flying home," but he'd eventually calm down.

On one such trip, when we got to Long Island, we planned to camp out on the beach in Montauk. We met a guy while surfing who owned a nearby bed-and-breakfast, and he offered us a room. We assumed it was free of charge. "Yes!" we cheered. "A bed." We went to the guy's place, and he told Sean and me that we could go up to our room and unpack. Meanwhile, he told Matt it was going to be $75 for the night. Sean was already asleep by the time Matt came up and said, "We're outta here. Let's get our stuff and go." The owner felt so bad he decided not to charge us. It was a good thing too, because it was the first bed Sean had seen in weeks and he was out cold.

On the way back home, we decided to spend a couple days in Cape Hatteras but ended up staying for almost two weeks. Each morning we walked to the beach and said, "No way! It's good *again.*" On July 3, 1986, at a place called Frisco Pier, we surfed the best waves I had ever seen on the East Coast. When a wave is powerful and hollow, the compression causes water to spray out the end of the tube, a phenomenon known as "spit." Getting spit out of a barrel is the ultimate in surfing, and I got a couple that day. Matt saw me come out of one and started freaking out. He screamed, "God, that looked like Hawaii," but there was one major difference: I was riding over sand rather than reef, so I had nothing to fear.

But we weren't there just for the surf; we had another reason for staying in Hatteras so long that summer. Matt was getting friendly with the desk clerk, a cute local girl, and wanted to hang out with her. He'd seen her a few times, but one night I remember he came back in a panic. He turned off the lights, jumped into bed, and told us to be quiet. Apparently, the girl had a boyfriend—a big, angry redneck who caught wind of Matt moving in on his turf. The whole night we thought this guy was going to come knocking on our door and kill us. The next day we packed up our bags and headed home.

MINOR THREAT

Even though I'd surf a pro event from time to time, I was consistently winning amateur events along both coasts. (I earned U.S. titles from 1984 through 1987.) At the Easter Surfing Festival in 1986, Todd Holland and I, although we were both amateurs, made it to the man-on-man final in the pro event. The waves were head-high and perfect, probably the best event we had ever seen. Winning the Festival meant you got bragging rights around Cocoa Beach for the rest of the year. For me, it was as big as the Op Pro in Huntington Beach, California. People (drunk, of course) were lined up along the Canaveral Pier, screaming their heads off for us. It was a close heat (I actually thought Todd had won), but I earned my first pro victory.

After that, it seemed like the top local pros started looking at me different, as if I was a threat rather than just a kid who could surf. I never felt any animosity from them, but I think they were a little frustrated. (I know if some kid half my age beat me, especially in good waves, I'd go nuts.) They still didn't consider me part of the elite crew at First Peak, so I was determined to prove to them I deserved a place in the lineup.

Later that year, in another pro-am, the Excalibur Cup at Sebastian, I wanted to make a lasting impression. All the top local pros were there, and the waves were head-high and wedging off the jetty—perfect. I came up against Sean in an early man-on-man heat and beat him. It was tough for him, especially as a teenager, because I was doing well and things weren't going great for him. Deep down, he was my biggest supporter, but it didn't always come out that way. We spent most of our time together, but there were times when he flat out said he hated me. We each wanted the same things out of surfing, but I was the one getting pictures in magazines and all the attention. The better I did, the harder it was for Sean, and it started to make us drift apart.

In the final, I faced Bill Johnson again. By then, Bill was charging big waves. I had seen pictures of him surfing Pipeline when it was big, so to me he was like a god. He had far more experience in competition and intimidated me with his aggressiveness. There was no way I could keep up with him when it came to paddling out, but I managed to get enough waves to beat him. First prize was a real sword made by some guy in England who was supposedly the best sword maker around. On the beach, the sword was sticking out of a big rock made of foam. I was supposed to pull it out, just like in the legend of Excalibur, but I didn't realize how heavy the sword was and couldn't get it to budge. My mind flashed to the scene in the movie *Excalibur*, in which only one person could pull the sword from the stone. For a brief moment, I figured I was the wrong person, but I put my foot on the rock for leverage and managed to pull it out. Having proven myself, I had no more problems catching waves at Sebastian.

Later that night, Heather Thomas from the 1980s TV show *The Fall Guy* came to the awards ceremony. She was one of the hottest blonde babes in Hollywood, and we were all excited to see her. She was dancing with people for charity, and some guy bought me a dance with her for winning. I don't remember what charity it was, but I do remember how embarrassed I felt because everyone was watching. A picture of us dancing ran in the next issue of *Surfing* magazine, and people at my school thought I was some kind of celebrity.

The more contests I won, the more I realized that I needed to step it up in bigger surf. I wanted to avoid being labeled as a small-wave guy. After running from Pipe with my tail between my legs, I was in no hurry to jump back into the North Shore arena. There was no need to travel six thousand miles to Hawaii until I graduated from my own backyard. I decided to ease my way into bigger waves and do it at my own pace.

STEPPING STONES

The Caribbean doesn't have the size and power of the North Shore, but it's a few steps up from Florida. Ever since my trip to Hawaii in 1984, I had been going to Barbados for spring break

with Sean, Todd Holland, and a few other guys. While I was there I rode the biggest waves of my young life (about six feet). Waves larger than a couple feet were so foreign to me that I didn't know what to do once I stood up. In all the surf movies I saw, when the waves were huge (twenty or more feet), the guys didn't do any moves, because just riding the wave straight to shore was exciting enough. To me, these waves were just as big, so I assumed the survival stance and held on for my life on a mere six-footer. To everyone in the water, I must have looked silly going straight on a wave that was so small. The guys I was with were maneuvering all around like it was a playground.

Sean and I spent Christmas 1985 at a place called Rincon in Puerto Rico and gained more experience with sizable surf. There were rocks at virtually every spot we surfed, and I was stressed that if I accidentally lost my board, it would end up getting smashed. I only had two boards with me, so once again, I thought about wearing two leashes but decided against it. The triple-overhead waves at Rincon were definitely out of my league. I didn't charge into waves, but I didn't run away from them either. I just sort of rode straight and hoped that I didn't look too dumb.

I made several trips to both Puerto Rico and Barbados as a teenager to compete in contests, and Sundek helped out with travel expenses. These experiences were just the gentle nudge I needed to get comfortable. They added to my surfing knowledge and gave me a feel for size and power, since bigger waves move faster and with more force. Most important, after a few trips to the Caribbean, I was no longer afraid of riding over a hunk of reef.

Surfing those islands was a great stepping stone, and Sean and I took advantage of it during nearly every school break. We missed a few days of school here and there, but it wasn't too big of a deal because we always made up the work.

VOYEUR BOY

The Association of Surfing Professionals World Tour (formerly International Professional Surfing) doesn't make many stops in Florida. Occasionally, a sponsor would cough up some money to bring the pros to town, but once everyone saw how bad the waves were, they usually didn't come back. In 1984, when I was twelve years old, the tour came to Singer Island, Florida, for an event called the Wave Wizards (even though there weren't any waves, and at one point, the contest sponsors had to hire a boat to cruise back and forth to kick up some wake). I was excited because I got a chance to surf with Tom Carroll when he wasn't competing. He checked out my surfboard and told me he couldn't believe how small it was. He spoke to me! Tom Carroll, my hero and soon to be world champion, actually took the time to say something to *me*. It was a big a boost to my ego, although to him I must have been just another giddy kid. Sean and I got our share of autographs at the Wave Wizards, but by the next year we were anxious to see more of professional surfing.

In the mid-1980s, if we wanted to see the pros at work, that meant traveling to one place every summer—California. The World Tour made annual stops at California's Huntington Beach and Oceanside, and Sean and I went every year to watch and learn from the pros. We'd stay in Huntington, so that we could go to the Op Pro, and hitch a ride to Oceanside for the Stubbies Pro.

The crowds at Huntington were huge, easily twenty thousand people. Along the pier, they were packed eight deep. Getting to see the pros in person was a magical experience. It was like going to any other type of professional sporting event as opposed to watching it on television. But since surfing is so much smaller than other sports, anyone can actually walk out on the field for a closer look, or in this case paddle out to the lineup for a closer look prior to competition. I'd go back to Florida and brag to all my friends, "I was there. I saw Tom Curren do this, and I heard Gary Elkerton say that."

The Stubbies Pro was filled with lots of kids like us, not to mention plenty of crazed groupies, so security was pretty tight. My friend Matty Liu from Hawaii knew some of the pros and convinced them to tell the security guards to let us through into the competitors' area. Once in, I recognized all the guys from the magazines. I studied everything—their boards, wetsuits, and gear. They probably thought I was a weirdo, looking to steal their boards or something. But I just wanted to see what went on behind the scenes in the life of real professional surfers. Sean and I weren't there for autographs. By then we were both teenagers, so we thought we were too cool for that.

In 1986, Sean and I got our own taste of stardom when Sundek sent us to do a surfing exhibition in a wave pool at Waterpark, USA in New Braunfels, Texas, near San Antonio. The waves, if you can call them that, were pitiful even by Cocoa Beach standards, maybe knee-high and barely breaking. We couldn't do much more than stand up and ride for a few feet before sinking. Not many people in that part of Texas had ever seen someone ride a surfboard, so fortunately it wasn't hard to make an impression. We were treated like surf stars. But with waves like that, it was easy to see why Middle America didn't take hold of the sport.

ALMOST READY FOR THE WORLD

If my progress in the U.S. team trials in Ventura, California, was any indication, it looked like my time in the Caribbean and California was paying off. In 1986, two years after getting left out of the running, I not only qualified for the team but won the event. I was going to England to represent my country in the World Amateur Championships.

Sean, on the other hand, wasn't so lucky. In a battle for the final team slot with Todd Holland, he became a victim of politics. A big rivalry was developing between the Eastern Surfing Association (ESA), which Sean and I supported, and the National Scholastic Surfing Association (NSSA), of which Todd was a member. In the late 1970s, the NSSA was started on the West Coast, and the organizations continually battled over whose surfers would represent the United States in the World Contest.

In the last trials event, Sean was in eight place in the overall standings, which would qualify him for the team. It came down to one six-man semifinal. If Todd finished first or second, he would eliminate my brother for the last slot. All the surfers in the twenty-minute heat, with the exception of Sean, were from the NSSA and had either already qualified for the team or couldn't make it. It seemed as if their director, Ian Cairns, instructed them to let Todd win, because they all came in after riding three waves rather than the allotted four. This left Todd a clear path through the heat and on to the team, while Sean was relegated to an alternate spot. I saw one of the guys come in early, and ran up to him to ask why he did that. He responded with a threat to pound me if I didn't mind my business. At the awards ceremony, there was so much tension between the ESA riders and coaches and the NSSA riders and coaches that I thought at any second a fight would break out. It wasn't the kids' fault—they were just doing what they were told. I went to England carrying a grudge against Todd and the rest of the NSSA.

England is a far cry from your typical surfing destination. I had no idea there were waves there, but the surf scene is surprisingly strong. In Newquay, where the contest was going to be held, there is a small slice of coast with a few stormy, overcast, freezing cold waves. Surfing is so out of place in such a proper Old World atmosphere that the surfing community has become a tight-knit group. There aren't a lot of them, but they stick together to make their voice heard on environmental concerns within the government. They put a lot of effort into keeping the ocean clean and safe.

As soon as the U.S. team arrived in Newquay, karma was thrown back at Ian's coup. We were all waiting for our boards to come off the plane, when Todd's somehow fell off the conveyor belt and was crushed into three pieces by a baggage truck. He'd have to ride a backup board.

There wasn't enough money in the sport at the time to put us up in a cheap hotel, so they put all the teams in a trailer park. Each trailer was big enough for four people, so Sean and I stayed with our friend Chris Brown and his dad, who were from California. It was September, and I didn't know what kind of weather to expect. I only brought a few changes of warm clothes, and it was the coldest, most blustery place I had ever been. Inside our trailer, there were coin-operated heaters. At night I put on every piece of clothing I had—T-shirts, sweaters, jeans, and a couple pairs of socks—and Chris's dad tucked us in and put a bunch of coins in the slot. Within an hour, our time was up and we froze through the rest of the night.

In the Open Division of the event, I advanced through several rounds and was headed for the finals when I was done in by team bias. When surfers are done with a heat, they aren't allowed to stand on their boards and ride them back to shore because it interferes with the judges who are trying to score the next heat. On the way in from one of my heats, I was riding on my knees, which is perfectly legal, when I fell off my board. One of the judges from another country saw me fall and figured I must have been standing up, so I was disqualified. It was a blatant rip-off, but I still had a shot of winning the Juniors' Division.

On the last day, the waves were pretty big. At fourteen years old, I was the second youngest kid in the contest. Shane Dorian, who was a few months younger than I, was the youngest. He was smaller than I was but fearless. He streaked across the biggest waves and kept eating it. I was scared out there and couldn't imagine performing at my best. I was afraid of getting caught by a set, so I pretended to not be able to paddle out too far. I stayed close to the beach and rode the smaller waves. It was a huge event and people from all over the world were seeing me surf for the first time, no doubt thinking, "Man, that Slater kid's a wuss."

More daunting than the surf was the famous Nicky Wood from Australia. He was a fifteen-year-old legend, the godson of four-time world champion pro surfer Mark Richards, and already had beaten some of the best surfers in the world. On the morning of our heat, Sean said, "I think you're gonna beat Nicky today. I saw him in a bar last night until two in the morning and fed him some beers." Sean may not have made the team, but he ended up being the most valuable player keeping Nicky out late drinking. I won the semifinal but had to face him again in the final.

That afternoon, the tide came in and the surf dropped just enough for me to have fun. I was up against Nicky, a Hawaiian named John Shimooka, and a Tahitian named Vetea David in the final. Vetea was a huge seventeen-year-old kid nicknamed "Poto." He didn't speak a word of English, and nobody outside Tahiti had ever heard of him. He grew up surfing dangerous reef breaks and was on fire the whole contest. Poto dominated, and Nicky finished second. I fell on two waves and placed third.

Without winning the World Contest, I didn't consider myself a successful competitor. Even though this was my first try, I was convinced that winning the event was the only way I could be assured of a professional career in surfing.

HUMBLED IN HAWAII

No matter what a surfer accomplishes the rest of the year, he isn't fully respected until he performs in Hawaii. Everyone who surfs knows this. After staying away for a year, I went back to the North Shore in 1986. I haven't missed a winter there since.

That year, and for the next couple of years, Sean and I stayed with another Sundek rider, Ken Bradshaw, a famous big-wave surfer who grew up playing football in Texas. He learned to surf in Galveston when he was in high school and fell in love with the sport. He quit school in 1969 and moved to California to surf. In 1972, he went to Hawaii to ride big waves and has been there ever since. He was one of my mentors when it came to learning to ride big waves, and he took his job very seriously. I had no choice but to improve. If I didn't, I'd have to find a new place to stay.

Ken's mission was to make me surf Sunset Beach, a popular big-wave spot right behind his house. The wave breaks a quarter of a mile out from the shore, and when you're there, it seems like the whole ocean is rising into each wave. I told him I wasn't ready for Sunset, so he said, "Okay, I'll take you to Little Sunset," which is a semisecret spot a couple miles down the coast. I had never heard of Little Sunset, so I couldn't argue.

By the time we made it out to the surf, I was so tired and scared that I wanted to go in to shore. Ken wasn't exactly the most compassionate guy, so he said, "You want to go in? Paddle straight in, NOW!" There was a set coming on the outside reef, but he didn't care. I paddled straight into the impact zone as a huge wave prepared to squish me. Ken's booming voice screamed for me to face the beach and hold on. When the wave hit me, I did two front flips and somehow held on to my board until I washed up to the beach. I had escaped death but not humiliation, because when I looked back out, everyone was riding waves as easily as cruising down the bunny slope. It was a humbling experience.

Even though I couldn't hang with Ken, there were plenty of smaller quality waves along the North Shore to help build confidence without threatening my life. So one day I went surfing with Adam Repogle, a friend from Santa Cruz, California, who was around my age and experience level. The waves at Sunset were big, so we walked right past it and on to a spot farther along the coast called Velzyland, which was more suited to our tastes. The waves were smaller, but the reef was razor sharp. On my last wave I tried to get barreled and lost my balance. I put out my hand in hopes of breaking my fall and hit the reef. A little hunk of coral got lodged in my palm. I didn't realize it was there until a few weeks later when I was sitting in school. The cut had sort of healed over, but it was still a little sore. I was playing around with it, when suddenly the piece of coral popped right out of my hand. I showed it to a girl sitting next to me and explained the story, but she wasn't impressed.

I turned fifteen the following year, and Ken finally dragged me out to the real Sunset. It was a day I'd now call "fun six-foot Sunset," but at the time it seemed like Mount Everest. I watched from the lineup as Ken, Sean, and my friend Alex Cox each grabbed a wave. They were paddling back out through the channel when a perfect peak came right to me. I heard them scream-

ing, "Yeah, yeah, yeah . . . aww." Stage fright got the better of me, and I pulled back. They were disappointed in me, but not as much as I was in myself. They paddled farther out and caught a bunch of waves, while I sat inside and picked up a few scraps, but nothing as good as the one that got away. The whole time, I paddled toward the channel to avoid getting clobbered by a set. What I didn't realize until several years later was that, at Sunset, it's actually more dangerous riding the inside reef. The waves there are more powerful due to a bend in the reef, as opposed to farther out to sea where the waves are more crumbly.

The fact that I paddled out at Sunset was a major accomplishment, and I was in no hurry to push myself over the edge. Competing and excelling in big Hawaiian surf was more of a long-term goal. As far as competitions went, I was up there at the top of the ladder, but since I wasn't comfortable in big surf, I still felt like I was on the bottom rung. I had many steps to climb before I could feel like I had made it to the top.

That summer, I won my first overseas event, the 1987 Pacific Cup, which was a step in the right direction. It pitted the best U.S. amateur surfers against the top amateurs in Australia and New Zealand. I had seen the world's best amateurs in England, but the talent level at every beach in Australia blew me away. We pulled up to Duranbah, on the Gold Coast, to perfect hollow peaks everywhere. The lineup was packed, and on every wave was a great surfer. I was overwhelmed and intimidated but somehow won both the Juniors' and Open Divisions of the event.

I felt like a man of the world. Yet I wasn't so daring as to stray from my three McDonald's meals per day to try the local favorites like meat pockets and Vegemite sandwiches, but my mind was opened in other ways. Jason Buttenshaw and Josh Palmateer, two of the best young Aussies of the day, gave me some beer and I got drunk on the beach for the first time. Most teenagers drank at least occasionally, and I wanted to know what

ESA TEAM/KELLY SLATER

the buzz was about. After a couple beers, I sat around with a goofy grin, staring at all the people who walked by. It wasn't a feeling I enjoyed, and I stayed away from drinking for a few years after that.

MINUTEMAN

In September 1987, I was driving home from the ESA Championships in Hatteras with Sean and our friend Brett Gardner. I had just won my sixth straight East Coast title, but that topic wasn't nearly as exciting as listening to Sean's and Brett's tales of sexual exploits. Suddenly, I realized the one thing I was missing. I hadn't ever had sex and blurted out, "Man, if I don't have sex in the next year I'm gonna go crazy."

Thankfully, I didn't have to wait long. I'll reserve the names to protect the innocent, but there was a girl, let's just call her Darla, whom I went to school with who had hooked up with a friend of mine. Darla and I kissed at a party one night, and she said she wanted to come to my house the next day. I told my friend Drew she was coming, and he assured me, "It's gonna happen, for sure." I was scared to death of intimate contact, but now there was no way out.

The next day, there was a knock at the front door. My mom was at work and Sean wasn't around, so Stephen and I had the run of the house. He was on one couch watching TV, and Darla and I settled on the other. She was all over me, and I thought, "Gosh, my brother's not even ten years old. I can't do this in front of him." I took her into my room. Just as things really got going, the party was over. Our school nickname is the Minutemen, and I'd be lucky if I lived up to that billing. I was ashamed at my speedy perform-ance and tried to conceal the evidence by stammering, "I can't do this. I've got to stop." I thought I had pulled a sly one, but as she was getting dressed, she put her hand in something wet on the side of the bed. "Ewww!" she shrieked, confirming that my cover was blown. I couldn't get her out of the house fast enough.

Two minutes later, my phone rang. "Did it happen?" Drew demanded. I tried to play it off, but he knew I was lying. "All right," I said. "I'll tell you everything if you promise not to tell anybody." I gave him all the details, and by the next morning, it may as well have been posted on the school marquee. Everybody knew I had sex, and I was no longer the shy, innocent kid I had been the day before. My classmates looked at me like I was a different person.

It felt good to think of myself as a Ladies' Man. I was certain that my wealth of experience enabled me to look at any girl and know if she went all the way. I thought I had an all-encompassing knowledge of the female gender. Obviously, I didn't.

MESSING WITH TEXAS

As soon as Tom Curren began to lose interest in competition after winning his second world title in 1987, the American surfing media was grasping for straws. That same year, I won a pretty big pro event (a stop on the Professional Surfing Association of America Tour) in a wave pool in Irvine, California. The waves were tiny and weak, and anyone over 120 pounds more or less sank to the bottom of the pool. Chris Brown and I weighed a combined 180 pounds at the time and finished first and second. A photo of me from the contest ran on the cover of *Surfing* magazine. They airbrushed some extra spray coming off my board to make it look as though I was going faster than I really was. The magazines started calling me the future world champion. Since I had won six East Coast titles, four U.S. Championships, and two NSSA Nationals, all eyes were focused on me. While the attention and faith in me was nice, I still had to prove I could do it. Before I could even think of turning pro, I had to win as an amateur at the highest level.

With the 1988 World Amateur Championships around the corner, here was my chance to show everyone I could perform under pressure. Since a new team is chosen to represent the United States every two years, I had to qualify for the team again. In November 1987, the team trials were held following the U.S. Championships in South Padre Island, Texas. Apparently, not everything is big in Texas, because the waves were nearly nonexistent.

Despite a healthy surfing population, Texas is hardly a surfy place. The only surfer I knew who was still living in Texas was Jay Bennett, who could fart for a minute straight. He got into a four-point farting stance, sucked air into his backside, and let it rip, announcing each one by name. "Here comes 'the Demon!'" We timed one effort at fifty-three seconds, a personal best. I don't know if all surfers from Texas have the same type of skill, but Jay stood out in any crowd.

For some reason unknown to me, that year the U.S. team was decided by combining results from the U.S. Championships with the results from the two trial events. The top twenty surfers made the team. I was at a disadvantage from the beginning, because the Men's and Juniors' competitors received twice the number of points that I got for winning the Boys' Division. The organizers figured the competition wasn't as strong for the kids, so we didn't deserve as much for winning.

I had a hard time getting used to surfing in Texas. The water was colder than what I was used to, so I was wearing a full-length wetsuit and booties, and had a thick leash attached to my board. I couldn't get going in the tiny surf with all my gear weighing me down, and I bombed in an early round of the first trials event. To make the team, I needed to finish first or second in the last event. I made the six-man final, but once again I was up against a guy I thought I had no chance of beating, Chris Billy from California. He was older, stronger, and had a board that was perfect for the tiny surf. In my mind, I was shooting for second.

This time, there was no fairy-tale ending. I surfed a terrible heat and finished fourth, leaving me as the second alternate for the team. I was asked to join the team in case somebody couldn't surf, but I declined. As competitive as I was, there was no way I could sit on the sidelines and watch the event. I couldn't stand losing in anything I tried, especially surfing. I felt I was improving, but I failed to qualify for the team, much less win the 1988 world title. Everyone was calling me the best amateur in America, but after Texas, I had serious doubts.

5

Prodigy

DICK CATRI AND MATT KECHELE, my earliest mentors, both told me I had the potential to make it big in surfing. But as a high school freshman in 1988, I was a four-feet-ten-inch, ninety-five pound, squeaky-voiced runt who was a year from reaching puberty and unable to bench-press his own weight. Needless to say, I didn't consider myself on the same level as top professionals.

During my sophomore year in school, I sprouted six inches and began talking and surfing more like a man. In March 1989, I went to Barbados for a pro-am, where I won the amateur event and finished second in the pro. There were a lot of good surfers in the contest, and the waves had some size to them. More important than how I finished was that my surfing had made an impression. Instead of feeling threatened by me, the older locals from my area now had a vested interest, sort of an ownership, in the way I was performing. Around town, friends were coming up to me saying they heard from pros who were there that I had out-performed everyone and was surfing like Tom Curren.

Surfer magazine did a nine-page profile on me that summer entitled "The Seduction of Kelly Slater," in which the writer Matt George more or less hailed me as the next Tom Curren. In the 1980s, every kid wanted to surf like Tom, and none more so than I. He set the standard. Before he came along, there had never been a professional men's world champion from America. Being compared to Tom was the highest honor.

After that, I was no longer thinking of surfing as mere recreation. I was beginning to realize it could be my career. It was my opportunity to set myself up for life, and I wasn't going to blow it.

STYLE BANDIT

Surfing without style is like music without rhythm. It has no flow. In the 1970s, surfing techniques were as diverse as the personalities. There were smooth surfers like Gerry Lopez and Michael Peterson who flowed with the wave, radical guys such as Buttons Kaluhiokalani and Larry Bertlemann who went wherever their minds could take them, and stylists like Rabbit Bartholomew and Barry Kanaiaupuni who surfed with more flair and focused on the way their body was positioned. It was interesting to see different lines drawn along the same wave, just like appreciating several artists depicting the same scene.

Like all surfers, my style was a product of my environment and the people I looked up to. Because of the short, sloppy waves, East Coast surfers didn't have much face to carve on, so we had to rely on quickness. We had a choppy style full of radical moves. The guys I admired in Florida—Matt Kechele, John Holeman, Charlie Kuhn, Bill Hartley, Pat Mulhern, and John Futch—were among the first surfers sliding their tails out, doing 360s, and try-

ing airs. It was an East Coast thing. I grew up bouncing around trying to fit moves into tiny places on the wave, and early on my style suffered as a result.

Magazines, videos, and traveling introduced me to a world of different surfing styles, and there were two surfers whose styles impacted me the most—Martin Potter and Tom Curren. Seeing Martin Potter blasting an aerial on the cover of *Surfing* magazine in 1984 when I was twelve years old changed my life. He was a South African with a cool green-and-yellow explosion airbrushed on his boards. He refused to hold back, even during a heat, and lost contests because he would try difficult maneuvers and fall. I respected that. He was someone I could relate to, and right away, I wanted to fly. Martin once said to me, "Kelly, I see a lot of me in you. When you see a lip, you just want to hit it."

Tom came along at the same time, and he had the ideal mix of flow, radical moves, and a perfect style honed on long California pointbreaks. Everybody would mimic his moves. I wanted to combine Potter's flair with Curren's flow. I even went through a stage where I'd try to strike Tom's trademark pose on every turn. He did this thing where, for no reason, he looked back after hitting the lip, and a lot of people copied it. It looks foolish today, but I thought I was killing it. As loyal as I was to my East Coast roots, I was determined to break free of the stereotype. I later found that trying to surf in a way that wasn't natural was a bad thing, but at least it helped smooth out my style.

The board you ride also has a lot to do with the way you surf. Shapers from different parts of the world tend to specialize in boards that work well where they live. East Coast boards are flatter and wider for generating speed where there is none, while other boards are curvier and narrower for speeding down the line on a steep wave. It should be simple for a sponsored surfer to get a new board, but for me it had become a hassle. Sundek agreed to pay for my boards, Matt would shape them, and someone else would glass them. During the summer of 1988, Al Merrick of

Channel Islands Surfboards in Santa Barbara, put the word out that he wanted to make me some boards. I had tried out the boards before because my friend Chris Brown rode them, and Chris and I had traded boards when we'd surf spots around Santa Barbara. The spots there are mainly pointbreaks, and Al's boards were perfect in those waves. It seemed to me that if I wanted to smooth out my own style, switching boards was a step in the right direction. Al is one of the most respected shapers around, so I jumped at the chance.

Al brought me up to stay at his house in Santa Barbara, and we clicked immediately. His wife was blown away by the fact that I took out the trash. A lot of surfers had stayed with them over the years, but I was the first one who ever voluntarily helped out around the house. Up until that point, I had only ridden boards that were made in Florida, so I felt a little scared and guilty for parting with Matt after four years to work with a West Coast shaper. But Al was making boards for Tom Curren, the best surfer in the world, and that was what I wanted to be. Al and I have been together ever since.

ON CENTER STAGE

By 1989 I had surfed plenty of contests in front of crowds, but the Op Pro in Huntington Beach was in a league of its own. Each summer somewhere around twenty thousand people packed onto the beach and pier for the event. That year Ocean Pacific invited the nation's top amateurs to compete in a separate division alongside the pros. It was billed as the Op Junior, and it stuck a bunch of nervous kids in front of the surfing world for the first time.

In my first heat of the contest, on a cold weekday morning, my back foot came off my board and I did a split. I was pretty flexible, and doing a split on land was easy, but doing it on my board while riding a wave was a different story. It felt like I ripped my hip in half. In reality, I tore a muscle in my hip, although I didn't have that confirmed until twelve years later when I finally had it examined by a doctor.

For most athletes, flexibility is at least as important as strength, and I was lucky enough to be born limber. From the moment I hurt my hip, I needed to use the flexibility in my back to compensate for the injury. (Because of this, I developed a hump on the lower left side of my back, and my friends started calling me "Camelback.") My back doesn't bend very well going forward, but Stephen and I can bend backward as far as we want. In fact, during the 1983 ESA Championships in Hatteras, Charlie Kuhn saw me sleeping with my body bent backward so that my feet were almost touching the back of my head like I was doing a back bend. It must have looked to him as though I was a limp bag of bones, because Charlie ran around hysterically shouting, "Kelly's dead. Kelly's dead."

Not only is stiffness an undesirable quality in surfing, it also increases the chances for injury. I'd never done any training beyond going surfing, and tearing a muscle impressed upon me the importance of keeping my body fit. I started taking yoga classes after the hip injury, which made me aware that I wasn't as flexible as I thought.

At the Junior Op, I advanced to the final against Rob Machado. I closed my eyes and hummed loudly, but it failed to make the crowd full of screaming fans disappear. Huntington had been a second home to me, so I had some support. Rob, on the other hand, was from California, so the other 98 percent of the crowd were in his corner.

Because the magazines had been hyping me, the pros were there to see if I could deliver, and right off the bat, I made a fool of myself. In the early 1980s, the Op Pro introduced a priority buoy in man-on-man heats to keep guys from paddling up one another's backs to catch waves. The rule was that the first surfer to paddle around the buoy had first choice of waves, and they more or less took turns from there. But there was one minor part to the rule that I hadn't heard. A surfer needed to ride a wave before paddling around the buoy. Until that happens, no priority can be awarded to either surfer. So basically, it's each man for himself until one of them rides the first wave. The heat started, and I immediately paddled around the buoy, thinking I'd receive first priority. I looked toward the colored marker atop the scaffolding, but it didn't indicate priority for either of us. I was furious and threw my hands in the air, cursing the judges incompetence. Rob was equally clueless, so I didn't feel too stupid. We each shrugged our shoulders, gave the other his space, and went about our business of catching waves without getting in each other's way. I managed to avoid further embarrassment, but I didn't surf great. At least I won the contest.

FAST TIMES AT COCOA BEACH HIGH

There were a lot of surfers in Cocoa Beach, but for some reason there weren't too many at my high school. In tenth grade, as captain of the Surf Club, which Sean had started a few years earlier, I was in charge of only a handful of people. There weren't enough surfers to form a circle, much less a clique. We had weekly meetings when I was in town, and we mostly sat around and looked at surf magazines and sometimes watched a video. The club eventually fell apart from lack of interest.

I got along with everyone at school and sort of bounced between groups. I made time for the Spanish and Booster Clubs, and in eleventh grade I played tennis. But my surf and sleep priorities didn't leave much time for extracurricular activities. I stayed up late watching *The Arsenio Hall Show*, woke up at 6:49 every morning, wiped my face with water, grabbed something from the kitchen, and ran to class before the tardy bell rang at 7:15.

I had a few serious girlfriends throughout high school, but they didn't like the idea of vying with surfing for my attention. With as much time as I spent traveling, it was difficult to maintain a relationship.

There were times when I wanted to switch to home school, so I could surf whenever I wanted, or go to California, where I could get out early for surf class, but I never seriously considered quitting school to turn pro. (I could have if I wanted to, because it was before the ASP introduced a rule that set a minimum-age requirement of eighteen for touring pros.) I realized from watching guys like Tom Carroll—who was almost thirty and still dominating at Pipe—that I was nowhere near my prime. I figured I had a few years to go before I reached my physical or mental peak.

Cocoa Beach High provided the stability I needed to keep me on track. Traveling for contests meant I always had work to make up, but I made a point not to get too far behind. Since I was doing well in school and in my sport, the principal was cooperative. The teachers were there to help me in class, and most of the time I understood things on my own. During my junior and senior years, I didn't take a book home. I finished my assignments in study hall so I wouldn't have to worry about them at night. I figured when I was at school, I would work, and as long as I got it all done, I wouldn't have to think about it when I was on the road.

MONEY

Hundreds of years ago, surfing was such an integral part of life in ancient Hawaii that people bet their homes, their crops, even their wives, on the results of a surf meet. But for the first half of the 1900s, the only contests you could find were paddle races for trophies and bragging rights. The first cash purses for competition were doled out in the 1960s. The best and most marketable athletes—guys like Californians Phil Edwards, Mickey Dora, Dewey Weber, and Corky Carroll, as well as East Coasters Gary Propper and Mike Tabeling—were paid a small salary to put their name on a board or to appear in magazine ads, which gradually increased from a couple hundred dollars to tens of thousands of dollars per year. It wasn't until 1976 that a legitimate pro tour was formed, and gradually an industry was formed to support it. Still, it wasn't until the 1980s that more than a handful of people at any one time were making a living simply from surfing.

When I started thinking about a career in the sport in the late 1980s, it had grown into a lucrative business. A lot of guys were making ends meet on the Professional Surfing Association of America (PSAA) Tour, which was created by Joey Buran in 1985, just after he won the Pipe Masters and quit surfing professionally. Joey was the first Californian to make his mark on the ASP tour,

and started the PSAA because he wanted young surfers to have opportunities to succeed domestically. Aside from those surfers, there were many others who were making a decent living on the World Tour. Even if they weren't winning, they could make around $20,000 a year through contest earnings and sponsor salaries, which was enough to buy a car and pay for a place to live. As an added bonus, they got to travel the world in the process.

The mid-1980s surfing boom turned into the early 1990s bust in the United States. All but the strongest companies folded, and the magazines, which are fueled by advertising, shrunk to less than half the size they had been a few years earlier. By 1989, Sundek wasn't doing much business and the company folded. My mom lost her job there and bounced between bartending and cleaning construction sites to have enough money to keep a roof over Stephen's and my head. During that time, I started getting offers from bigger companies. It seemed crazy to me that I, a seventeen-year-old kid, would need a manager, but no one in my family knew anything about money.

I'd known Bryan Taylor since he spotted Sean and me in a Sundek ad three years earlier. He was a young talent agent with no ties to the surfing industry. Sensing an opportunity, he got in touch with my mom and asked if he could take us out to eat the next time we were in Huntington, California. At the time, I was wary about what he wanted from a fourteen-year-old kid, but a free dinner at Sizzler was worth hearing him out. I didn't expect anything beyond the free meal. But in 1989 when I needed someone to work out a contract for me, my mom gave Bryan the go-ahead.

He worked out deals for me to wear Ocean Pacific clothing and Rip Curl wetsuits, and just like that I was making a decent living. They were both really stable companies, and they made the best offers at that time. I was still an amateur but must have made at least as much as my high school teachers. I bought my own car, a brand-

new Honda Civic, with cash. After having to save my Sundek earnings for weeks just to get a new bike, this was splurging.

My mom had sacrificed a lot to get me to where I was. After we left the house on Aucila Drive, my mom, Sean, Stephen, and I were in and out of several places for a few years. Even though she remarried in 1987 to a boat mechanic named Walker Rivers, we weren't much better off financially. We needed a base, so I bought a house on Thirteenth Street in Cocoa Beach. The house was pretty much the same as most other homes around town—a three-bedroom cinder block ranch house built in the 1960s. It was overpriced, run-down, and we had to gut it and rebuild it, which turned out to be more trouble than it was worth.

After buying a car and house, the next step was to get a bank account. Since I wasn't old enough to open one on my own, my mom and I opened one together. I put all my contest winnings there and gave my mom free reign over it. My success became my family's success. We had lived without money for such a long time that my mom used the added income to make things good for all of us.

SEARCHING FOR TOM CURREN

Within a few months of getting sponsored by Op, I was questioning the decision. Op has always been a huge company, pulling in more money than anyone else in the industry. Of course, the company did so by catering to nonsurfers, who outnumber actual surfers by a hundred to one. I had nothing in common with the company, the people running it, or the vision they had. My whole life was surfing, but they seemed to be on the outside looking in. When I walked through the massive warehouse to pick out some clothes, I only found one pair of shorts I liked. It was a horrible feeling knowing I could pick whatever I wanted and that I didn't want anything. My deal with them was only for a year, and, well, they did have Tom Curren, so I stuck it out.

Tom grew up in Santa Barbara, California, and rode for Op from the time he turned pro in 1982. Since he was my favorite surfer, one of my goals in life was to get to know him. Soon after I signed with the company, Tom picked me up in Huntington and took me to the Op offices, which were about a half an hour inland, to meet some of the employees. He is a nice guy, but he isn't what you'd call sociable. Driving down the freeway on our big day out, he didn't seem to be paying attention to where we were going. I said, "Look, if you don't get out of this lane, you're gonna have to turn here." He looked at me like I was crazy and said, "Do you think I don't know how to drive, kid?" I was already nervous, but after that I was praying for the passenger seat to swallow me whole. The anxiety was nothing I had ever experienced. It was like being around a girl you really like: You act goofy and say all the wrong things.

As a signing bonus, Op sent me to stay with Tom for a couple weeks in France right after the Op Pro. I was going to be starting my junior year in school, and for me, or for any teenage surfer, it was the ultimate European vacation. Tom was living in a town called Biarritz on the southwest coast of France with his wife, Marie, and their newborn baby girl, so it was a slight imposition having some strange kid staying at the house.

I had never traveled internationally by myself. Tom and I had different flights and were supposed to meet up at the airport in Paris before flying on to Biarritz. After three hours spent in the Paris airport trying to find my connecting flight with no sign of Tom, I went on without him. I landed in Biarritz with no clue where he lived. Biarritz is a romantic town with beautiful architecture, an amazing countryside, and beaches. There's a ritzy casino right on the sand, and the waves break in front of buildings that are hundreds of years old. Surfers come out of the water in their wetsuits and stand in front of one of the most expensive hotels in the world, with people clad in expensive suits and dresses getting into chauffeured limousines.

Stranded in the airport, I didn't speak a lick of French, and I didn't have Marie's number or any money other than a little change. I traded it in for some francs and tried to call home. Stephen answered and said, "Oh, hi Kelly, I'll get Mom," and the phone died. I sat in the airport for seven hours, until the last flight of the day came in from Paris. Tom thought I was lost, and he came off the flight looking awfully stressed. He was relieved and a little pissed to see me, so we didn't get off to the best start.

Tom wasn't totally comfortable with letting me into his home, so he set me up in a hotel across the street. After two days, he let me sleep on his couch, but it wasn't like we were best pals. I actually felt closer to his wife, Marie. She was really friendly and, since she had traveled around the world with Tom from the time she was eighteen, sympathized with my feelings of being in a strange place. Tom and I only surfed together three times in the two weeks I was there. The rest of the time I surfed alone while Tom went off to play music. Or I watched his baby daughter so he could surf when Marie was away at work. I was learning from the master all right, learning how to change diapers.

The waves were perfect at the beach breaks around Tom's house, but surfing with Tom was more difficult than talking to him. I was having trouble getting used to a new board and felt like a complete beginner. Meanwhile, Tom was in his prime and ripping. When we got in the car after our first session together, he said, "You know, when you ride different waves, you have to approach them in different ways. You have to read the curve of the wave. You can't always do the same off-the-lip." He was right, and that simple tip still sticks in my head. But at the time, I was so embarrassed I wanted to hide under a rock.

On one of my last days the waves were particularly big, and I sat on the beach with Marie's entire family as Tom surfed a heavy shore break behind his house for hours. It was more than double overhead and whomping on the sand. No one else thought about paddling out, least of all me, but watching him let me know how much I still needed to improve.

The day I left France, Tom was surfing in the Rip Curl Pro in Hossegor. When he dropped me off at the airport, I said, "Go win this one," and he did. I felt like, yeah, I told him to do that.

CHUMP OF THE HILL

Armed with the secrets from Superman's hidden sanctuary, I returned home for a few months of school before my annual trek to the North Shore. Tom's expertise, combined with a few more inches and pounds, made me ready to continue delving into larger surf. The only problem was that my friends like Brock Little, Todd Chesser, and Shane Dorian were already way ahead of me.

Back when the older guys tried to coax me into surfing big waves it was easy to resist; I could always play the youth card, claiming, "Hey, I'm just a kid." But when my peers started doing it, I started to run out of excuses. While I was in high school, I spent my Christmas vacations at the home of my friend Ronald Hill at the infamous Hill House. I met Ronald in 1984 during my first trip to Hawaii, and my circle of friends and I crashed at his house in the winter. His parents, Cory and Senior, didn't seem to mind. The deal at the Hill House was this: No one paid rent, everyone cleaned up after himself, and at night the place was quiet. At any one time, there were twenty young guys from all over the country scattered around their floor and all eighty of their boards in the garage. We were allowed to ride any of them.

It seemed like the perfect accommodations, but they came at a price. When the waves got big, we had to go surfing. The peer pressure among friends was intense.

No matter how bad he surfed in small waves, Brock Little had been riding big waves his whole life and was the ruler of the Hill House. The Hills had a boxing ring in the backyard and he could knock any of us out. He also rode waves that we couldn't imagine. At the time, Waimea Bay was considered the ultimate big wave. When Brock was seventeen, he was riding Waimea by himself—at night. Well, almost. The Hills had home videos of him taking off on a twenty-five-foot wave that closed out from one end of the bay to the other. This was the first wave of the set, and he kicked out just in time to see the rest of the waves about to break on his head. He got thrashed around and blacked out underwater two times before gathering his senses. Because it was so big and the currents so strong, he had to swim around the bay twice before making it back to the beach. That's what happens if you don't swim in next to the rocks, the current sweeps you out to the middle of the bay, and you have to swim toward the impact zone and try again. To this day, I haven't had to do it, but Brock would do it for fun. He didn't have a breaking point. He was king and everyone else found a spot on the floor.

Brock pushed everyone. Todd Chesser and Shane Dorian were right behind him, riding surf that could kill them. Most of our other friends were in there as well, but those three led the charge. It took me a long time to get my head around the thought that I might enjoy big waves, but I was making small steps. A person can't jump from a three-foot wave to a twelve-foot wave overnight and expect to get the timing and the approach right. I had to surf it in my mind before I'd ride it.

Brock claims that when he pushed me it was because he was watching out for me. Years later, he still laughs and tells me,

"When it got big, you were a pussy." He'd be like, "Come on, get your ass out there." He figured I was going to stick with riding little waves my whole life. He claims it was from the heart when he'd tell me it was safe to go out in big waves, that it was genuine.

JINXED IN JAPAN

Japan is full of amazing surf, but for some reason it's never during contests. There is every type of wave imaginable and it gets huge swells during typhoon season. In Chiba, where the 1990 World Amateur Championships were held, I was almost guaranteed small waves. There the stage was set for what I hoped would be the perfect ending to my amateur career—a world title. I knew it was my final test before turning pro, and it was one I thought I could pass without studying.

On my way to Japan, I stopped at Rob Machado's house in Cardiff, California. He was also a member of the U.S. team, and we were becoming close friends so we decided to travel to Japan together. It was the first time I stayed with him, and we played Ping-Pong for two solid days. Rob is a Ping-Pong master, and the competition on the table was as fierce as any of our heats in the water. When we got to our tiny Japanese hotel room, we rigged together a table and played Ping-Pong the entire trip. Eventually, we grew bored with table tennis and resorted to hitting each other with the ball. If either of us gave the other guy a body welt, we scored a point. It turned from Ping-Pong into BW, Body Welt.

The small waves on the final day of the event were right up my alley, and I was determined to finish the job. I put so much pressure on myself that it kept me from surfing freely. In the semifinal, one heat away from fulfilling my final objective, I had a great heat but somehow lost to fellow American Taylor Knox and Heifara Tahutina, a Tahitian who went on to win the event. Everyone who watched the heat from the beach thought I had advanced, but the judges have the only opinions that count. And they didn't see it my way.

For the entire event, it seemed like the other teams were out to get me. My teammate Pat O'Connell saw everything and explains it better than I could. "Kelly was getting gang-raped in his heats. They were siccing goons on him, so he'd catch crummy waves and still advance. He was that much better than everyone else. In one heat, it was Kelly and three Brazilians, the most aggressive competitors you can imagine. They were all over him, and somehow he won. He ended up losing in the semifinal, but he shouldn't have. Kelly does a different type of surfing. It's difficult to put a number to what he was doing. He was busting aerials and reverses and nobody knew how to judge that. He was way outside the box."

On one hand, since it was my last chance at a world title, I was devastated. Any potential sponsors would figure, "If he can't win an amateur title, how can he win a pro title?" On the other hand, I didn't think it was a clear indication of talent. There is so much bias in amateur surfing, with judges pushing certain competitors, that I was fed up with the whole thing.

I DON'T EVEN CARE

In July 1990, just after my junior year in high school, I turned pro. Even though I didn't have a world title, I figured it would motivate me to try harder, because I still felt like I had something to prove. There is nothing formal about the transition; anyone can be a pro surfer simply by entering a professional event. There was no press conference (I didn't know what one was), and I didn't have a sponsor. My contracts with Op and Rip Curl wet suits had expired the same month, so I was on my own. If I didn't win contests, I didn't make any money.

Bryan Taylor was negotiating on my behalf with three interested companies—Op, Gotcha, and Quiksilver. Each potential sponsor was leery of my failures in the World Contest and doubted my ability to perform in Hawaii.

While conversations of my worthiness were taking place all over Orange County, California, the Life's a Beach Klassic came to Oceanside. I sent my entry fee to the ASP, then I turned up at the pier in Oceanside, and surfed my first event as a pro, scrapping with 150 other trialists for a piece of the pie—a total purse of $75,000.

At every stop on the tour at that time, a trials event was held to determine which sixteen surfers would face the top thirty-two seeds. It was run pretty much like a tennis tournament. I had no ratings points and was placed in the pretrials, another series of heats that were necessary at events with a lot of competitors. I advanced through seven heats and was one of forty-eight surfers in the main event.

In the second round of the main event, I faced Martin Potter, who was the reigning world champion. Scared to death of "Pottz," I paddled down the beach to the opposite end of the surfing area so I could catch waves by myself. I was winning for most of the heat, but he posted a near perfect score on his last ride to turn it around. Losing in the second round meant I finished tied for seventeenth place, which felt like an accomplishment. When Pottz went on to win the event, it made my loss easier to swallow. At the awards presentation, he said, "I knew after I beat Kelly that I could win this contest." To mention me among all his opponents was a huge compliment.

As Pottz tells it, "I remember going through the heat sheet and when I saw Kelly's name, I got nervous! Being in Kelly's heat does strange things to you. It can either completely crush you or it can make you perform to a level unknown to yourself. Fortunately, that day, luck was on my side."

The negotiations for my first pro contract had turned into a bidding war. I had a good meeting with the owners at Gotcha. They had just put out *Surfers: The Movie,* which in my opinion is one of the greatest surf movies of all time. It captures all the elements of the sport and made me proud to be a surfer. The grassroots vibe at Gotcha was something I would have been proud to be associated with, and Quiksilver was equally desirable, but neither had offers that were in the same ballpark as Op.

I wanted to be with a company whose image and clothes I liked. However, Op's proposal was so substantial that it looked like I was going to be stuck with them.

Turning pro was a big step, and dealing with the business side of my career got to be the furthest thing from my mind. I was tired of worrying about getting the best deal and wanted to get away from the chaos to go surfing. So I took a vacation to Mexico with some friends.

Before leaving, I got a pair of trunks from some of Rob Machado's friends who owned a screen-printing company. They had stenciled the words "I don't even care" across the seat of the pants. It was a phrase they used all the time, and since I didn't have a sponsor, it didn't matter what kind of trunks I wore.

Surfer magazine took a photo of me surfing in them and ran it with a story concerning my contract negotiations. I remember that an instant after the shot was taken, I fell and landed on a longboarder who was paddling out. I came up just in time for the guy's board to nail me in the side of the head, smacking me back to my senses. It was like someone shook me and said, "Wake up, kid!" Suddenly, I cared.

My tow board and I.

Testing the waters with my daughter, Taylor, to see if she will love surfing the way I do.

Before I got into golf, playing pool occupied much of my downtime on tour.

We used photos like these to help create the real-life illustrations in the Kelly Slater Pro Surfer video game.

I haven't mastered this . . . yet.

Okay, so I stole this cutback from Tom Curren. He's my hero. What can I say?

After scaring the hell out of me for years, Backdoor Pipe feels like my backyard.

This was a real gloomy day, but thanks to flash photography, this shot made the cover of *Surfing* magazine for the August 2000 issue.

Opening ceremonies for the Quiksilver in Memory of Eddie Aikau contest.
Being invited to this event was one of my greatest accomplishments in surfing.

My generation basically took the
moves of our predecessors and
did them above the lip of the wave.

Borrowing a move from skateboarding: a lien air.

Cloudbreak 2002: This is where I learned to translate small wave maneuvers on to big waves back in 1990.

Bottom turns don't get as much attention as other aspects of riding waves, but they form the foundation for good surfing.

Another average day in Cocoa Beach, Florida—I wish!

QUIKSILVER TO THE RESCUE

When I got back to California, Bryan called me out of the blue and said, "You're going to ride for Quiksilver. They made a great offer at the last minute, and you're with them." The agreement would pay me six figures annually for three years and make me among the five highest paid surfers in world. I was speechless but breathing a huge sigh of relief. When it came down to serious negotiations, Op couldn't rationalize paying me what they paid Curren, which was fine with me. Rather than suck it up and deal with Op for a few more years, I was with a company every surfer wanted to ride for. It wasn't as big of a company as it is now, but both my brother Sean and Matt Kechele rode for Quiksilver, as well as a lot of my friends and surfers I admired.

Quiksilver wanted to be my only sponsor (other than Channel Islands, Al's surfboard company), so that meant I wouldn't have a bunch of logos battling for space on my board and I wouldn't appear in anyone else's ads. Tom Carroll, the two-time world champion from Australia, had signed an exclusive, million dollar, five-year deal with Quiksilver in 1989, and the company found that exclusivity gave it the most bang for its buck.

A few years later Peter Townend—the 1976 world surfing champion, contest commentator, and publisher of *Surfing* magazine—passed out a questionnaire to school-aged kids. There were a bunch of questions about surfing, and one asked the kids to name the sponsors of several famous surfers. Out of twenty surfers, I was the only one who was correctly matched with a sponsor by every kid, thus proving the merits of exclusivity. Since then, a lot of companies have signed surfers to exclusive deals.

With the uncertainty behind me, I went into my first real Op Pro in July 1990 as a Quiksilver rider. I hadn't signed the contract yet, but we had already agreed on the deal. They were paying me more than I expected to make, so there was pressure to prove their investment wasn't a waste. Having won the Op Junior in 1989, people expected me to step right up and challenge Curren, but I didn't get the chance. In the last round of the trials, I inadvertently dropped into a wave in front of another competitor and drew an interference call from the judges. When that happens, the offending surfer is only scored on his top two waves instead of three, so I failed to make the main event, and finished tied for fifty-seventh place.

There was no time to mope; I was off to France the next week for the Quiksilver Lacanau Pro and determined to make amends. As soon as it started, the excitement of being in France and competing against the best surfers in the world made me forget about the Op Pro in Huntington.

I expected the crowds in France to be more formal and laid back than in California, but I couldn't have been more mistaken. The French are fanatical about surfing. Thousands of diehard fans from Paris and other big cities fly into quaint little beach towns along the southwest coast like Biarritz and Hossegor to watch the contests. They all want to take close-up pictures and don't understand the concept of personal space. When a competitor comes to the beach after a heat, thousands of people are wading in waist-deep water with their pens and autograph books, pushing him, grabbing his board, and marking his arms with pens as they try to get him to sign something. By the end of the season, many pro surfers never want to write their names again.

I've noticed lately that, in a relatively short period of time, the talent level of European surfers has risen dramatically. It used to be a joke in terms of how many people were in the water and how few knew what they were doing. I could surf a perfect wave with dozens of clueless beginners bobbing through the lineup. Now the French have pretty much caught up.

After several rounds of trials, I again met up with Martin

Potter in round two of the Lacanau Pro main event. This time I pulled it together and won. He wasn't too happy about losing and was screaming in the water after the heat. When I got to the beach, it seemed like a thousand people were surrounding me, and I couldn't move in any direction. The fans pleaded with me, "Oh, sign, sign, sign, autograph." I was so happy to beat Potter that I would've stood there until dark. Nothing else mattered.

I was on a roll and beat Nicky Wood and Tom Carroll in the next two rounds to come up against Tom Curren in the semifinal. After such an impressive run, it felt like I was on a level with the best surfers, but then again Curren was in his own league.

Before paddling out, I saw Tom's wife, Marie, on the beach. She said, "I hope you surf good, Kelly, but I really want Tom to win," as if she were asking me not to beat him. She didn't have to worry. Tom went crazy, and before it was over, I was begging him, "Man, slow down. Give me a chance." He was on a mission. He had just come out of semiretirement to win his third world title, and his focus was amazing. There was no way he was going to lose. I wasn't quite giving up, but on some level, I didn't want to beat him. Finishing third in such a big event felt as good or better than winning anything else.

It became apparent after surfing against Tom that I needed to develop confidence in my own approach. To hear I was surfing like Curren was still a huge compliment, but I didn't want to be seen as a clone. If you follow someone completely, you can only become less than what he is. It took eight years before I beat Tom in a heat. I was always nervous surfing against him, and it took me that long to get comfortable with the position I was in. To me, he is still the ultimate stylist.

After the Lacanau Pro, I surfed the Rip Curl Pro (which would eventually be my first World Championship Tour win two years later) in Hossegor. If I were to do well enough in that event, I could possibly win the Sud Ouest Surf Trophee, which was the best placed surfer in the three French events. I had my sights set on trying to win it, which caused me to miss my first week of school as a senior. But I needed a good placing at this event to have a chance. I had the wave to win against Californian Brad Gerlach as the time wound down, but I fell after hearing him yell "F*$k!" really loud—and I was out with a 17th and no chance.

The World Tour continued through Europe without me, and I returned to Florida to begin my senior year at Cocoa Beach High.

IN BLACK AND WHITE

The Professional Surfing Association of America (PSAA), which was peaking in 1990 in terms of prize money, prestige, and coverage, was gearing up for its premiere event, the Body Glove Surfbout at Lower Trestles in San Clemente, California, that would take place in September. Ever since I was a kid, Lowers has been my favorite wave on the West Coast. I desperately wanted to do well but just getting in the event was a story in itself.

The PSAA had its own ranking system separate from the ASP. I hadn't surfed any PSAA events that year, and a surfer had to be in the Top 100 of the ratings just to get into the Lowers event. It is such a great wave and so crowded that everyone wants the chance to ride it in a heat with only three other guys at a time.

Earlier that summer, I was at a party at Pat O'Connell's house in Laguna, where I was probably the only sober person in the place. Everyone was running off a diving board into the pool, and as I went to jump, I saw something coming at me from the side. It was Hank, a surf photographer who checks in around six feet tall and two hundred pounds, and our heads hit in midair. He sank to the bottom, and I thought I broke my neck. The music was blasting, and nobody was paying attention. I could barely breathe, and no one heard me whispering for help. Hank was out cold at the bottom of the pool, and I went under and dragged him to the shallow end before somebody finally helped pull him out. He was delirious and didn't remember a thing. I was okay other than a sore neck, but that was the end of a good time, which was a blessing in disguise.

I spent the night with a friend in San Clemente, and the next morning when I woke up I realized the pier where a PSAA contest was just getting under way was only a few blocks away. Seeing my chance, I borrowed some trunks and a board, and got into a heat. I finished fifth in the event and earned just enough points to make it to Lowers. (Thanks, Pat.)

Just a few weeks into my senior year, I returned to California to compete at Lowers. Quiksilver was planning a short promotional video called *Kelly Slater: In Black and White,* something to let people know I was its new rider. The company needed to shoot some fresh footage and the perfect waves provided a golden opportunity. I signed my Quiksilver contract right on the beach and set my sights on winning the event.

I was staying with a guy named Richard Woolcott—who later started and now owns Volcom—in Newport Beach, a half an hour north of San Clemente. John Freeman worked for Quiksilver and was in charge of putting together the movie. He filmed everything I did, from my heats to sleeping on the floor, to eating cereal, while Richard interviewed me.

At the Body Glove Surfbout, I made sure not to lose. I advanced through seven rounds on the way to the final. I was up against my good friend, Chris Brown, which made it a close heat. I honestly would have been happy if either of us won, but fortunately for the sake of the video, I got the nod and a check worth $30,000.

Peter Townend commentated the event and said later, "Kelly was going so much faster than everybody else at Trestles, like he was in a Ferrari and everyone else was in a Ford. The thin, narrow boards he was working on with Al Merrick were making it happen. Kelly had more influence on surfboard design than anybody realizes. There were other guys beginning to ride in areas on the wave no one ever thought possible, but he was taking it to the extreme. In the old days, if you went outside the curl line it wasn't cool. Now, because of Kelly, that's the place you have to go if you want to score points."

We had some good footage from Trestles, but Richard convinced Quiksilver to hold out for more from the winter season in Hawaii. Considering how little I had accomplished so far on the North Shore, it was a gamble. I'd only have two weeks during Christmas vacation to spend on the Islands, and even if it were two months, there was no guarantee that I would perform well. While the rest of the surfing world was heading to Oahu and was getting used to the big waves, I was headed back home. Instead of establishing my place in the lineup at Pipeline, it was back to my school desk in Cocoa Beach.

YOU WON'T GO

If Mr. Ballantine's third-bell English class couldn't keep my interest, nothing could. He was my favorite teacher of all time (tied with my fourth grade teacher, Miss Stroman). He was one of those rare individuals who put his heart into his work and knew how to draw the best out of his students.

My classmates' biggest concerns were how to score a six-pack, a date for the party that weekend, or a passing grade on the

upcoming math test, and even though I was thinking about some of those things, I had a lot more to worry about.

I was eighteen years old and felt like the weight of the world was on my shoulders. Not only was I supporting my family and beginning a career but also having the added pressure to perform in Hawaii gave me a deadline for surfing big waves. I'd always learned at my own pace, but that was a luxury I no longer had. People were waiting for me to fail. As heavy as the expectations of others were, they were nothing compared to the pressure I put on myself.

Fortunately, Quiksilver sent me to Tavarua, Fiji, over Thanksgiving, mainly to gather footage for the movie but also to serve as a North Shore tune-up. It wasn't Hawaii, but the tiny Fijian island offered some heavy reef waves. Each day, the surf grew bigger, and the final day was the most intense surf I had ridden.

My last morning on the island, I was up early and amped to surf. I got tired of waiting for the whole crew to get ready for the boat ride out to the main spot, Cloudbreak. There was perfect six-foot surf at Restaurants, a smaller, cleaner wave within paddling distance of the island. I wasn't afraid of the ten- to twelve-foot surf out at Cloudbreak, but I couldn't see passing up some of the best surf I'd ever seen at Restaurants. I went to Cloudbreak that afternoon, but by then it was too overcast to shoot photos.

People love to gossip, and rumors quickly spread that I hadn't charged on the biggest day at Cloudbreak. Dan Merkel, a photographer I had admired growing up, went straight to Hawaii and told everyone I had chickened out. As word of this filtered back to Cocoa Beach, I couldn't wait to prove him and everyone else wrong. I hadn't charged in Tavarua, but I hadn't backed down either. I was confident in my abilities, and that was all I needed.

By the middle of December, school was out and I was headed toward my destiny. As usual, I spent the holidays with my friends in Hawaii instead of with my family. It had been years since my family had all been together for a holiday, so I didn't miss being in Florida.

A good friend from San Diego, Benji Weatherly, moved into a house directly in front of Pipe with his family, and it was the gathering spot for our generation. There was a trampoline in the yard overlooking the lineup, and everyone hung out there whenever we weren't surfing. When Pipe was breaking, we went out, took our wipeouts, went back to Benji's for a Band-Aid, and paddled back out. Before I knew it, it wasn't even Pipeline anymore. It was my backyard. How can it be scary when it's your backyard?

One of the local guys we surfed with was Jack Johnson. He lived on the beach at Pipe, and his family took me in as one of their own. He witnessed my transformation firsthand and remembers it well.

When asked about it, he says, "Before I knew Kelly, I remember him coming over and surfing at the sandbars. My friends and I were the up-and-coming kids from Hawaii, and we were all riding big surf. To make ourselves feel better, we'd be like, 'Aww, he rips, but he can't surf big waves. He's from the East Coast.' Around 1990, he submerged himself in our group and got to the level of all the crazy kids on the North Shore. We played this thing called 'You Won't Go,' where we'd convince each other to take off on ridiculous waves. Usually, we'd just do it on a wave that was questionable, but every once in a while it'd be a wave that was impossible. Pretty soon, he was taking off deeper than us. Within a couple years, he was taking waves nobody else wanted. We had another game called 'BDPC,' the Backdoor Paddle-out Contest. There's a perfect channel for paddling out next to Pipe, but at Backdoor you're charging right through the surf over a shallow reef. Nobody paddles out at Backdoor because it's so much easier to go around. We did it just for the challenge. Walking down the beach, somebody would say 'BDPC,' and it was on. There were different rules depending on the day. If it were just medium surf, you'd have to paddle out fins first. If it was only four-feet, you had to turn your board upside down. You could pull leashes and everything. Whoever got out first was the winner. That's how he got comfortable."

If anything went down around Pipe, we knew about it. We were learning about the spots, our equipment, and sharing our experiences. Every day, the whole crew—Rob Machado, Shane Dorian, Ross Williams, Kalani Robb, Taylor Knox, Pat O'Connell, Conan Hayes, the Malloy brothers, Timmy Curran, and a bunch of other guys—congregated at Benji's to shoot video with Rob's friend from high school, Taylor Steele. My brother Sean was around a little, but by this point Sean wasn't really focused on surfing too much. At night, the peanut gallery gathered around the television to see who had wimped out. If the video showed that someone took the easy way out of a difficult situation, he was heckled to no end. There was huge pressure among us to go for it, and we were constantly pushing the whole group to improve.

We all wanted to surf with power, but none of us had the muscle yet to back it up. Power was something that would come in time, so we approached waves with agility and finesse. To compensate, we rode boards with far less volume. They were narrower and thinner than what everyone else was riding. The boards allowed us to fit into more critical positions on the wave, and we pushed one another to get as radical as possible.

On stormy days, my friends and I had the lineup at Pipe to ourselves, but otherwise there was the crowd to contend with. Wanting to catch some set waves was one thing; having people let you was another. The only way to prove yourself as a surfer is through commitment, in this case dropping into a ten-foot wave with only a few feet of water between you and the reef—lunacy.

My plan for showing the crowd I was serious was to paddle out on my biggest board and take off deeper than anyone. The locals saw me paddling and went anyway, but my theory was that sooner or later they'd let me have some to myself. I must have gotten dropped in on fifty or sixty times. Each time, I got caught behind the wave and took a beating. But eventually it worked.

One day, while we were filming the Quiksilver video, I started catching my own waves and actually getting barreled. I wouldn't say I was attacking Pipe, but it was the first day people recognized that I could surf real waves. I had one real bad wipeout. The wind caught me as I was trying to drop in and went over with the lip of a good-size wave, but I discovered it wasn't the end of the world. I actually popped up in about three seconds and hadn't even hit the reef.

The two weeks flew by, and it was soon time to get back to school. I hadn't won any contests or been the best guy in the water, but I paddled out and gave it a go. It wasn't a feeling of accomplishment as much as one of anticipation; I knew that next season I'd return ready to compete with confidence. If I hadn't had the pressure to perform on the North Shore, I doubt my

learning curve would have been so steep. Who knows, I might still be trying to overcome my fear of big waves or actually, maybe that never ends.

Only a month after I got home from Hawaii, *In Black and White* premiered in front of much of the surfing world at the Surf Expo in Orlando, Florida. I hadn't been in many surf movies before that, and all of a sudden there was a movie entirely about me. I still didn't like being the center of attention, but I was starting to get used to it. Everyone seemed to like the movie, and it became Quiksilver's best-selling video ever.

In Black and White did a lot more for my career than I realized at the time. Up until then, a lot of people still hadn't seen me surf. I don't think I was doing anything revolutionary; I was basically taking moves I'd seen other guys do and pushing them further. Instead of doing a standard off-the-lip, I'd try to hit it and slide my tail around. When four-time world champion Mark Richards, the surfer with the most wins in history at the time, saw the video, he said, "I was struck with how good Kelly actually was. He was doing radical maneuvers. I thought, this guy's gonna wreak a fair bit of havoc if he can do that sort of stuff in a contest situation. Kelly was the classic combination—freakish free-surfing with a vision for bringing his act on the pro tour without toning it down because he's wearing a contest jersey. That, and he had the lethal competitive attitude of a great white shark."

CROSSING THE BRIDGE

While school kept me from winning many surf contests, it put me in the running for other, more superficial honors. During my senior year, I was voted Best Looking and Homecoming King of my school. I have no idea what it means to be Homecoming King, other than I got a little trophy and the right to dance with the Homecoming Queen. Since I wasn't a jock, it was surprising that I won. I was also nominated for Prom King, but you can't win them all.

In 1990, *People* magazine chose me as one of its "50 Most Beautiful People." The issue featured a wide range of individuals, from athletes to musicians to artists, so it was an honor to be recognized by such an American institution as *People*. I wish I had been part of the "50 Most Interesting People" or "50 Greatest Athletes," but the magazine didn't give me a choice.

For the photo shoot, a photographer from *People* came to Cocoa Beach, but I wasn't about to have my picture taken in front of anyone I knew. We drove down every street until we found an area of beach with nobody on it. I knew that millions of people would read the magazine, but they didn't need to see me pose.

The mainstream media can be dangerous. They don't understand our sport and have a way of making surfers look silly. *Seventeen* ran a mini bio on me and put more emphasis on my green eyes and the fact that I was an Aquarius rather than my surfing accomplishments. My friends at school weren't the most understanding when it came to that sort of thing. Their teasing gave me a complex, and I decided not to return any more calls from teen magazines. The girls at my school didn't think my fame was a big deal. They'd known me most of my life, so it wasn't like they started paying attention to me when I showed up in a magazine. I remember that a lot of the older guys around town started coming up to talk to me a lot more. They all had a story about the time they changed my diaper or baby-sat for me. I know we never had any male baby-sitters, but I was nice about it and gave them the benefit of the doubt.

A couple months before graduation, I was jumping on a trampoline at school. A friend of mine bet me six dollars I couldn't do a back flip off the trampoline and land on the floor. I accepted the challenge but landed awkwardly and banged my knee on the bas-

Cocoa Beach High School

Cocoa Beach   Florida

This certifies that

Robert Kelly Slater

having satisfactorily completed all requirements of law
and standards for high school graduation as prescribed
by the State Board of Education and the District School
Board is hereby awarded this

Diploma

by order of the Brevard County District School Board
Given at Cocoa Beach, in the State of Florida, this 7th day of June, 1991

Abraham S. Ainsworth   Kathy Carlson
Superintendent of Schools   Chairman, School Board
                    Leslie Patricia Vana
                    Principal

ketball court. I didn't get the six dollars,
and worse yet, I tore my meniscus, the car-
tilage beneath my kneecap. I was out of the
water for three weeks, but it should have been
longer. Definitely not worth the challenge.

Graduation was an event I wouldn't have missed for anything. A lot of people never make it through high school, especially around Cocoa Beach. It's easy to become shortsighted and
think you can surf forever, without preparing yourself for the
future. If you can't finish school, there probably aren't a lot of
things in life you *can* finish.

At Cocoa Beach High, there was a little bridge out front that
we had to walk across as we picked up our diplomas at graduation. Every day at lunch, people hung out on it, but in all my
years of high school I never walked over that bridge. It was a rite
of passage, and I wanted to wait until I graduated.

Out of 130 students, I ranked seventh in my class. I had a 3.4
GPA, but including my honors courses, it was a 4.0. Math was
my favorite subject. I still think about taking college courses, but
I don't know if I'll ever get a degree.

CALLED UP TO THE MAJORS

With my diploma in hand, I joined the 1991 ASP World Tour with one goal in mind—to finish in the Top 44 and qualify for the World Championship Tour. Judging from the results I had the year before, I'd gained strength and confidence at a quicker rate than most guys on tour. I felt I would be able to make it. It was the last year of the old trials system. In 1992, the ASP would switch to a two-tiered system that was made up of the World Qualifying Series and the World Championship Tour. Because of school, I started from scratch midway through the year, so it was like letting everyone else run halfway around the track before I took off.

I made a few quarterfinals along the way (one in Huntington and two in France), but also floundered in a couple events. In October 1991, I faced a difficult decision. There were two events in Brazil just prior to the Hawaiian Triple Crown. I could either go down to Brazil and secure some valuable ratings points to further my chances of qualifying for the World Tour, or I could go to Hawaii and compete in an event that offered no points, only the opportunity to get comfortable with competing in big surf. I had heard horror stories about homicidal drug dealers who roamed around the contests in Brazil, so it seemed like a scary and foreign place. The choice between facing big waves or a gun to my head wasn't an easy one, but I chose big waves.

The contest in Hawaii was the XCEL Pro at Sunset Beach. Sunset is a tricky spot that breaks a quarter of a mile out at sea, and it's easy to get caught out of position and smashed by a giant rogue peak. The surf was ten feet for the event, which doesn't sound too intimidating, except Hawaiians use the modest scale. In actuality, it was at least four times over my head, bigger than anything I'd surfed there.

In my first heat, I followed the lead of my friend Todd

Chesser because I really didn't know where to pick off waves in the vast lineup. That probably wasn't the smartest thing to do because Todd always liked to take chances. I had a lot of respect for him, especially in big surf. I took my share of beatings, but I also got a few good rides. We made it through a couple heats together, and then Todd lost out. I was coming up against guys whom I had watched surfing big waves since I was a kid—Mark Foo, Davey Miller, Tony Moniz, Mike Latronic, all of whom were mostly local Hawaiian guys—and I was beating them. The contest went on for a couple days, and the first day I was really just feeling my way around the lineup.

The next day, in my quarterfinals heat, something clicked. Looking back, it wasn't even huge Sunset. Today, I'd surf it without a leash. Back then it was kind of scary. I was riding a 7'2" and I'd never ridden a board that big in a contest. I took off on one wave and tried to get in the tube but got smashed. The wave knocked me underwater and all the fear I had built up about big waves was right there. I came up and my first thought was, "Wow, that wasn't bad at all." I still had more breath and hadn't even come close to drowning. It was a pretty good-size wave, and I expected it to be a lot scarier. It was the end of my heat, and I sat up on my board. Instead of paddling in, I just sat there with the biggest grin on my face. The lineup was so spread out that no one was within shouting distance of me, and I just started screaming, "Woo-hoo!" I said to myself. "I'm doing this. I'm f—king doing this!"

I didn't want people to think I had a fear of big surf in the first place, so I didn't verbalize it to anyone except my brother Sean. He was in Hawaii that winter and I confided in him what I had experienced at Sunset. I felt I could look at Sean after surfing a session when the waves were big and smile, and he'd know that I was saying, "Hey, I can surf big waves now."

The following week was the Hawaiian Triple Crown, which

is possibly more prestigious than the world title since it takes place exclusively in heavy surf. Because of their familiarity with the conditions, Hawaiians almost always win. I made a point of surfing all three events, but my focus was on Pipe as it sometimes determines the world title.

For the first event of the Triple Crown, the Wyland Pro at Haleiwa, the waves were massive and getting bigger all day. The waves at Haleiwa usually break from left to right according to the formation of the reef, but that day huge waves were peeling across in the opposite direction from way outside the normal takeoff spot. I was paddling for my life and witnessed some of the scariest wipeouts I've ever seen. The waves required riding a bigger board than I normally would because it gave me more speed while paddling. My brand-new 7'9" was totally foreign to me. Still, I advanced through a few heats, then lost in the third round. I was bummed not to make it to the final because the waves were about half the size of the previous days. They would have been a walk in the park.

Pipe had become my backyard, so I felt confident going in to my first Pipe Masters, which is the second event of the Triple Crown. The history, prestige, and drama make it the world's greatest surf contest, and to finally get to compete after so many years of watching it was a dream come true. Since competitions require surfers to catch waves in a limited amount of time, I took some chances that day and had some heavy wipeouts. I remember one in particular in which I hit the water so hard my head was ringing. When I came up, my board was broken in half, each of the halves was bent in half again, and one of my fins was smashed flat against the board. I swam in, dragging the remnants of my board behind me, and grabbed a backup from Sean. As we ran back down the beach, he said, "Man, don't ever do that again!"

A couple years earlier I wouldn't have considered attempting such a wave. But in the back of my mind, I could hear my friends saying, "You won't go." It seemed the judges, the media, and the thousands of spectators were saying the same thing, and there was no way I was going to back down. My childhood preparation of falling off surf swings and getting run over by cars had me ready for any sort of bodily abuse, and, believe it or not, once you actually do it, it's not as bad as it looks. Not that I looked forward to getting pounded, but the challenge of pulling through a difficult situation kept me going back for more.

In the quarterfinals, I was losing and in desperate need of a wave. A big, nasty one came through that nobody wanted, but it was my only chance. As I dropped in, it jacked up and tried to buck me off. I somehow managed to land at the bottom and sneak into the barrel without being decapitated by the lip. A few seconds later, the wave spit like a fire hose and sent me flying into the channel to safety. I wasn't thinking about it as I was doing it, but it was the gnarliest wave of my life. It was enough to get me into the semis, and when I saw it on video, I realized I was lucky to be alive. Tom Carroll later said it was one of the heaviest waves he'd seen ridden at Pipe.

I was close, just short of the final, finishing fifth in my first Pipe Masters. The final was so exciting that I didn't mind sitting on the beach watching, especially Tom Carroll, who got first place. He was so committed that he was doing things no one had ever seen at Pipeline—making unbelievably late takeoffs and cranking powerful turns on giant waves.

In the final contest at Sunset, I fell one heat short of the main event. I've never been much of a threat there. Luckily, I made it through the one heat I needed, and everything worked exactly as planned. I made it just far enough to finish forty-third in the year-end ASP ratings, ensuring me a seed for 1992.

My primary goal was accomplished, but I had one more mission before beginning my world title quest—the Australian Pro Junior. Every talented Australian surfer, such as Tom Carroll, Gary Elkerton, Barton Lynch, Mark Occhilupo, and Luke Egan, began his career with a win at the Pro Junior. It's an event no overseas surfer had ever been able to place first in. School had kept me from competing prior to 1992, and this would be my only chance. Ross Williams, Shane Dorian, and I flew over with hopes of putting an end to the Aussie dominance.

It was a tough contest, but I was on a roll and advanced through a couple close heats. The Australian surfers complained about the judging, claiming I was overscored, but the judges were all Australian. When the field came down to two finalists, Shane and I were the ones left standing. Either way an American would win. We thought about surfing the final switchfoot, just goofing around and having fun, but decided it would be disrespectful. Still, we wanted to celebrate and ended up riding our first waves switchfoot before getting serious. I heard that Terry Fitzgerald, the event sponsor, wanted to come out and strangle us. He was on the beach screaming, "What are those guys doing? They're making a fool of me!" We didn't intend it to be a slap in the face. It was a celebration, but they didn't think it was funny.

We didn't realize the significance at the time, but the event had been Australia's pride and joy for seventeen years. No American had won it before or since. With the exception of Tom Curren, Aussies had dominated pro surfing since its inception, but our crew was coming of age. The writing was on the wall, and they were grumbling Down Under.

After winning the Pro Junior, I was having dinner with an Australian friend of mine, Stuart "Stretch" Cooper, a rep for Quiksilver in Sydney. He owned two apartments and was talking about buying a third. I told him I was interested in some property as well, and we decided to go in together. After dinner, we walked down the street, saw an apartment, and decided to buy it. It remained unfurnished for a long time, but whenever I competed in Australia, I was surfing for furniture. Stuart would say, "All right, if you get through this heat, we get a sofa."

6

Rookie

THE ASSOCIATION OF SURFING PROFESSIONALS World Tour is like a yearlong pleasure cruise to some of the most beautiful spots on the planet. It's eight months of traveling to Australia, Africa, Europe, Japan, Brazil, and Hawaii. But as I prepared for my first full tour in the beginning of April 1992, I was overwhelmed with affection for my hometown. Having spent the last several years surfing either Sebastian or in front of my house when I was home, I made a point of going back to the Islander Hut for a farewell session.

Little remained of the scene. A sleazy bar occupied the building where my family spent its final days as a group. A boardwalk ran along the dunes where I once played, and I knew that the encroachment of condos would soon wipe away any trace of my childhood playground. Cocoa Beach as a whole wouldn't change, but surfing was about to take on a different meaning in my life.

I knew I was ready for the tour, but I didn't know if the tour was ready for me. Judging surfing, like figure skating or gymnastics, is subjective, but there had to be a happy medium. Obviously if someone goes all out and falls, a judge can't give him a high

score. If another guy is surfing conservatively but catching the biggest waves and not falling, he's usually going to win. But if a guy takes off on an average wave, reads the lines right, and gets radical, he should also have the potential for scoring a perfect ride. The brand of surfing my friends and I were doing was an extreme change from what was going on at the time, and we didn't know if the judges would like it—but it wasn't going to stop us from trying. At the time, most pros surfed differently when they were in heats than when they were just out for fun. In heats they were afraid to try anything new. Even though their style was smooth and powerful, it became boring to watch at times. My friends and I surfed contests the way we free-surfed—trying big moves in critical positions. The media dubbed us "the New School," building a distinction from the ranks of established pros.

Everyone knew we could do the fancy tricks, but the question was, "Did we stand a chance against the gods of the sport?" Tom Curren, Tom Carroll, Martin Potter, Gary Elkerton, and Mark Occhilupo were the big guns. If we were going to make a name for ourselves, we would have to take on these guys, our heroes, and win.

Most of my friends, who were already phenomenal surfers, were still getting their contest acts together on the Bud Tour, which took the place of the old PSAA. So I was traveling with Australians— Shane Herring, Shane Powell, and Todd Prestage. At the time, there weren't many Americans on the World Tour. There were a few older Californians, but I didn't know them very well. And even though Todd Holland lived right down the street from me in Cocoa Beach, we had remained on shaky terms since the incident at the 1986 U.S. team trials involving my brother. Besides, he listened to country music, so I couldn't travel with him.

The changing of the guard transcended nationality. The young Australians were coming to America to compete on the Bud Tour and forming bonds with the surfers. We were all pushing one another, and the national lines were blurred by the camaraderie of a new generation. I saw Shane Powell beat Tom Curren in France and I was stoked. To see a young guy doing airs and beating Curren was great, because it meant a different type of surfing was moving in.

Even though I held no grudges against surfers from other countries, I felt a bit of responsibility to regain the world title for America. Nationalism was a far bigger deal in the early 1980s, when guys would make brash statements and have to back them up. The way the magazines portrayed it back then, Tom Curren represented America against the rest of the world. We all took pride in his achievements. He was *our* world champion. I was barely twenty years old and only eight months out of high school, and yet to make my mark, but the media was already making me out to be the next symbol of American surfing.

Most believed it would happen eventually but didn't think I was ready to go all the way, especially when it came to Hawaii. In my mind, there was no reason I couldn't win straight off. I had beaten some of the top guys, and the world title was nothing more than stringing together a bunch of good heats. I gave myself a much better chance than other people did.

DEBUTING DOWN UNDER

The ASP World Championship Tour consists of forty-eight surfers competing in an average of ten events around the world. Forty-four of those competitors qualified the previous year by finishing either in the Top 28 of the WCT or the Top 16 of the World Qualifying Series, which is a string of smaller events that are open to anyone. The other four are wild cards chosen by the event sponsor. Points are awarded at each event, and the season starts in March and finishes up in Hawaii sometime in December. Consistency, more than anything, is a trait shared by all world champions. One must be able to adapt to any conditions at any time, because the waves from day to day and country to country vary greatly.

The quest began at the legendary Easter Contest at Bells Beach, in southern Australia. It's the longest running professional event in the world, and one that was usually won by Australians. Since it started in 1973, only Americans Jeff Hakman and Tom Curren had broken the local stronghold. I had dreams of standing atop the podium, ringing the coveted bell that was the winner's trophy. Bells is a cold, gray place, and I was in for a rude awakening.

I may have been the valedictorian of "the New School," but my style of surfing didn't seem to fit on Bells's long, slow-moving rights. I had trouble from the beginning. In my very first heat, I was up against Tom Curren and Todd Holland. The waves were barely over knee-high, and the high tide meant that not many waves would even break. Todd was an intense competitor. He wanted to win; it didn't matter whether it was me or the next guy.

He got off to a quick start in the heat, and Tom an even quicker one. Three-man heats don't use the priority buoy, so there is a lot of hassling for waves. The guy who is farthest back on the breaking wave has the right of way. Todd was so focused on making sure he beat me that he was willing to paddle all the way back to Florida, just to keep me from getting the inside position. Every time I was sitting out the farthest, he paddled right around me. I was intimidated, starved for waves, and finished last in the heat. Former top pro surfer Derek Hynd, from Australia, covered all the contests for *Surfer* magazine, and of my opening performance, he wrote, "Appearing gun-shy of his sturdy Florida rival, Slater all but lay down with legs in the air." He was basically right. I thought, "Oh well, next heat."

That one didn't go much better. I finished thirtieth out of forty-eight surfers in my first event. I looked at the ratings and saw that I was thirtieth in the world. With so much pressure to start strong, someone else in my position might have been heartbroken, but I wasn't. It was thirteen places higher than I had finished the previous year, so I was stoked. After a miserable performance, I was doing better in the ratings than I'd ever done. If I got a decent result in the next contest, I'd move up.

From Bells, which is way out in the country, our next stop was the Coke Classic at North Narrabeen in Sydney. Even though it was only a few hundred miles from Bells, it was worlds away. Bells is considered a grassroots contest that's put on by surfers, for surfers, so it centers only on surfing. Most other events were like circuses, with bikini contests and other events going on at the same time. I was shocked by the difference. The waves in Sydney were better suited to my surfing, and I made the final against Shane Herring. He won, but the result lifted me to fourth in the ratings. One good contest, and I was number four in the world.

BREAK ON THROUGH

I had won a handful of heats in the first few events, but I didn't feel like I hit my stride until I went up against Martin Potter in the fourth contest at Reunion Island, a tiny French territory off Madagascar with a great left that breaks over a shallow reef. After falling a few times to start the heat, I finally put it together and finished strong. Every one of my turns felt perfectly timed and executed. In the next round, the quarterfinals against an Australian named Mike Rommelse, I scored a total of 28.5 out of 30 possible points and ran away with the heat. I felt like I finally had showed my potential, but no one was there to see it. It was raining so hard that no one except the judges showed up.

My semifinal taught me a valuable lesson about pacing myself. After two such decisive victories, I was tired and fell on wave after wave against Richard Marsh. Richard, another young surfer from Australia, went on to win the event. I realized I needed to think of a contest as a long-distance run. To beat somebody, I didn't have to demoralize him, just outscore him by a tenth of a point and save something for the next round. Instead, I used up all my artillery early, something I see all the time on tour. It was a frustrating loss, because after such a great heat, I thought I was going to win that contest.

There were three competitions in France, so that gave me several chances to try to put together a complete event. I had been competing in Europe for a few seasons, so I knew the breaks pretty well. In late summer and early fall, the west coast of France

ASSOCIATION of SURFING PROFESSIONALS
1992 "WCT" Ratings After Event #5 the LACANAU PRO-FRANCE

1992 Rat No#	UPDATED 23-Aug-92 Name	From	1992 Total Pts	1992 "WCT"Tour $us	Career Money $US	'91 Rat No#	1992 Seed Pts	Evt 1 Plc	Evt 2 Plc	Evt 3 Plc	Evt 4 Plc	Evt 5 Plc	Evt 6 Plc	Evt 7 Plc	Evt 8 Plc	Evt 9 Plc	Evt 10 Plc	Evt 11 Plc	No# Evts Surfed
1	Slater,Kelly	USA	3550	$25,480	$56,530	43	3820	30	2	17	3	2							5
2	Hardman,Damien	Aus	3545	$22,600	$374,160	1	4545	3	3	9	5	5							5
3	Herring,Shane	Aus	3500	$33,000	$61,870	36	3805	9	1	9	9	9							5
4	Macaulay,Dave	Aus	3425	$18,100	$239,125	12	3887	5	3	5	9	5							5
5	Bain,Rob	Aus	3090	$12,500	$229,672	9	3590	9	9	5	9	3							5
6	Elkerton,Gary	Aus	2980	$15,000	$281,515	11	3455	3	9	2	33	17							5
7	Garcia,Sunny	Haw	2970	$24,500	$187,595	6	3553	9		1	2	5							4
8	Lynch,Barton	Aus	2890	$11,700	$371,705	5	3500	17	9	5	3	17							5
9	Marsh,Richard	Aus	2825	$21,600	$148,675	20	3210	9	18	33	1	9							5
10	Collins,Richie	USA	2760	$21,400	$191,345	10	3248	1	33	9	9	17							5
11	Ray,Tony	Aus	2630	$21,400	$96,320	40	2915	33	9	33	17	1							5
12	Hoy,Matt	Aus	2520	$10,200	$71,970	27	2870	20	9	9	9	17							5
13	Padaratz,Flavio	Brz	2515	$10,800	$109,725	17	2915	27	5	17	17	9							5
14	Curren,Tom	USA	2405	$10,900	$447,355	25	2765	5	46	3	17	9							5
15	Gouveia,Fabio	Brz	2365	$12,420	$128,083	13	2815	21	5	33	33	5							5
16	Jaquias,Kaipo	Haw	2360	$9,800	$47,480	38	2655	26	9	17	17	9							5
17	Andino,Dino	USA	2305	$9,500	$36,625	39	2595	5	24	17	17	17							5
18	Law,Simon	Aus	2270	$10,100	$118,550	21	2650	9	29	9	5	33							5
19	Powell,Shane	Aus	2250	$9,800	$48,265	33	2570		31	3	17	3							4
20	Potter,Martin	GB	2215	$11,900	$365,275	7	2770	2	34		5	17							4
20	Wilson,Graham	Aus	2215	$10,200	$141,190	29	2555	31	5	17	33	17							5
22	Clarke-Jones,Ross	Aus	2150	$9,500	$100,925	37	2450	5	41	17	9	17							5
23	Egan,Luke	Aus	2030	$8,800	$116,215	19	2420	28	17	17	9	33							5
24	Anderson,Greg	Aus	1945	$8,400	$129,055	26	2300	19	22	33	17	17							5
25	Rommelse,Mike	Aus	1940	$9,200	$65,675	24	2305	48	27	9	17	9							5
26	Shimooka,John	Haw	1935	$8,600	$81,585	42	2210	9	20	33	33	17							5
27	David,Vetea	Tah	1905	$9,100	$107,505	22	2280	9	36	33	5	33							5
28	Winton,Glen	Aus	1810	$8,600	$234,865	23	2180	44	21	17	9	33							5
29	Page,Rob	Aus	1790	$8,800	$118,295	34	2105	41	9	33	17	33							5
30	Wood,Nicky	Aus	1775	$8,800	$185,645	18	2170	23	44	9	33	9							5
31	Carroll,Tom	Aus	1730	$7,800	$440,029	3	2460	9	9		33	33							4
32	Ellis,Bryce	Aus	1725	$8,600	$163,335	16	2138	39	30	9	33	17							5
33	Byles,Jeremy	Aus	1710	$8,200	$34,270	41	1990	47	19	17	33	17							5
34	Barry,Michael	Aus	1690	$8,400	$46,465	44	1955	34	25	33	33	9							5
35	Thomas,Marty	Haw	1610	$8,700	$148,665	14	2048	32	39	5	33	33							5
36	Holland,Todd	USA	1570	$8,000	$164,950	8	2098	22	45	33	17	17							5
37	Hedemann,Hans	Haw	1485	$8,000	$205,965	35	1795	18	32	33	33	33							5
38	Bedford-Brown,Stuart	Aus	1465	$7,800	$119,510	28	1810	40	40	17	17	33							5
39	Kerr,Rod	Aus	1430	$7,600	$67,880	31	1760	35	35	17	33	33							5
40	Ho,Derek	Haw	1370	$7,800	$268,810	4	2040	29	43	33	17	33							5
41	Horan,Cheyne	Aus	1340	$7,800	$331,255	30	1675	42	47	33	17	17							5
42	Sainsbury,Mark	Aus	1200	$6,400	$75,325	45	1460	36	23	33	33								4
43	Thorson,Mitch	Aus	1075	$6,400	$142,505	32	1400	43	48	17		17							4
44	Booth,Jeff	USA	1040	$4,600	$125,325	15	1465			17	17	33							3
45	Munro,Shaun	Aus	1020	$5,000	$40,020	46	1275	25	37			17							3
46	Spooner,Jake	Aus	915	$4,000	$15,625	51	1145		5										1
47	Gerlach,Brad	USA	765	$3,800	$218,795	2	1625	24	28										2
48	Strong,Justin	SAfr	720	$4,200	$24,745		720			33	33	33							3
49	Tostee,Pierre	SAfr	640	$3,000	$26,505		640			17	33								2
50	Parsons,Mike	USA	465	$2,200	$151,055	103	514		26										1
51	Branson,Matt	Aus	405	$3,200	$54,165	47	655	45	38										2
52	Jenkins,Joey	USA	400	$1,600	$1,600		400				17								1
52	Robin,Frederic(am)	Reun	400	$0	$0		400				17								1
52	Rahme,Noel	SAfr	400	$1,600	$12,260		400		17										1

gets some of the world's best surf. Perfect beach breaks will sometimes work for weeks on end. But it *is* the Atlantic, and flat spells can last for just as long. That year, we had a little of each.

In the first event of the French leg, the Lacanau Pro, I made the final against Tony Ray, an unheralded Australian. I surfed really well the whole contest and thought, "Wow, I've beaten five tough opponents to get here. I can win this final for sure." Tony smoked me. On waves that looked like crap, he found barrels and turned them into eights. The tide was really low and most waves closed out, but he had no trouble comboing me, leaving me in need of not just one, but two good waves to retake the lead. When that happens, you've pretty much had your butt kicked.

When I walked up the beach, there was Derek Hynd, shaking his head. He said, "So how long's it gonna be?" I didn't know what he was talking about and gave him a puzzled look. "Till you win one of these things," he said. I was wondering the same, but I wasn't too bummed. After making, and losing, two finals that season, I realized how much I needed to work on maintaining my focus. By finishing near the top in three of the first five events, I moved into first place in the ratings.

The next week in Hossegor I made the final again and my opponent was Gary Elkerton. He had come close to winning a couple world titles and wasn't too happy to see a bunch of new kids nosing around at his party. He was a big guy who felt that surfing should be based on power and have weight divisions like boxing, so he had every intention of squashing little ol' me like a Bordeaux grape.

Given our differences in size (Gary had about forty pounds on me) and method (I surfed with finesse; he was all about power), the double-overhead storm surf clearly favored Elkerton. The wind was blowing, it was cold, and you couldn't hear the announcers from the water. Vetea David, a friend of mine from Tahiti, who was also on tour, was there with his mother. She was a remarkably kind three-hundred-pound woman who wrapped a towel around me to keep me warm. I had a way of gravitating toward close families like the Davids whenever I was away from home, and I still do. Contests can be stressful, and since my family was back in Florida, having this kind of support made me feel comfortable. She massaged my feet and back, sheltered me from the elements, and told me over and over, "You're gonna win this contest, I just feel it." (She unfortunately passed away in an auto accident in Tahiti in 2001.)

Seven minutes before the start of the final, I began to paddle out, because the surf was so big it took me a long time, about thirteen minutes. They held the start of the heat for me until I could get out there, and Elkerton was fuming. He had paddled out early, was ready, and had to wait for me in the lineup. It threw off his momentum, and he was making a big fuss in the water. He later said, "It was a mission to get out. I was already in position by the time Kelly hit the water, and it was really hard to stay in the good spot. I had to let five perfect waves go by. I was shocked that they held up the final for him. In all my years of competition, I've never seen a surfer get that kind of treatment. If you didn't leave the beach on time, you were out!"

I got only two good waves in the final and came in thinking, "Aw God, I got so close again. Too bad I didn't win that one." The French spectators were coming up to me, patting me on the back, saying, "Yeah, good job." But they're just fans, and they have no idea whether I won or not. As I got closer to the competitors' area, I saw that everyone was cheering for me.

Even though I didn't have a strong third wave, my other two were longer, bigger, and packed with maneuvers, so they were enough to beat Elkerton. He protested the delayed start, and I felt so bad for him that I would have had no problem redoing the final. The contest directors told him too bad, so on August 31, 1992, I had won my first World Tour event. It seemed like it had taken forever. Before I stepped onstage to receive my trophy and check for $14,000, I called my mom back in Cocoa Beach. It became a tradition that every time I won, she was the first person I called, even if it meant the awards presentation would have to wait.

There's a bar in Hossegor called Rock Food where everyone goes after the contest, and the place can get out of control. Danny Kwock from Quiksilver showed up later in the night with Bob

McKnight, the company's CEO. By then, my friends and I had our shirts off, and beers were being sprayed everywhere. I was letting off a bit of steam, and I ran up and head-butted Danny. They were completely sober, so they just looked at me like, "Whoa, what happened to our guy?"

I was on a roll and wanted to distance myself from the pack the next week in Biarritz, but it was not to be. The waves were too small—even by Florida standards—to hold the quarterfinals. France is a great place, but after three weeks you've usually had more than enough baguettes and red wine to last an entire year. With no guarantee of surf, it was too much trouble to change everybody's travel reservations to wait around for some swell. It sounds like a poor excuse for pro athletes, but this isn't tennis or golf. We were surfing for a few thousand dollars, not a few million. The contest was canceled, and each quarterfinalist received fifth place points. Of course, the waves came up the next day.

By October of 1992, I definitely had something to lose. The idea of leading in the world ratings had time to sink in, and the pressure hit. Magazines were asking, "Can the young guy do it?" For the first time, I felt I would be letting people down if I failed to win the world title. I was on top, and I went from playing offense to playing defense. I had something to protect. With four events remaining, all I had to do was not screw up to win it. It's difficult to surf freely when you're thinking like that.

SOMETHING TO LOSE

The next two contests were held in Japan. Japanese people are absolutely crazy about the sport. Because of import taxes, boards cost as much as $1,800, four times what one would pay in the United States for the same thing. Still, the Japanese surfers all want boards by the best shapers. I've done promos there where department stores paid me ridiculous sums of money for an hour of signing autographs. It's an exclusive gathering, where they only allow fifty of their best customers in the door. The fans there are the most appreciative and most unusually dressed in the world. It's an ongoing contest to see who can wear the highest heels to the beach. I have a friend who works for a Japanese surf magazine who collects pictures of them and then sends to me.

The waves, as usual for Japanese events, were pretty bad, but I surfed one of the best heats of my life in the quarterfinals of the Marui Pro at Hebara Beach. Unfortunately, I made another rookie mistake. My opponent was Sunny Garcia, one of the Hawaiians I met way back at the 1984 U.S. Championships. At one point during our heat, Sunny had wave priority, which he obtained by paddling around the priority buoy after the last exchange of waves. He had his choice of the next good wave to come through, and I couldn't stand in his way. He started paddling for a wave, and I took a few strokes toward it to make sure he caught it. I didn't drop in on him, but it didn't matter. He stood up and pointed at me like crazy to get the judges' attention. I was called for a paddling interference, meaning I'd only be scored on two rides rather than three. Each of my waves scored in the nine-point range, so I almost beat him anyway. Sunny thought I had something going on with the judges for them to give me such big scores.

It was a crucial time in the season, and to lose on such an unfair call was tough. I came in punching my board over a silly mistake. Rules are rules, so the ASP Rulebook became my bible. I studied it from cover to cover. The rule was subsequently changed so that a rider has to actually interfere with the other surfer before being penalized.

The next event, the Miyazaki Pro, again had small surf. I made the final against Martin Potter. I was within range of catching him toward the end of the heat but couldn't find a wave, giving Pottz his last win on tour. Still, finishing second was almost enough to clinch the world title. All I had to do was show up in Brazil for the next to last event and wait for the other guys to lose. The title was more or less in the bag.

THE BOY KING

It was my first time in Brazil, and since I knew nothing about the place, I was scared to leave my hotel room. Brazilians are passionate about sports, be it surfing, soccer, or jujitsu, and they are extremely supportive of the pros who come to town. Because of this, especially in Rio, I got my first glimpse of the price of fame. A couple years earlier I could have walked up the beach without being recognized, but now I had to be escorted to and from my heats by eight bodyguards. Under these circumstances, surfing became more stressful—even frightening.

Aside from the overwhelming crowds, I wiped out on a wave in the shore break and broke my favorite board during my first heat—the one I had ridden for much of the year, including my win in France. Sunny Garcia happened to be watching the heat and quickly paddled one of his boards to me. It was a boat compared to what I had been riding, and I lost the heat, which wasn't too bad. Round one really doesn't matter, except that the winners get to leapfrog into round three.

Ironically, Sunny was the last contender who could catch me in the ASP ratings for the year, and he had a heat just before mine in the fourth round against Australian Matt Hoy. I tried not to think about the circumstances, but just before my heat with Tom Carroll, the commentators announced that Sunny had lost. It would have been nice to surf my way to the title instead of waiting for someone to hand it to me, but just like that, I was the new world champion. No matter what happened in the rest of the contest, or at the year's final event, the Pipe Masters, Sunny and the rest of my competitors could not overtake my lead.

So much of my life was geared toward this moment, that when it came, I didn't know how to react. At age twenty, I was the youngest men's champ in history. I wanted to celebrate, but I felt I was too young to have already reached the pinnacle of the sport. Tom gave me a hug and congratulated me, but it still didn't seem real. I couldn't believe I won the world title ahead of my heroes—Tom Carroll, Tom Curren, and Martin Potter.

It seemed unreal, but after competing against them, I realized that they had their own faults. I thought Curren rode too many wacky boards and Carroll's boards were too big. Potter was still making silly mistakes that were costing him heats, and Elkerton toned his surfing down to try to fit the criteria. In fact, I was quoted in several major magazines saying as much. I wasn't being cocky; I just hated to see those guys make mistakes and couldn't see keeping it to myself.

Australian Mark Occhilupo was also in a really bad place in 1992; his erratic behavior was turning a lot of his friends into enemies. Back in 1984, Mark had burst on the scene at seventeen years old. He surged to the top of the World Tour ratings, but because he wasn't mentally prepared for success at that age, and the responsibility and stress that came with it, he burned out on traveling and competition. Without proper guidance at a young age, it's difficult for people to develop their full potential. At the Lacanau Pro in 1992, I was carrying my pool cue down the street to meet some friends to play a game. Occy tried to run over me on his bicycle, then started yelling at me. He was in a karate stance saying, "You got a karate stick, huh? You wanna go? I'll go ya right now." He hadn't slept in a week and was going off the deep end. He buried all his boards in the sand and the beach-cleaning tractor ran over them. It got so bad he was asking directions to Australia so he could jump in the water and swim home. He all but quit surfing shortly thereafter, and it would be a few years before anyone in the world of surfing heard from him again.

There are so many outside influences on the tour, where young guys are thrust into the role of rock stars with no preparation. Everyone wants you to think they're your friends. People are handing you free drinks in bars and girls are falling all over you. If you don't have a good foundation, it's easy to get lost. My friend Shane Herring was leading the tour for a good part of 1992. He had a rough upbringing and couldn't handle the freedom of being on tour. Over the course of the year, he fell apart and his career on the World Tour was pretty much over.

VALIDATION

It was strange to think that I had won the world title, and the biggest event of the year, the Pipe Masters, was still to come. The ratings weren't important, but I desperately wanted to validate my achievement with a good showing. I knew what it would take to finish the job. My ability was there; I just had to stay focused and catch waves. If I didn't, people would hold it over my head. And even worse, I would let myself down.

The distractions began in my first heat of the Pipe Masters, when Hawaiian Liam MacNamara and Californian Jeff Booth got into a fight. Liam is an aggressive Pipe local who tries to catch every wave in a heat. He paddled up Jeff's back to get a wave and speared him with the nose of his board. Jeff turned around and started punching Liam in the head, but Liam was wearing a helmet for protection from the reef. As it turned out, the helmet protected him from Jeff. They were screaming back and forth, and I yelled, "Why don't you guys just shut up." Liam said, "What, do you want some too?" It was comic relief. Jeff only needed a two-point ride to advance and finish the season in the Top 16, but he was too caught up in Liam's aggressive tactics. They almost squared off again on the beach. The lifeguards, who acted as water patrol for the event, knew Liam's reputation as a hassler and after the heat claimed not to have seen anything. I won the heat and advanced with Liam.

It wasn't classic Pipe, the waves were not perfect by any means, but it was pretty good in size. Sunny Garcia dominated the four-man final from the start. I was fighting for second with Liam and Australian Barton Lynch. About halfway into it, Sunny took a bad wipeout and was rushed off to the hospital. Sunny had been hurt three times that day, and was still leading in the final minutes. By then I wasn't worried about proving anything. Making the final was enough. I had convinced myself I could surf in big waves and wasn't worried about what others were thinking. It seemed it was his contest to win, and I was content to let it be.

But I could only control myself, and Liam was determined to win. He said, "Let's make sure an Australian doesn't win, and we bring this thing back to Hawaii." I suggested we let Sunny win, but Liam wanted no part of that, because he thought he was ahead.

I wasn't about to roll over for Liam, and with three minutes to go, I grabbed a crummy little wave and got the three points I needed to win my first Pipe Masters.

Even though all my drive and determination went into preparing for Pipeline, I honestly never thought I would win an event in Hawaii. I was comfortable at Pipe, but winning was a privilege reserved for experienced guys like Dane Kealoha, Shaun Tomson, and Tom Carroll. To say it was overwhelming is an understatement. It was more of a dream than reality.

At the ASP banquet the following night, I dedicated my world title to Mark Sainsbury, a friend from Australia who died a few months earlier of a brain aneurysm while surfing. He was only twenty-six years old. Mark won the 1986 World Contest in England and was a top-ranked pro after that. It's heartbreaking to lose someone whom you've known and competed against for years, especially at such a young age.

On a lighter note, I had made a promise earlier in the year to sing "the Star-Spangled Banner" if I found myself in that position. I love it when the national anthem is played as athletes receive their Olympic medals, but that sort of thing doesn't happen in a small-time sport like surfing. True to my word, I asked the crowd to stand up and join me. It was embarrassing, but a lot of people sang along.

I went home to Cocoa Beach, and the first thing I did was surf with Sean. We had been on different schedules since he turned pro. By the time I started competing on the World Tour, Sean had already settled on surfing the domestic tour. We'd meet up every now and then but were nowhere near as close as we had been as kids. We were sitting in the water at Thirteenth Street after I won the world title, and he looked over and splashed me. He said, "You won it. You're the world champion, you little f—ker. I can't believe you." He has a funny way of expressing his emotions, so for him that was like giving me a hug and saying congratulations.

Being so focused on competition, I didn't have time to think about what winning a world title would mean until it happened. I wasn't able to enjoy the ride, so to speak. It was difficult to feel the enjoyment of meeting people and seeing new places. I felt like a robot, constantly thinking about how to improve my ratings. Spending time with my friends was great, but my mind never stopped devising ways to win. Plenty of other guys in the Top 5 could have won, but my focus put me over the top.

I had fantasized that winning a world title would keep me from ever having to face life's problems. My unfulfilled side told me that winning made me a better person, and I needed that title for affirmation. Deep down, it didn't change me or make me any happier. In fact, it can sometimes deepen the lows you feel when things get out of hand in life. The only thing I had now was my name on a plaque.

Even getting my face on a box of Wheaties, the mark of any successful athlete, was beyond my reach. The guys at *Eastern Surf* magazine in Florida printed the address to General Mills so readers would send their pleas to put me on the box. I didn't know it at the time, but Bryan, my manager, was also in contact with the company. They told him, "We only feature genuine athletes on our boxes." To them, I was just a beach bum.

7

Things Fall Apart

ONE SUNNY SEPTEMBER MORNING in 1992 on a
beach somewhere in southern California, I woke up in my van,
stepped out onto the beach, and went surfing. After meeting a
pretty lifeguard and teaching her how to surf, the day got ugly. A
gang of heavy locals, who called themselves "the Shooters,"
started hassling me for surfing at what they considered to be their
spot, and their leader challenged me to a surf-off. I wasn't backing down, but it turned out to be a trap. The Shooters had run
barbed wire across the lineup, and I ran into it and nearly
drowned. Fortunately, David Hasselhoff happened to be cruising
past in his lifeguard jeep and came to my rescue. "Stay still," he
commanded. "Don't move. I got you!"

Okay, it wasn't *me* he saved, but Jimmy Slade, my television
character on *Baywatch*. It was my acting debut, an episode titled
"Tequila Bay." Being on the show was something I did against

my better judgment. I was naive to the bigger picture, but my manager, Bryan, and my mom thought it would be a great boost for my career. It happened so quickly that I didn't have time to stop it.

BAYWATCH

When I was in first grade, Steve Martin was my hero, and I wanted to be an actor. After that my aspirations for TV and movies took a backseat to surfing. I was in a couple plays in school, but I always forgot my lines.

In the beginning of 1992, Bryan said he was trying to get me on a TV show, and I brushed it off with a "Yeah, yeah. Sure." If it happened, I figured I could turn it down at that time.

Soon after, I was called in to do a reading for a television show called *Baywatch*. I didn't know much about the show, except that people watched it for the slow-motion shots of girls with big boobs running down the beach in tiny bathing suits. I had heard people making fun of it, but I'd honestly never seen it. I read lines for a character named Jimmy Slade. Jimmy was a surfer who lived in the back of his van and had dreams of turning pro. I did a horrible job, partly on purpose but also because I was a little nervous. When I finished, they said, "Okay, great. You got the job." I was thinking, "What kind of show is this?" There must have been people who could have read it a lot better than I did. I later found out that they created the part just for me. Next thing I knew, I was Jimmy Slade, with a contract for two seasons on the show.

A few months later in April, after the opening leg of the 1992 ASP World Championship Tour in Australia, the producers wanted me to come back for a photo shoot. I didn't want to go, and I really tried to miss my flight. I called Bryan, who was in California, from my condo and kept him on the phone as long as I could, asking, "Do I really have to go?" To Bryan, who didn't surf and knew very little about the culture of the sport, the show made perfect sense. As far as he was concerned, it was exposure outside of surfing, which was what he felt I needed. I could tell I would get a lot of shit from other surfers when they saw how silly the show was, and I wanted to get out of it early. Our phone conversation was tense. He thought I was too young to make smart business decisions and convinced me to give *Baywatch* a try.

I was with Bruce Raymond, the managing director for Quiksilver, and he called the airlines to ask them to hold the flight. They did, but I barely made it. The shoot was the next morning, and it went all day. I was introduced to cast members Dave Charvet, Pamela Anderson, and Nicole Eggert—the other youngsters on the show. Bryan met me there and when he saw Pamela, he pointed her out and warned me that she was bad news. He said I should stay away from her. I already had a girlfriend and wasn't interested, plus Pam was going out with Dave Charvet anyway.

We started taping in April 1992, and the producers more or less handed me a script and yelled, "Action." Everyone else there had some acting experience except me. I felt like a deer in the headlights, but I did my best. Luckily, the scenes weren't too complex.

There were all sorts of silly shots, like dreamy love scenes with Nicole Eggert and me. Nicole played the part of Summer, my character's girlfriend, so in one episode we had to swim in a pool, hold hands, and fondle each other. Since my character was a player, in another episode, I had to kiss her and another girl in a matter of minutes. The other girl was trying to get Jimmy Slade a sponsorship deal so he could surf more contests and get free clothes, so he kissed her even though Nicole's character was supposed to be his girlfriend. He wasn't faithful to her, because he was blinded by his dreams of turning pro. Soon I had all the kissing and fondling I could take. I really wanted to get off the show.

On the set, I became friends with Pamela and a few other actors, but I didn't hang out with the cast when I wasn't working. Being a celebrity wasn't one of my goals, and it was difficult to avoid the publicity that went with the show. My anxiety about being a part of such a silly program kept me from feeling like one of the gang, so whenever we were shooting on the beach I met guys who were surfing nearby and invited them over for a free lunch.

It was obvious to me that *Baywatch* was cheesy from the moment I set foot on the set, but I had no idea it would send shock waves through the surfing community. As far as many of my fellow surfers were concerned, I was selling out the sport. My role was an easy way for people to take a shot at me, and I found myself ducking for cover.

In January 1993, my portrait ran on the cover of *Surfer* magazine next to the headline "The 'Baywatch' Kid Pulls It Off." The magazine was complimentary of my surfing and congratulatory of my being the world champion but wrote several less than flattering references to my other job. Tony Hawk's older brother Steve was the editor of *Surfer* at the time, and I was a little upset that he let the article run that way.

I spent the whole time looking for an excuse to get off the show. My friends knew that *Baywatch* was a sore spot for me, so they didn't bother joking about it. When they realized how much more attention I was getting from girls for being on television, they didn't think it was so bad. From time to time other surfers would poke fun by paddling up to me in the water and saying, "Hey, Jimmy Slade." My friends would calm me down and say, "Aw, forget that guy."

I'VE FALLEN AND I CAN'T GET UP

I had been dating a girl named Bree Pontorno for about a year, and her parents were pressuring us to get married. We had some relationship issues that I thought still needed to be ironed out, but I wasn't prepared to lose her. I thought getting engaged was the answer, so I bought Bree the four-karat diamond ring she wanted and took her on a trip to Barbados in March 1993 to ask her to marry me. She was seventeen, and I had just turned twenty-one a month earlier. My heart wasn't into the idea of settling down at that age, but I cared about Bree and didn't want to let her down. It was a volatile situation that was getting out of control.

She was pushing me to set a date, and it seemed as if the marriage was more important to her than I was. She wanted to buy a house on the Intercoastal Waterway in Fort Lauderdale so that we could put down roots in South Florida, but things were moving too quickly for me. With so much time spent traveling, I wasn't ready to commit to another house payment. I was still paying for my house in Cocoa Beach.

On the surface, it looked like everything in my life was coming together, but in reality it was all falling apart. The façade of a

world title being the cure for all my troubles quickly vanished. As the 1993 ASP tour got under way in April at Bells, my frustrations due to *Baywatch* and my engagement were eating away at my concentration. I was in danger of succumbing to my own set of pressures. When I'm surfing at my potential, I feel like I can score a perfect ten-point ride at any time. But I've never felt comfortable at Bells and I was up against Barton Lynch, who had beaten me several times. I lost to him in the quarterfinals and started the tour with a fifth place finish.

A few days later at the next event, the Coke Classic in Sydney, my old knee injury from the trampoline debacle in high school was giving me fits. It hadn't bothered me for a while, but those injuries don't just go away. I lost my first heat and had to surf in round two (the losers' round, since winners skipped ahead to round three) against Isaac Kaneshiro, an unassuming dark horse from Hawaii who had beaten me in the U.S. Championships in 1989. Each time I finished a crummy wave, I turned around to see him riding one that was twice as big with more opportunities for maneuvers. I still managed to keep up with him, and it came down to the last minute, but Isaac picked off the winning wave.

I was so discouraged coming out of that heat. It was the first time I placed thirty-third in my career, which is last place on the World Championship Tour. (Now most surfers refer to it as "dirty turd" not thirty-third.) My life was based around competition, so it was hard to take that loss. In addition to my personal problems, I was now worried about dropping in the ratings.

As I came out of the water after losing to Isaac, I head-butted my board out of frustration. A sequence of it ran in *Tracks,* an Australian surf magazine. There is a phenomenon in Australia known as "the Tall Poppy Syndrome," a tendency to attack and "cut down" visibly successful people. The term originated from the way we cut down the strongest specimen from a flower garden for display. Basically, some surfers want to knock down who-ever's on top. I was a young American world champion who was failing to live up to their expectations. Plus, being on *Baywatch*, the ultimate cheeseball all-American show, made me Public Enemy Number One in Australia. I was embarrassed by the negative press and vowed to keep any future emotional outbursts private.

JIMMY SLADE R.I.P.

Fortunately, I was involved with one mainstream project that year that was true to my surfing roots. Bruce Brown was putting together a sequel to his classic 1966 surf movie, *The Endless Summer*. I was considered for the lead, which was an honor, but given my very busy competition schedule, I wasn't the best guy for the job. Bruce ended up hiring Pat O'Connell, who was a great choice for the part. Pat is funny, outgoing, and he wasn't dead-set on competition at the time. Bruce still wanted me in the film, and we were set to shoot a segment in Tavarua, Fiji, soon after I left Australia at the end of April.

Before I could surf in the movie, I had to see someone about my knee. I met with an arthroscopic surgeon while I was still in Australia. He pressed his thumbs into my kneecap, and it hurt like hell. He said, "I know exactly what it is. We'll operate the day after tomorrow." Two days later I was in the operating room, where surgeons removed some loose tissue from my knee. I woke up from the anesthesia and turned green. The rest of the day was spent hovering around the toilet. People were knocking on the door, asking "Are you okay?" And all I could say was "Leave me alone." In the cramped hospital bathroom, I struggled to keep my leg straight as I slept on the floor.

The next day, my knee felt so much better that I walked a mile back to the apartment I'd purchased in Sydney. I spent the next week icing and massaging my knee. After six days, which was the longest I had been out of the water since the original injury, I went surfing. My knee was still sore, but the source of the pain was gone. On the tenth day, I left for Fiji, Tahiti, and New Zealand to film *The Endless Summer 2*. Tom Carroll, Jeff Booth, and I surfed big, perfect waves in Tavarua for five days. Somehow I managed not to make my knee worse, and it's been fine since.

With my knee fixed, I turned my attention to my other problems. *Baywatch* was hanging over me like a black cloud, and it was time to get out of the rain. There was so much pressure to be true to my roots from surfers everywhere, and if there were benefits the show would provide for my future, I was tired of feeling like the one surfer in the world who was selling out.

In South Africa that July, I was surfing a small event in perfect eight-foot waves at one of the premier pointbreaks in the world, a place called Jeffreys Bay. Despite the political problems there over the years, the area is magical. As soon as I got there, I borrowed a bike from the family I was staying with and rode it around town to check the area out. I came down to the beach and saw flamingos flying overhead, dolphins riding waves, whales breeching, and penguins swimming, not to mention perfect waves that seemed to peel forever. After the event, I had to leave for a *Baywatch* shoot. As I was walking away from the flawless surf a person sees only a handful of times in life, I decided it was the last straw. No matter what, this was the end of Jimmy Slade. I tried to get Bryan to make excuses for me, to tell them my schedule was too busy. He said, "Just stick with it. You need this."

Again I got to California just in time to film, and it just so happened that the episode we were shooting took the absurdity to new heights. Jimmy Slade was surfing with Dave Charvet's character, Matt Brody, and they both lost their boards, which happened to get washed into a cave where a giant octopus was waiting. No one had known for the last twenty years why surfboards were disappearing, but it was because the octopus was stockpiling them in his cave.

Things were tense on the set because my fellow cast members could sense that I thought the story was really stupid. Acting was Dave Charvet's main job, and I wasn't taking it seriously. We were practicing a scene in which we were supposed to fight the octopus, and Dave was reading his lines with sincerity, saying, "We gotta get outta here. What are we gonna do?" Sarcastically, I replied, "Oh no, it's a *Baywatch*-topus." We were friends, but Dave started cussing at me and came charging. We got into a fight, and the water safety guys pulled us apart.

Dave was frustrated, screaming, "This is my job." I was frustrated too, saying, "This is mine too, but I don't want it to be." I went to Doug Schwartz, the producer, and said, "Look, I can't do this anymore. This is not me. It's not what I want to do. It's not who I want to be. It doesn't feel good, and I want to be off the show."

He was cool about it and wrote me out of the next script. In my last show, Jimmy's girlfriend, Summer, was held hostage in a lifeguard tower, and he tried to climb up and save her. I don't know what he was planning to do once he got there. The kidnapper had a gun and he shot Jimmy, who freaked out and moved to Hawaii.

I never thought getting shot could feel so good. It was too late to undo the damage acting on such a corny show had done to my image and to surfing, but at least it was over. Looking back, I see that doing the show supplied me with some of the fame I have today. Because of it, a lot of people recognize my name and I am afforded opportunities outside the surfing industry. In the end, Bryan and my mom were probably right—it was good for my career. Still, I wouldn't be kicking myself if I'd passed on the chance.

George Greenough, one of my heroes in the world of surfboard design, was quoted on the cover of an Australian magazine saying that if he ever met me, he would say, "Hey, you're the guy who fought the octopus on *Baywatch*." When I saw that quote, and imagined George saying it to me, I was so bummed. Because of the show I had hurt my credibility with some surfers. But what the hell was George Greenough doing watching *Baywatch* anyway?

NEAR-FATAL ATTRACTION

By the time I got to France in the middle of August 1993 to begin the European leg of the world tour, I was losing my mind.

There was a woman whom I'd met in France in 1991 during my first season on tour when I had been traveling there with a crew of young Australians. We had a loft in our rented apartment reserved for bringing home girls, and everyone else slept downstairs. One of the guys brought a girl home one night, and we woke up to check her out. After they finished whatever they were doing, somebody yelled up, "Swing ya mates," Australian slang for, "Ask her if she wants to hook up with any of your friends."

We walked up to the loft and the lights came on, and it wasn't a pretty sight. "Oh no," we realized. "She's not cute at all." In fact, she was hideous. She had to be forty years old, and next to the bed was a baby carrier with an infant in it. This crazed groupie was traveling with her baby! Still thinking we were interested she went into her purse and pulled out an ASP ratings list. She looked at each of us, saying, "What's the names? Are they on here?" She barely spoke English, but we knew what she was saying. If we were on the list, she wanted to get to know us.

I couldn't believe there were surfing groupies like that in the world. Fortunately, it had been my first year on tour, and I wasn't on the list. I just said, "Oh well, too bad for me." The other guys were saying the same thing. "Nope. Not me. I'm not on there either."

She started showing up at the contest and soon set her radar on me. In 1992, before my second year competing on the French leg, I received a lot of attention from the media. She screamed my name on the beach and held signs that said things like "I love Kelly Slater" and "E=MC2." (I still can't figure out the "E=MC2" part.) She'd walked in front of me holding up these signs like she was the head of my fan club or something, not even looking at me.

During the summer of 1993, she went to Australia, found out where my apartment was and slept out front in a van with her child. Luckily, I wasn't there at the time. My roommate Stretch informed the police that she was stalking the apartment, and she was deported. If she got inside the apartment, she probably would have boiled my rabbit, just like in the movie *Fatal Attraction*.

When I went back to France that summer for the contests, she was there. She slept on the ground outside my front door, so in the morning I couldn't leave my hotel without stepping over her. She wrote "E=MC2" and "I love Kelly" in lipstick all over our elevator, on our door, and all around the contest. I lost early in the event and was hoping to get the next flight out of Europe. She followed me to the airport, and there were no flights out for a couple days. I sat there, wondering what to do as she snapped pictures of me from two feet away. I wanted to beat her senseless, but I couldn't bring myself to hit a woman. Finally, the police threw her out.

I ran into her again the next night, this time in a bar. I asked her politely to leave me alone, but she wouldn't. After three years of her stalking me, I was sick of it. Out of desperation, I dumped a beer on her head. I thought it was pretty funny, and the next thing I knew she smacked me across the face. I grabbed her by the arms and told her to stay away from me.

Afterward, I went outside the bar to call my mom for some motherly advice. I was on the phone when up walked Psycho with six guys. I could make out enough of what she was saying to realize she was explaining to them how I'd been disrespectful to French women. I told my mom I had to go. It was an enclosed phone booth, and I tried to call the police. The station was right down the street, but they didn't speak English. I thought, "Okay, I'm screwed," as I stepped out of the booth.

The guys surrounded me, and I figured the best thing to do was kick the biggest guy between the legs and run. As I was sizing them up, the largest guy came at me, saying in broken English, "What are you doing to this woman?" I said, "You guys have no idea what this woman's been doing to me for the last three years." They started pushing me, and just as I was about to make my move, a car came screeching sideways onto the sidewalk, just like a scene from a movie. Tom Carroll and another friend of mine from Australia named Ross Clarke Jones were driving up and saw what was happening. They jumped out of the car just as some other friends of mine came walking up, and the tables turned in my favor. Ross went crazy and scared all six guys away.

I was thinking irrationally. I backed the woman against a wall outside the bar, and there was a twelve-foot drop on the other side. If her three-year-old son hadn't been there, hitting me in the legs and yelling at me to stop, I may have done something foolish. It brought me back to reality, and I let her go. That was the last I saw of her.

My home life was equally stressful. After talking with Bree's family, I was convinced that buying the house in South Florida was a good investment. I felt that not buying it would cause more trouble in our relationship. The Realtor began putting together all the necessary paperwork for the house, and I called my bank to transfer money for a down payment. The bank informed me the account was overdrawn. I was broke. I had made more than a million dollars and had nothing to show for it. My mother and I were awful at managing money and we were unknowingly spending more than I was making. My manager asked where the money was going, and I had no idea.

Bree and my mom didn't get along and stopped talking to each other. I tried to smooth things over between them, but there was only so much I could do while I was traveling in Europe. Their feud, the new home, the engagement, I was broke, and everything else that came with it was worrying me, and my mind was everywhere but where it needed to be.

I can't lay the blame for my money problems with anyone but myself. When I was younger, I never expected to be rich. I grew up without money, and I didn't know how to manage it once it started coming in. How to save and invest, and whom to trust, are all things you learn when you have money. This was the heads up I needed to start paying attention. I took responsibility for my finances and cleared things up with my bank. I'm still learning about how to manage money, and I think I'll have it figured out eventually. But it was a tough way to learn a lesson.

BACK TO BASICS

If you polled every surfer in the world, you'd be lucky if one in ten could name the current world champion. Relatively few surfers care about competition, and even fewer—perhaps one in a hundred—actually compete. For most, putting on a contest jersey is a traumatic experience. It brings out the worst in people and brings to mind feelings of failure, greed, and deceit.

When I was losing in contests, I hated them too. I had no confidence in my surfing, my boards, or my competition skills. I started to believe that my world title was a fluke, and I didn't belong alongside my heroes. In France I had a fifth at Lacanau, a seventeenth at Hossegor, and another thirty-third in Biarritz. I felt the same as I did when the year started off, if not worse. With four contests to go in the 1993 season, I was in twenty-fifth place. Defending the world title was the furthest thing from my mind. I was just hoping I could stay on the tour, and my seed was in serious jeopardy.

I remembered how competition had taken my mind off my

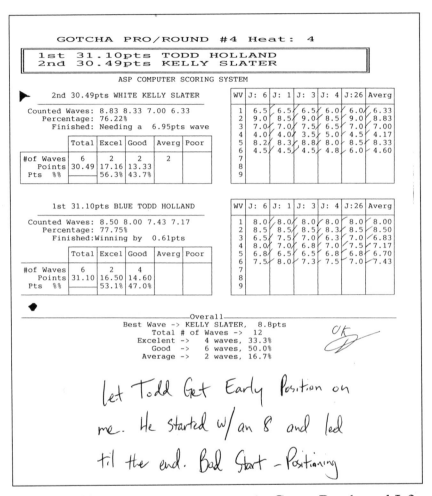

```
          GOTCHA  PRO/ROUND  #4  Heat:  4

    1st  31.10pts  TODD  HOLLAND
    2nd  30.49pts  KELLY  SLATER
              ASP COMPUTER SCORING SYSTEM
```

▶ 2nd 30.49pts WHITE KELLY SLATER

Counted Waves: 8.83 8.33 7.00 6.33
Percentage: 76.22%
Finished: Needing a 6.95pts wave

	Total	Excel	Good	Averg	Poor
#of Waves	6	2	2	2	
Points	30.49	17.16	13.33		
Pts %%		56.3%	43.7%		

WV	J: 6	J: 1	J: 3	J: 4	J:26	Averg
1	6.5	6.5	6.5	6.0	6.0	6.33
2	9.0	8.5	9.0	8.5	9.0	8.83
3	7.0	7.0	7.5	6.5	7.0	7.00
4	4.0	4.0	3.5	5.0	4.5	4.17
5	8.2	8.3	8.8	8.0	8.5	8.33
6	4.5	4.5	4.5	4.8	6.0	4.60
7						
8						
9						

1st 31.10pts BLUE TODD HOLLAND

Counted Waves: 8.50 8.00 7.43 7.17
Percentage: 77.75%
Finished:Winning by 0.61pts

	Total	Excel	Good	Averg	Poor
#of Waves	6	2	4		
Points	31.10	16.50	14.60		
Pts %%		53.1%	47.0%		

WV	J: 6	J: 1	J: 3	J: 4	J:26	Averg
1	8.0	8.0	8.0	8.0	8.0	8.00
2	8.5	8.5	8.3	8.5	8.5	8.50
3	6.5	7.5	7.0	6.3	7.0	6.83
4	8.0	7.0	6.8	7.0	7.5	7.17
5	6.8	6.5	6.5	6.8	6.8	6.70
6	7.5	8.0	7.3	7.5	7.0	7.43
7						
8						
9						

```
─────────────────Overall─────────────────
       Best Wave -> KELLY SLATER,  8.8pts
          Total # of Waves ->  12
        Excelent ->   4 waves, 33.3%
            Good  ->   6 waves, 50.0%
         Average ->   2 waves, 16.7%
```

Let Todd Get Early Position on me. He started w/ an 8 and led til the end. Bad Start - Positioning

family problems as a young teenager in Cocoa Beach, and I figured it could work again. It wouldn't necessarily make me happy, but anything was better than being miserable *and* losing. My competitive nature took over, and if the other areas of my life had to wait, so be it.

There were specific reasons why I had been losing heats, and I set out to find them. I got a folder and kept every judge's sheet from when I lost to try to pinpoint my mistakes. The sheets contain each judge's score from every wave ridden, so it's easy to figure out where I went wrong. While the losses were still fresh in my head, I wrote the reasons for losing on each sheet, including all the stats from each contest—highest wave scores, highest heat scores, anything to get my focus back on surfing.

Sometimes I'd get six or eight waves and lose. Other times I'd get four waves and win by a long shot. Only three waves were counted toward each surfer's final tally, so it's a good idea to be selective. I had to pay more attention to the conditions, and make sure I was in the right spot at the right time. I would figure out where to sit and which wave in the set was the best. Everybody on tour has the ability to win at any time, so it comes down to understanding the conditions and getting the best waves. Patience is a virtue, even in surfing.

By the time I got to Japan in October, something snapped in me and I thought, "I've got to turn things around and get some results." A lot of people from Quiksilver were there for me, but Tom Carroll helped the most. He had been on the World Tour for fifteen seasons and had overcome his share of adversity, including several serious injuries. He was sort of my big brother on tour and helped get me focused on surfing again.

I put together four good contests in a row to finish out the season. In Japan, I placed ninth in the Miyazaki Pro and won in the Marui Pro in Chiba, which was the richest purse of the year, earning me $25,000 and a new car. My ratings were on the rise, and by the time I left Japan, I was ranked twelfth. With a quarterfinal finish in Brazil, I moved into ninth. I had no chance of winning the world title, but with the tour finishing at Pipeline, I was determined to finish with a bang.

While I wasn't in the running, five guys still had a chance at winning the world title at Pipeline. It came down to the final, and Derek Ho had a chance to become the first Hawaiian world champ. All he had to do was finish first or second to pass Gary Elkerton, so the pressure was intense. The other finalists, Jeff Booth, Larry Rios, and myself, all rode for Quiksilver, but that day was about Hawaii more than anything else. Derek wore a look of focused determination that said, "Don't get in my way." I can't see rolling over for anybody, so thankfully the fact that Derek didn't need to get first to win the title meant I could go all out.

We gave Derek his space, but I wanted to win. I went out looking to catch waves at Backdoor, the right-breaking end of Pipeline, but they weren't coming. I thought I saw one and paddled around Derek, and at the last second I decided to go left. It was my best wave of the heat, but I was pushing my luck in a big way. It felt like the whole crowd on the beach was gritting its teeth, waiting for Derek's reaction. It's disrespectful to paddle around someone, no matter what, and call him off a wave, but Derek was doing so well he didn't care. It was a close heat, but he won. I finished second, moving me into a tie for fifth in the final World Tour standings.

All I could think about was how great it must have felt for Derek to come from behind and win in such dramatic fashion. It was the ultimate surfing trifecta—winning at Pipeline, earning

the Hawaiian Triple Crown, and securing the world title. I wanted to do the same.

WE'RE IN BUSINESS

Most former competitive surfers end up facing financial hardships somewhere along the line. There just isn't any sort of retirement plan in riding waves. In baseball or other high profile-sports, guys are getting signing bonuses of several million dollars, enough to live comfortably for the rest of their lives without lifting a finger. I was making considerably more money than any other surfer, but I hadn't received any real signing bonus other than a new pair of trunks.

After the mishap with the bank, I started planning for my future. There was always a chance that I'd get seriously hurt and not be able to surf. If that happened, I wouldn't have anything to fall back on. So at the end of 1993, Bryan and I worked out a deal with Quiksilver to include in my new contract. The company agreed to put up some money for me to start my own business. A friend of mine in Florida named Kurt Wilson was experimenting with surfboard traction pads and sent me a bunch to try. Traction pads take the place of wax—which can smear off or get slippery—on the tail of a board. The first models in the early 1980s were nothing more than the rubber strips in a bathtub. Eventually, the pads had arched bars for extra foot support and a small lip along the back that keeps your foot from slipping off. When the opportunity arose to start my own company, Kurt's idea was a perfect match. Bryan wanted to call it "K-Stick," but I didn't like the sound of it. Just as we were going to sign the papers, I came up with "K-Grip," a name I could live with.

8

Changing of the Guard

BECAUSE MY PERSONAL LIFE took a backseat to competition, in February of 1994, Bree and I ended our engagement. I knew it was for the best, but I was heartbroken. Luckily, my mind was occupied with contests, which kept me from sitting around and moping. I redirected my emotions into surfing. My only focus became refining my skills and becoming a better competitor. I was determined to win everything in sight. Surfing was my savior, and competition was the ultimate escape.

There was a lot of downtime between heats, and a hobby was just the thing to recharge my batteries, so I took up drawing. I wanted to do caricatures of every surfer and turn it into an autograph book, but I only drew a few of them before I grew tired of the idea. In elementary school, I was into art because my mom sculpted and painted. There was always wood, paint, and clay around our house. I made a couple surf paintings that I was really proud of. I entered them in a local Cocoa Beach art show and won.

For my graduation in 1991, Cocoa Beach High School used my artwork on the cover of the graduation program. I drew a guy jumping over the graduation bridge with a four-leaf clover in one hand and his tassel moving from one side to the other.

The 1994 ASP World Tour came around again at the end of March and it was back to Australia. I was anxious to build on the

momentum I gained at the end of 1993. Since I was newly single, I decided to use some waterproof paint pens that Rob Machado had with him to draw a girl on one of my boards. I decided to draw Stephanie Seymour—she was a popular supermodel at the time. Shane Dorian saw her image on my board and suggested I draw women on all my boards. I started to draw other models and my dream girls, and soon I had a harem. They were my new girlies. They went surfing with me, and I had the perfect relationship with each of them—stress-free.

While I was on tour, my little brother, Stephen, turned sixteen on March 6, so I decided to bring him out to Australia as my present to him. After years of refusing to surf, he finally took it up when he was fifteen. He was hanging out at the beach when a guy he knew asked him to keep an eye on his longboard while he went to get something to eat. Stephen decided to paddle out on it and catch a wave. He stood up on his first try and instantly fell in love. Longboarding is completely different than shortboard surfing. Riding a longboard is all about style and flow, whereas shortboarders try to get as radical as possible. Stephen started surfing all the time; I guess he was trying to make up for all the years he'd missed. He wasn't as into shortboarding, mostly because Sean and I rode them and he wanted to be different. Within a year of learning to surf, he was pulling off amazing moves. Needless to say, he was thrilled to be going to Australia.

There was great surf during the first event at Bells Beach, and Winkipop, the next beach over, had the best day I've ever seen there. Whenever we weren't competing in heats, most of us went over to Winkipop to surf. The waves were six feet and perfect. I begged Stephen to go surfing with me, but he refused. He was intimidated by all the pros in the water, and still wasn't biting on the twenty bucks. He surfed a lot during the trip, but with only a year of experience he wasn't ready for anything too serious.

I'd never had a good result at Bells, but I went into the event with plenty of confidence. I was determined to keep my mind occupied with thoughts of winning so that I wouldn't have to think about Bree. If I lost, my mind would have started wandering . . . and, well, losing wasn't an option.

Gary Elkerton and I met in the semifinals, and the waves were pumping. It was one of the highest scoring heats of the year. He had me on the ropes. I needed a great ride in the final minutes. A small wave came through, and Gary let it go, thinking it wasn't very good. I didn't get that choice. I had to take it, because I knew I needed to go all out. I rode the wave with reckless abandon, pushing myself to the verge of spinning out on each turn. It was my best ride of the event, and I won by half a point. Elkerton was pissed, not at me but at the judges for giving me the score I needed to win. He charged the judges' stand and berated them—a move he had become known for. Sometimes he did it after he won, just to make a point. I've always thought that the more of a scene you make about losing, the more people remember it.

In the final I was up against Martin Potter, and there was a lot of hype on the beach since it was a clash of former world champions. Unfortunately, we looked like a couple of amateurs. We each fell on our first few waves. In most events, I paced myself so I'd have something left for the final, but it took everything I had to get past Elkerton and I had nothing left for Potter. Despite this, I won for the first time at Bells, and I haven't had a good result there since. Afterward, when I watched a video of the final, it looked as if Pottz beat me. But the judges thought otherwise, and who am I to argue?

Bells set the tone for the rest of the year. For years it had been up in the air as to whether the New School's tricks were enough to outperform the Old School's power. As much as I hoped my approach was a good mix of the two styles, the surfing media as well as the older guys on tour went out of their way to label me as a New Schooler. They didn't take us seriously, so whenever I, or one of my peers, faced any of the old guard in a heat, it became increasingly important for us to win. We wanted respect.

Finally, after a three-year struggle, the changing of the guard became official during the 1994 World Tour. The veteran competitors were still there, but no longer did you see them winning events. It was almost as if they had punched their time cards and kicked back on their La-Z-Boys with the remote control and beer in hand. I had been holding my own in the winner's circle for two years as I waited for my friends to get to the party. When they arrived, I couldn't have been happier. It finally felt like I was part of a group, rather than an outsider among Old Schoolers. As each new kid made his mark, we fed off the other's success. If I lost a contest, I'd pull for my friends to win.

At the Marui Pro in Japan in May 1994, Rob Machado dominated for the first time in a World Championship Tour contest. He surfed much faster in the small waves than everyone else in the event. After the final, I ran down the beach with some of our friends, picked him up and carried him to the podium on our shoulders. He barely weighed a hundred pounds, so it wasn't much work. For me, it was an awakening. All our childhood dreams were happening. We worked our whole lives to be pro surfers and compete with our heroes, and now we were winning the biggest events in the world. In my mind, we were in the middle of the biggest leap in performance and surfboard design since the generation that laid the foundation for pro surfing in the mid-1970s.

COMING TO AMERICA

It was amazing, but in my two full seasons on the WCT tour, there hadn't been a single mainland event. Ocean Pacific had withdrawn its support for the Op Pro in 1991 due to the recession, and no one had stepped in to fill the void. And while competing and winning around the world is nice, it means so much more to be able to do it in front of friends and sponsors.

The World Tour returned to Huntington Beach, California, in August of 1994, so I finally got to have a home field advantage against the international pros. Instead of the Op Pro, it was called the U.S. Open and funded by various sponsors. Even though the name changed, the excitement of surfing in front of huge crowds screaming from the pier and the beach was the same. Quiksilver is right down the street, and having spent my summers in Huntington as a kid, the beach almost felt like home.

Huntington usually has the worst waves, but from a U.S. media standpoint it has always been a very important event to win. Nearly the entire American surfing industry and media are located within an hour of the pier, so almost every surfer in the United States is watching.

I did well early on, but in the man-on-man final I faced a Californian, Shane Beschen. I beat Shane at Huntington in the NSSA Nationals back in 1987, so he had plenty of time to plan his revenge.

He caught all the best waves and was killing me for most of the heat. I was hoping Shane wouldn't combo me and toward the end, I managed to get myself within striking distance, meaning I no longer needed a combination of waves but one single perfect score to win. Unfortunately, in the small, crumbly, and wind-blown waves, that was next to impossible.

Out of nowhere, the best wave I had seen all day came to me with only a minute to go. I could feel the crowd's excitement. It was just like when I used to watch Tom Curren and Mark Occhilupo in the same situation. I pulled into the tube, came out and did an aerial, and rode the whitewater to the beach. There was no way I could have surfed it any better. The crowd went absolutely loony. Everyone, including me, expected the judges to score it a 10, but it came through as a 9.6. I got second, but I was stoked with the way it ended by coming down to the wire. Shane was one of the fresh faces on the ASP tour, and anything was better than seeing another dinosaur on top.

One reason for the success of Shane Beschen, Rob Machado, Taylor Knox, Shane Dorian, and other young American surfers at the time was the strength of the domestic tour. The Bud Tour was still a big deal in the United States. It offered good money with minimal traveling and heaps of valuable points toward the World Qualifying Series. It definitely gave them an opportunity to polish their contest act while surfing against the best guys in the nation.

Still trying to make up for my bad year in 1993 by keeping my head in competition, I surfed on the Bud Tour whenever I was at home. Rob Machado and I had several clashes in California, with each of us winning a fair share of events. During one event in Rob's hometown of Seaside, California, we were so into playing Ping-Pong at his house that we almost missed our heats. We must have played ten straight games the morning of the last contest, but I wasn't quitting until I beat Rob. It didn't happen, so I took out my aggravation in the surf and beat him in the final.

Bree and I had tried to work things out for the first half of 1994, but by August, around the time I left for the European leg of the tour, we finally realized we were beating our heads against a wall and called it quits. I was filled with anger and used it to my advantage when I won the Lacanau Pro in France for my second victory of the season.

The next week in Hossegor, France, I surfed an expression session the day before the final. The ASP sometimes runs expression sessions in the middle of an event so that surfers can win cash prizes for performing certain individual maneuvers, and the go-for-broke attitude is always a crowd pleaser. The ocean in Hossegor was sort of dirty that year, not the kind of thing you want your body getting into. Californian Mike Parsons wiped out and cut his head open on his board, and two waves later I fell and split the webbing between my toes the same way. The lifeguards threw us on an ATV and drove us to their office. They stitched up Mike and me right there with no painkillers. The lifeguard said, "Well, eef we geev you de novocaine, it would by five or six pokes you would feel, but dees way you only feel four pokes' cause we do in and out and you have a steetch." If you've ever had someone pull your toes apart while stitching the webbing back together, you know it's medieval torture.

I felt a little queasy the next day. I was going from hot flashes to cold sweats and puking my guts out. Apparently, the nasty water pouring through my open wound was a bad thing and made me sick. Even though I had a comfortable lead in the ASP ratings, I wasn't above the occupational hazards that afflict fre-

quent travelers. I lost the final to Brazilian Flavio Padaratz and returned to the beach completely drained.

Shane Dorian and I had to check out of our room and drive to the next event a short way down the coast in Biarritz, but I couldn't move. Shane had to pack my stuff, carry my bags, drag me to the car, strap my boards on, drive us to Biarritz, and check us in. I felt sick the entire week and finished seventeenth in the event, my worst showing all year. When you get sick on the road, it makes traveling a nightmare.

The worst part of being a pro surfer is never feeling rooted in one place. As soon as you get comfortable in one location, you're off to the next contest. You have to be ready for flights to be canceled and delays of every kind. Sometimes you can't shower for days and you're living on planes and in airports. It's hard to feel like you belong anywhere, to live a normal family life and develop real relationships. My life's nothing to complain about, but in terms of travel there are a lot of things I wish were better. Too bad I don't make enough money to have my own plane.

I spend more than half the year traveling, and the only thing that makes this sort of lifestyle possible is my network of surrogate families around the world. The 1994 World Tour was my fourth time competing at a lot of the spots on tour, and in that time I'd been fortunate enough to have met and been taken in by loving families that provided me a warm meal, companionship, and roof over my head. A lot of surfers burn out on the travel and miss home, but these families help feel comfortable anywhere I go.

Good waves are only so fulfilling if you don't have some kind of family support. Ever since I started traveling at age twelve, I've been more interested in getting to know the locals at each spot than sitting in a generic hotel room watching *Beavis and Butt-head* between sessions. I can show up at any beach in the world and see somebody I know. I'll go somewhere and, instead of leaving right after the contest, hang around with my friends until I

have to be somewhere else. There is so much to learn from other cultures, and as a surfer I have a unique opportunity to experience a lot of places. To me, that's living.

LAYING DOWN ON THE JOB

When it comes to other forms of riding waves, surfers are notoriously closed-minded. A lot of guys feel that if they aren't riding a modern shortboard, they're not real surfers and don't deserve to catch waves. Bodyboarders and bodysurfers are often regarded as nothing more than speed bumps in the lineup. As a teenager, I felt that way too, but traveling opened my eyes to different equipment, or sometimes no equipment at all.

Most surfers will bodysurf out of necessity. If you aren't tied to your board with a leash, it will usually wash up on the beach after a wipeout. Hitching a ride with a wave is easier than swimming to the beach to retrieve the board. All you need to do is take a couple strokes to get into the wave, and let your body be taken to shore. Until I took a trip to the Mentawai Islands in Indonesia in 1994 for a Quiksilver video, that was all bodysurfing meant to me. Don King (not to be confused with the boxing promoter) is the greatest water photographer of all time and one of the best bodysurfers around. During the trip to the Mentawais, he bodysurfed when he wasn't shooting photos, which inspired Keoni Watson (a friend I met in Hawaii back in 1984) and me to try it. We ripped some wood off a sunken charter boat and made hand guns, little wooden planks that would help us plane across the water. We both fell in love with it and ditched our surfboards for one session each day. We learned how to get barreled, execute different postures, and have fun on pretty much any wave.

That winter in Hawaii, every day Pipe broke, we bodysurfed. It was great training—probably the best cardiovascular workout we got—since we were moving all the time just to stay afloat. We stopped wearing leashes when we surfed so we could practice bodysurfing to our boards after a wipeout. Even when the waves are horrible, bodysurfing can still be a blast. The sensation of speed, even on a tiny wave, is incredible, much more intimate than riding a surfboard.

All serious bodysurfers wear fins to help them swim faster and control their direction. Keoni Watson, Strider Wasilewski, and I bodysurfed a huge day at Pipe without swim fins. There were massive sets breaking way out on the second reef, which was a quarter of a mile out at sea. We figured that by not wearing fins, we would increase our learning curve. It was sort of the old school method of bodysurfing. Instead of propelling us forward, the current was sweeping us out to sea. We barely made it back to shore. The lifeguard at Pipe was a guy named Mark Cunningham, who is one of the most respected watermen ever. He's won the World Bodysurfing Championships at Pipeline countless times and is known for going out on days that are considered too dangerous to surf. He could swim out to Pipe and catch a wave with his eyes closed, and to prove it he sometimes surfed it at night. It's hard enough to surf there during the day when you can see what's going on, but to do it at night borders on psychotic.

Mark came running down the beach to rescue us. When he realized who it was, he said, "Aww, you knuckleheads. I should have known it was you guys. You're coming with me, right now." He took us to his shed nearby and got each of us a pair of swim fins.

Since then, I've wanted to enter the Pipeline Bodysurfing Classic. The best bodysurfers in the world compete in the event each year, which is usually won by either Mark Cunningham or Mike Stewart, who also happens to be one of the best body-boarders ever. In February 2002, I was in Oahu and finally got my chance. It was really strange competing in a different sport after so many years of only surfing. The judging criteria is pretty much the same—the competitor who catches the best waves and completes the most radical maneuvers for the longest functional distance is deemed the winner, but I had no idea who most of the competitors were or if I could beat them. I just went out and had fun. There were thirty-some guys in the contest, and I advanced through a few rounds but lost in the semifinals. I was almost happy I didn't make the finals, because I knew Mike and Mark would destroy me—they're untouchable.

SHUTTING OUT THE COMPETITION

There are some years when the surfing conditions don't come together, even in Hawaii. The weather systems are too far away to create swells or the wind blows onshore and tears the surf to bits. The waves in Hawaii were so flat in December 1994 that on some days we couldn't even bodysurf. Each day our crew hung around Jack Johnson's parents' house on the beach near Pipeline looking for things to do.

Jack was in film school and got the idea to make a short film, *Mr. Slater Goes to Work,* which showed me going about my daily business. I put on a three-piece suit of Jack's, grabbed an old door that was lying around in his dad's shed, and went to work. I carried the door down the beach at Pipeline to surf it. I didn't do it so much for the movie as I did it to prove that I could surf on a door. It was one of those "You Won't Go" type of deals. I couldn't back down to a challenge.

The waves were barely breaking, and the shape of the door—a thin, wide rectangle with no bottom contour—made it nearly impossible to catch one of the tiny ripples. I kept falling but refused to give up. After about an hour, I caught a little wave and wasn't standing for two seconds before I nose-dived into the water. The door eventually became waterlogged and wouldn't stay afloat. I've heard people say, "He's so good he could ride a barn door." After seeing how hard it really is, I now know they'd have to be extremely good.

The waves were so bad that winter that the Pipe Masters used its entire two-week waiting period just hoping for some kind of pulse, which never arrived. On the final day, we finished the contest at Ehukai Beach Park in head-high mush that was no bigger than what I rode as a twelve-year-old grommet. This average day would decide the world title, so you can guess who had the advantage.

Australian Shane Powell was in second place, and he was the only person with a chance to catch me in the ratings. He had to make the final to hold on to a shot at overtaking me for the season. I sat on the beach watching his semifinal heat, trying to put a hex on him. He lost, and I reclaimed the title. Even though the Coke Classic, the final event of the year, was the biggest contest in terms of prize money and points, my lead was insurmountable. I went on to win my second Pipe Masters, although I'd hardly go around claiming it considering the conditions. As it turned out,

Shane won in Australia, and came within two hundred points of catching me. After such a miserable December, in January 1995 Hawaii was the best month of surf I've ever seen. Unfortunately, all of the contests had long since finished.

I soon found out that my mission to win all the major events in 1994 was accomplished. I won the World Championship Tour, the World Qualifying Series, and for the first time, the Surfer Poll, an annual popularity contest among the readers of *Surfer*. As teenagers, Sean and I religiously filled out our ballots each year and couldn't wait for the magazine to print the results to see if our favorites won. If readers guessed the Top 10 men's finishers and Top 5 women correctly, they earned a trip to Hawaii. Some guy named Walt Novak always won, and he already lived in Hawaii. Maybe they gave him a ticket to Maui instead.

Surfer puts on a huge party to present the Surfer Poll awards, and with all the pros, legends, beautiful girls, and industry big-wigs, it's a who's who of surfing. Looking at the photos in the magazine back in Cocoa Beach made me feel like I was there.

They stopped having the banquet in the mid-1980s to cut costs, so when I debuted at number ten in 1991 there was no party. I finished second to Tom Curren the next two years and started winning first place in 1994. It wasn't the same without the banquet, and I'd have to wait until the next year before *Surfer* decided to bring back the ceremony. Going to the party brought back the memories of waiting by the mailbox, wondering if Sean and I had picked the winners.

I won the Surfer Poll every year from 1994 to 2001. Well, almost every year. In 2000, I lost to some guy named Crazy Randall, the mascot for . . . Lost, a clothing company that prides itself on being dysfunctional. The company campaigned around the country, offering free T-shirts for everyone who cast a ballot for Randall, and he won. In light of the circumstances, *Surfer* gave me the award, since I was the next highest vote-getter.

Despite my popularity among the general public, I got the feeling my competitors weren't too happy with me. At the ASP awards banquet in Sydney at the beginning of 1995, I was crowned champion of both the World Championship Tour and the World Qualifying Series, and my competitors were obviously tired of me winning. Since I was in Australia, I didn't have much support anyway. I felt lonely.

According to former world champ Barton Lynch of Australia, people were definitely sick of my face: "During our era, roughly 1983 to 1993, there were a lot of guys with the potential to win. When Kelly came along, there were great surfers, but none of them were ever able to live up to their potential because of his dominance. When he came on, people in the sport were saying, 'An American world champion. It's the thing we need. It's gonna turn the sport around. We're gonna be millionaires. It'll be fantastic.' Then, a couple years into it, they're saying, 'Christ, we need some other people. He's killing the sport.'"

9

Big Time

I NOW KNOW HOW ELVIS FELT. If his death were a hoax, if he just got sick of dealing with people and staged the whole thing so he could live in peace, I wouldn't blame him. Surfing is so small that my experiences are a fraction of his, but the feeling's the same.

It happened so fast, and in Australia of all places, where everyone surfs and world champions grow on trees. In March 1994, after losing in the quarterfinals of the Kirra Pro, a World Qualifying Series event on the Gold Coast, I decided to check out the rest of the contest. Big mistake.

The contests had always been so casual that I didn't mind when people asked to take a picture with me or get an autograph. As a grommet, I'd been something of an autograph hound whenever the pros came to Florida, so I understood that young surfers wanted to meet the current world champ. I would have been bummed if they hadn't. But hysterically crying girls? Where did they come from? *Baywatch* had put my face on every television on earth, and my private life was finished.

I stopped to sign a few programs for a couple of kids who came up to me on the beach, and the crowd got bigger and bigger. Before I knew it, there was no escape. I was at the center of a couple hundred people, and I was scared. They were grabbing me, and angry parents were yelling for me to sign something for their kids. Finally, the event's security guards helped me get to my car so I could leave, but the army of teenage girls didn't give up. They chanted, even cried, my name. They banged on the windows and shook the car until I eventually pulled away. It was pandemonium. Surfers never got that kind of attention, and none of my friends on tour could relate to it.

Rabid fans soon became a regular occurrence in places like France, Japan, even California. Their timing couldn't have been worse. I wanted less attention, not more.

LOST IN LOVE

I can sum up my somewhat checkered love life quite easily. We learn from the examples set for us early on in life, and I think it's safe to say that my parents weren't exactly an example of a healthy relationship. Considering that and my nomadic lifestyle, it's no wonder that I've had several less than perfect relationships.

I had to find out on my own what a healthy relationship is— no slight to my parents. It's like if you were taught that cooking is opening the microwave and popping in a TV dinner, and suddenly somebody asks you to cook a seven-course meal. You won't know how to cook it. You can try, maybe even get help from books, but it's practice that makes it perfect.

Believe it or not, when I was on *Baywatch*, I wasn't attracted to Pam Anderson. People find that hard to believe, but it's true. After I quit the show, we didn't keep in touch. But in 1994, a few months after Bree and I ended our engagement, I ran into Pam in Hawaii. She was shooting a TV special, and we clicked immediately. We started dating, but we weren't exclusive. I'd see her whenever I was in California. Since we weren't serious, we didn't make a big deal about it or tell anyone. We wanted to keep it out of the media. Getting involved with somebody far more popular than I was probably wasn't the best idea. She was getting a lot of attention because of *Baywatch,* and that was exactly the kind of news coverage I was trying to stay away from.

In January 1995, I went to Australia for the Coke Classic held at Manly Beach in Sydney. Coincidentally, Pam was hired by Coca-Cola to make an appearance at the same contest. A photo was taken of us when we happened to be standing together and it ran in a local newspaper and a few gossip magazines. The caption implied we were an item, and as the photo spread through Australia, then back to the States, it freaked me out.

I cared about Pamela as a friend, but when I was with her, I was reminded of my connection to *Baywatch.* I wanted to be taken seriously in my career, and my credibility as a surfer was more important than any relationship. Plus, having just gotten out of one serious relationship, getting into another with someone in her position was out of the question. Pam wanted more than I could give her. She was looking to settle down and start a family, but for me at twenty-two, it was the furthest thing from my mind.

A few days after news of our relationship spread throughout the United States, I explained to her how I felt. Within a week of our conversation, she met and then married Tommy Lee. Unfortunately, my ties to her put me back in the spotlight, and my privacy was a thing of the past. I wasn't ready for the life of a public figure, but I didn't have a choice.

I'M TOO SEXY

After all the media attention, modeling opportunities began coming my way. I wasn't breaking my neck to pursue them, but I was no longer a shy teenager. Given the opportunity, I was happy to make a few quick bucks smiling for a camera.

Interview magazine got a hold of me and asked to do an article on me. I had Stephanie Gibbs, the wife of my old coach Bruce Walker, set it up. Stephanie ran a modeling agency in Florida and asked a photographer named Bruce Weber to take the photos for the feature. I didn't realize at the time that Bruce was a famous fashion photographer and that most models would rip one another's eyes out for a shoot with him. The pictures came out really well, and I ended up on the cover of *Interview* with a headline that read, "Kelly Slater: Half Fish, Total Dish," whatever that means.

After the shoot, Bruce took some photos of me wearing Versace stuff for a catalog. I agreed to it, because I figured no one would see it other than buyers for boutiques. I had heard of Versace, but the fashion world was still foreign to me and I wasn't aware of their style of advertising. I had to pose in a pair of tighty-whities, and as embarrassed as I was, Bruce did a good job of easing my anxiety. Next thing you know, the photos of me in Versace underwear are on the back cover of a bunch of magazines. That was more of me than I wanted to reveal, and I called Stephanie and told her to make them stop running the ad. According to Stephanie, the company was shocked, saying any model would kill for that opportunity. I asked her to politely let them know that I was not a "model," and would appreciate if that were the end of it—and it was.

Other lucrative offers came along, such as the Cool Water cologne campaign, but I was too busy to pose and leery of straying too far from my surfing roots.

I wasn't too crazy about modeling, but I did like female models,

specifically Helena Christensen. Shane Dorian and I thought she was hot, and when we roomed together along the southwest coast of France in 1995, we covered our walls with pictures of her that we pulled from magazines. Really, it was Shane that had the huge crush on her; it just sort of wore off on me. We'd stare at her pictures on the walls, wondering what it would be like to meet her. I soon got my chance.

A friend of mine in Paris owns a modeling agency and asked me to come over for a photo shoot that summer. Even though I wasn't gung ho on modeling, I figured it couldn't hurt to have a nice portfolio in case something great came my way. After a photo shoot one night, I went to a trendy club with some friends. After spending twenty-eight bucks on two drinks, I was broke and ready for bed. As I headed up the stairs to the bathroom before leaving, a group of people came stumbling down the stairs and bumped into me. It was Michael Hutchence of INXS, Bono of U2, and, lo and behold, Helena Christensen.

She was with Michael, so I didn't want to act too stupid. Michael was a friend of Tom Carroll's, so I introduced myself. I said, "My name's Kelly. I'm a surfer from Florida and just wanted to say hi." He made fun of me by saying, "Hey, Kelly . . . surfer." I thought, "Great, could you be any more stuck on yourself?" As soon as I told him I knew Tom, he became really friendly and offered to buy me a drink.

Even though INXS and U2 were two of my favorite bands growing up, I was more interested in Helena, and spent the next two hours talking to her—so much for going home. I told her about a picture I drew of her and asked if she would autograph it. I said I would leave it at the modeling agency the next day and would pick it up after she had a chance to sign it. When she said she also wanted a picture of me, I found it odd, considering I thought she didn't know who I was. When she saw my look of surprise, she leaned over the table and said, "Kelly, it's not the size of the wave.

It's what you do on it that counts." Whoa, maybe she did know who I was? All of a sudden I felt like a celebrity myself. That was the end of the evening, but I went back home and had some pleasant dreams. I never actually got the autograph from her, though.

I was starting to get recognized by people even when I wasn't on the beach, even in Paris, where I expected to be anonymous. A group of ten Italian guys stopped me as I was walking along a little street. Their faces lit up when they saw me, and they said, "Kelly Slater, *Alerte à Malibu*." That's cool, I thought, Malibu must be the only surf spot they've heard of, but I wasn't so lucky. It wasn't my surfing accomplishments they were familiar with—*Alerte à Malibu* is French for *Baywatch*. Even in the middle of Europe, I couldn't get away from the show.

When I got back to Florida in October, I was watching the Huntington event on television, even though it had taken place back in August. (Surfing still hasn't warranted live television coverage; we're lucky if it shows up months after it happens.) The producers had decided to interview people from the crowd and ask who their favorite surfers were. One kid was teed off at me, and called me a sellout for doing *Baywatch*. He suggested that even my relationship with Quiksilver went against the soul of the sport. It was the first time I heard my life discussed in public by complete strangers, and it hurt. I cared what people thought of me and was desperate to change their perceptions at any cost.

I decided that maybe I needed to part ways with Quiksilver to become more soulful. Tom Curren had received respect from surfers everywhere when in 1991 he turned his back on his sponsor and rode a board with no logos. It proved that all he wanted to do was go surfing, and I wanted to prove the same thing. If winning contests couldn't prove I was a real surfer, then I was willing to sacrifice my sponsorship to regain that credibility.

I had a long talk with Danny Kwock, Quiksilver's vice president of marketing, and told him I needed to be true to my roots. I told him of my plans to leave Quiksilver. The company had always stood behind me in all my decisions, and Danny offered to help me through this difficult time. He convinced me that other people could say what they want, but only I could determine if I was a sellout. I heeded his advice, and stuck it out with Quiksilver. It never really had anything to do with them.

THREE-HORSE RACE

Mark Richards was the most accomplished professional surfer in the world. The great M.R. won four consecutive world titles between 1979 and 1982. He once said, "Competition doesn't always determine the best surfer. It rarely does." Considering he had won more titles than any other man, it was a strange thing for him to say, but he's right. There are so many variables when you're dealing with nature that nothing is certain. It's difficult to account for subjective judging, an unpredictable playing field, and fate. Combined with never being home, it's enough to drive a competitor mad. Burnout is a common occurrence among the best of us.

Many great surfers never are successful in competitions; sadly, they fail to grasp the system well enough to reach their competitive potential. They are exciting to watch, especially in good waves, but there is more to competition than great surfing. As much as I was determined to push the performance envelope, I wasn't going to be one of the surfers that refused to work within the structures of contests.

Competitive surfing is basic: the object is to outscore one's opponent. But the complexities are endless. Attention to detail makes a great surfer into a great competitor. There are all sorts of things you can do to prepare, from training to designing better equipment, to getting experience in different situations, to learning a wave's break and your opponent's strengths and weaknesses. As I became more focused in my career, I spent absurd amounts of time fine-tuning each piece of the puzzle and trying to eliminate all the variables, but some things are beyond anyone's control.

I couldn't live with the notion that much of winning contests comes down to dumb luck. It was imperative for me to win the world title in 1995 to feel like a true world champion. I didn't tell anyone, but in the back of my mind, I was gunning for Mark Richards's record.

In my typical fashion, I started with a ninth at Bells, followed by a third in Japan. The next event was the Quiksilver Pro in Grajagan, Indonesia. Grajagan was a real crossroads for professional surfing, because the ASP was under pressure to rearrange the tour. They wanted to skip the crummy beach breaks and have contests in adventurous locations (although walking down the beach in Huntington can be as adventurous as anything I've experienced). Grajagan was one of those places. It's part of Plengkung National Forest in Java, well off the beaten path. We stayed in huts that are ten feet off the ground, beyond the reach of Javanese tigers, wild boars, man-size lizards, green mambo snakes (which if they bite you, can kill you in two minutes), and every other wild thing that lurks in the jungle. Well, almost everything.

Giant rats are always on the prowl, something I was used to from my old house in Cocoa Beach. In Indonesia, they sneak in and eat anything that isn't hung by a string from the ceiling. On my first trip there, I had some chocolate in a closed tin can, and while I was napping, they dragged it to the corner and opened the lid. They're not stupid. They know you're going to come after them, so they pull their loot next to their hole for a quick escape. I slept with a bamboo stick to fend off the intruders.

The logistics of setting up an ASP contest in such a far-off place are overwhelming. Getting there is trouble enough. You have to fly from California to Sydney, which takes fourteen hours, and from Sydney to Bali, which is another seven hours. From Bali, the bus ride to the boat docks takes around five hours. The tide has to be high to get the boat out of the dock, and that ride lasts another twenty minutes to get to the harbor at Grajagan. Throw in layovers, and it's easily a two-day trip. The waves break a quarter of a mile from land, so a scaffold for the judges must be constructed on the reef. It doesn't seem worth the trouble until you see the waves. The wind blows light offshore every day, and it grooms the surface to perfection. It was double to triple overhead for the entire event, the best surf we'd ever had for an ASP contest.

I made the final against Jeff Booth. Jeff and I both rode for Quiksilver, which was great for the company after all the planning that went into the event. As I paddled out, I got pounded by sets for ten minutes. Unlike my first win against Gary Elkerton in Hossegor, France, in 1992, this heat started without me. Jeff already had a wave and was back out to the lineup before I made it out. Luckily, on my first wave I got five barrels, setting the tone for the rest of the final. I scored a perfect ten on that wave and backed it up with a couple of other good rides to earn a magical, memorable win.

The season turned into a three-man race between Sunny Garcia, who won at Bells, Rob Machado, who won in Japan, and me.

The next event was in July on Reunion Island off the southern coast of Africa, and in the fourth round I met my old nemesis Gary Elkerton. Again, we were faced with a symbolic clash between generations. It was Old School Australians versus New School Americans, and he was frothing to get back at me for the loss at Hossegor. We'd had a few heats since then, and each time I found a way to hold him off. On the beach, it was as if there were a line drawn in the sand. It was obvious which guys supported Elkerton, and he had a whole crew getting him psyched up.

The waves were pumping at Reunion, and I was rattled by his aggressiveness. I had the waves to beat him, but I fell a few times out of nervousness and lost. It was a huge win for the old guys and a bit of retribution for Elkerton. His buddies were pouring beer on his head and screaming like mad, as if he had won the whole contest, even though it was only the fourth round. I was pissed that they were making such a big deal of it. Gary was clearly over the moon and walked straight up to me and said,

"Good heat, mate. Tough luck." It takes a while to swallow a loss like that, and I hadn't had time to deal with it yet. I felt Elkerton was sort of throwing it in my face to antagonize me. I looked at him and said, "F—k you." Obviously, I overreacted, but at the time I was caught up in the emotion. My mind was on the bigger picture—the ASP ratings—so losing to anyone was unacceptable.

When I really thought about it later, I felt honored that guys felt they won something by beating me in a heat. Seeing the reaction from his friends on the beach, it made me realize just how bad guys wanted to beat me.

I was back in Huntington, California, in August for the U.S. Open and made it to the man-on-man final against Rob Machado. It seemed like every single person on the beach was pulling for Rob and booing me. The waves were tiny, and I broke the nose off my board. The crowd got their wish as Rob absolutely smoked me. It's tough when you feel like no one is on your side. It sure would be nice if the tour went to Florida once in a while. There probably wouldn't be any waves, but at least I'd have some people cheering for me.

We returned to Europe directly after the Huntington event in August. I had consistent results (ninth at Lacanau, third in Hossegor, and fifth at Biarritz), but lost ground in the standings to Sunny and Rob, who each won an event in France. Europe is always the meat and potatoes of the tour because it hosts so many contests. Every heat is do-or-die. I had a couple really close ones and was cursing the judges but mostly myself for not taking advantage of the situations. This race was too close for comfort, especially since I was up against Rob.

Rob and I were good friends, but by this time the world title race was starting to wear on our friendship. I remember when we met in 1985 at the U.S. Championships at Sebastian Inlet in Florida. Rob came walking up to me with his dad, Jim, who said, "Hey, Kelly. I'm Jim Machado. This is my son, Rob. Do you mind taking a picture with us?" Rob was really embarrassed, but we hit it off right away. By 1995, we were pretty much best friends. We traveled together and had the same manager.

The Rio International Pro in Brazil during October set the stage for the final event at Pipe. A good showing would bring me close to the other guys and relieve some pressure, but there was a chance—if Rob or Sunny won—that I would fall from contention. In the quarterfinals, I faced Barton Lynch, who was thirty-two and barely hanging on to his career. Since he was well past his prime it seemed like an easy draw, but Barton was a crafty competitor. He knew how to get into my head by ignoring me and acting totally nonchalant before a heat. I had a mental block when it came to surfing against him that went all the way back to our first meeting in 1989 at the Aloe Up Cup in New Smyrna Beach, Florida. I was a seventeen-year-old amateur, and Barton was the reigning world champion. He was pretty content with his career even back then, so the night before our heat, he was at a party blind drunk, smoking cigars and carousing with a bunch of girls. I walked into the party and was shocked to see that he wasn't worried about the heat. I didn't party because I wanted to be in top form the next day. He showed up for the contest tired and hungover, and was still able to beat me.

In Brazil six years later, he still knew how to throw me off my game, and he beat me. If Sunny went on to win the event, my title hopes were finished. Sunny and Barton met in the final, and Barton became the oldest surfer to win a WCT contest. More important for me, it kept me in the running. With only one event left for the year, the Pipe Masters, my winning the title was a long shot. By the time I got home to Florida, I all but resigned myself to losing.

YOU DROPPED A BOMB ON ME

On the morning of October 17, 1995, I was sleeping comfortably in my new condo in Cocoa Beach. Even though I was only spending a couple months a year in Florida, I thought I should have my own place. My mom got a place with her husband and Stephen lived with them. Sean and a few of his friends were living in the old house I bought for my family.

Outside, it was pouring rain. It was the sort of morning where you don't want to get out of bed. The phone rang, and I picked it up and found that it was Tamara, a girl I had dated that summer in Fort Lauderdale. Since we weren't an item any longer, I knew she wasn't calling just to say hi. She told me we needed to talk and that she was driving up immediately.

The weather turned the three-hour drive into four-and-a-half hours of misery. I didn't have cable TV, didn't have a car, and there was no surf. All I could do was sit and wait. She didn't say what to expect, and she didn't have to. I told my mom she was coming, and as moms do, feared the worst. "Oh my God, Kelly. She's got AIDS." I told her to calm down and that I had a hunch Tamara was coming to tell me she was pregnant. Relieved, my mom said, "Oh. Well that's okay."

Tamara eventually arrived and confirmed my fear. She explained our options by saying, "I'm ready to have a child, so I'm going to keep the baby. I can do this on my own if you don't want to be involved. Or we can try to work things out between us. If that won't work, we can remain apart and both be parents." Choices A and B were out of the question. We weren't a couple anymore, and we weren't going to be. Still, I couldn't imagine having a child and not being a part of his or her life, so it was an easy decision. I told her that I wanted to be involved in raising our child, and thanked her for coming to tell me. The rain had let up by that time, and she returned home.

After she left, I sat and thought for a long while. As a kid, I thought of twenty-three as a good age to start a family, but now that I was there, the idea seemed another ten years off. I was still a kid myself. Until that day, I had one responsibility, which was to win surf contests. I'd never had a real job or paid a bill, but it was time to grow up. Things were different now. I was going to be a father.

As hard as this pill was to swallow, it relieved pressure in other ways by putting things in perspective. Compared to being a parent, ratings seem unimportant. I can't say I was no longer worried about the upcoming finale at Pipeline, but it definitely had a new spin.

SHIT 'N' ROSES

I considered every possible scenario and knew exactly what it would take for me to win the world title. I was in third place. For me to come out on top would take a minor miracle. I had to win at Pipe, which was conceivable. But if Rob made it to the final or Sunny advanced through two heats, I wouldn't be able to catch them no matter how I finished in the event. Sunny had won the Hawaiian Triple Crown three consecutive seasons leading up to 1995 and would be surfing in his own backyard with all of Hawaii cheering for him. Since he was in the lead, it was his title to win or lose. He hadn't finished less than ninth all year, and everyone thought he would dominate at Pipe.

Surfer magazine interviewed Rob, Sunny, and me in October, two months before Pipeline. I was the last to be interviewed and was told what the other guys had said. Sunny sounded arrogant, saying, "There's no way I would bet against me," while Rob didn't know the point standings and didn't care. I said that, most likely, I'm not going to win the world title, and I needed to be comfortable with that. In my mind, I approached it like I already lost. My mom and Bryan Taylor liked to say that I could fall into a pile of shit and come out smelling like a rose. Going into Pipeline, things definitely looked shitty.

By the time we got to Hawaii at the end of November, there

was already a ton of hype surrounding the event. A friend of mine named Peter King, a former pro surfer from San Diego, hosted a show on MTV at the time called *Sandblast* and convinced the network to go to Hawaii to shoot its "Ultimate Winter Vacation." It was sort of like spring break, and they used the showdown at Pipe as a backdrop. Everywhere we turned, there was press on the beach.

It had been a grueling war between Rob, Sunny, and me. We each set up camp within a quarter of a mile radius of one another for the North Shore winter season. Rob rented a place at Backdoor, Sunny was staying at the famous Gerry Lopez house at Pipe, and I was over at the Johnson's at Ehukai. It was too stressful to hang out with Rob, so I pretty much stayed away from his house. We shared a lot of the same friends, and since he had never won a world title, it seemed like most of them were in his corner. I got the feeling that people were ready to see a new world champion, whether it was Rob or Sunny. I was a little hurt, but having people root against me only made me try that much harder. It would have been nice to have people sitting on my deck and screaming for me, but I still had a job to do.

As soon as the contest began, a wrench was thrown into the machine. Twenty-nine-year-old Mark Occhilupo, after spending a few years sitting on the sofa, was superfit again and surfing in the 1995 Pipe Masters trials. He was so dominant that even with an interference he advanced to the main event. Since he came in as the lowest seed, he was matched against the number one seed, Sunny. If Sunny lost, there would be one less variable I'd need to worry about.

There was nothing I could do except get out my pom-poms and silently cheer for Occy. I was too nervous to watch. Had I not been in the next heat, I would have left the beach. All of Hawaii wanted Sunny to win, and there were rumors that Occy might not even paddle out for fear of his life. It was *that* tense. He was

escorted to the water's edge by security to prevent him being taken out by an angry Hawaiian. I tried to focus on getting ready for my heat, but every time I looked up, Sunny was falling and Occy was getting barreled. My pile of shit was starting to smell pretty good.

When Occy realized he was winning, he got frazzled and did everything in his power to lose. This contest was as important for his comeback as it was for any of us, but it wasn't worth the beating he stood to take for eliminating Hawaii's favorite son. Not here, not now. Occy paddled to the shoulder and was coaching Sunny into waves, trying desperately not to win. It was enough for Occy to know that he still had it; he didn't want to go through with winning. But short of scaling the judges' tower and running off with the scoring sheets, Occy was too far ahead to lose. In the end, the crowd was too shocked to react, and Occy got away before the people on the beach came to their senses.

With Sunny out of the picture, the ball landed in my court.

Winning the title was back within my control. Rob was on my side of the draw. All I needed to do was keep winning.

On the morning of December 19, 1995, before rolling out of bed to check Pipeline, I took a minute to consider my options. I could lose my quarterfinal heat to Hawaiian Kalani Robb and walk away with a couple thousand bucks in prize money and a huge missed opportunity. Or, I could win the contest and pocket nearly a hundred grand in contest earnings and bonuses, win my third world title, and seal the Triple Crown.

Up to that point, most of the pressure I had experienced in my career—from learning to surf big waves to winning world titles, to being seen as a sellout to the sport—had to do with long-term achievements. I had time to work solutions out in my head. But now there was so much riding on a single day of surfing. The stakes were greater than anything I had encountered before. I wished there was nothing on the line, that it was strictly for fun, but there were points, money, and careers in the balance.

I became more focused than ever. I knew I had to be on every good wave and couldn't give my opponents the slightest opportunity to beat me. Even though competitive surfing leaves a lot to chance, in my mind there was no way I could lose.

After beating Kalani Robb in the quarterfinals, my next heat was against Rob Machado. If Rob won, he was the champ. If I won, Rob was still the champ unless I won the final.

Pipeline was classic, with offshore winds and eight-foot peaks breaking in both directions. Rob and I agreed to take turns in the lineup rather than hassling for waves, so we did rock-paper-scissors to see who would go first, and I won. It helped relieve some tension, and by the time we reached the lineup, we couldn't help but laugh at the situation. Here we were, two best friends, riding perfect waves in front of the entire surfing world for the title. It was like slap-boxing with your best friend for the heavy-weight championship. We couldn't dream up a better scenario.

As the heat progressed, the scores became secondary to the enjoyment of the moment. Our friends may have been divided in their support on the beach, but the situation brought Rob and me closer than ever. I went left on one wave and kicked out in time to see Rob cruising into a perfect barrel. He came flying out and I sat upright in the channel, and I stuck my hand in the air for a high-five. He did a little cut back to set it up and slapped my hand as he rode past.

Without a doubt, that heat was the pinnacle of my career. The best part was that all our friends saw how much fun we were having, and it brought everyone back together. It proved that in the heat of competition, you don't have to hate your opponent to perform at the top level. It's not even about the other person so much as doing your best. The whole beach was sharing in the feeling, except maybe Sunny.

The judges were splitting hairs to pick a winner. At the time, it was the highest scoring heat in ASP history. The rights were a tad longer, so they were offering longer rides. I stuck to riding Backdoor for much of the heat, and I came out on top. Unless my momentum carried me through against Occy in the final, it was all for nothing.

For Occy, victory meant a perfect comeback, and seeing how nervous he was to be thrust back in the limelight gave me an advantage. He was still one of my heroes, so I felt I owed him something. As we paddled out for the final, I said, "Occy, this heat's as important for you as it is for me. Don't think twice about anything else. Just go for it." Looking back, it sounds as corny as Rocky and Mr. T, but he knew what I meant.

I've always been fascinated by Occy's surfing, but something he said way back in 1984 stuck in my head. He was quoted in a surf magazine saying something to the tune of, "It's time we get serious and stop these American wankers." I was only twelve, but as an American I took it personally, never forgot it, and carried a grudge every time we met in a heat.

The match with Rob took most of my energy, and I struggled to maintain a lead in the final. Occy seemed to have used up his magic as well, and I won the heat. It couldn't have been scripted better, but my bed of roses was bittersweet. A very small part of me wanted to see Sunny earn a world title. And another part of me wanted to see Rob and his family share in that as well, since they had been a second family to me for many years. In the final standings, I beat Rob by only eighty points; it was the closest race in ASP history.

DONNIE SOLOMON

Even though my apprehension in big waves had disappeared, I still took only what I considered to be calculated risks. Many of the guys I surfed with were complete madmen. On Thanksgiving Day 1995, Todd Chesser, Shane Dorian, and Ross Williams paddled into some the biggest waves I had ever seen nearly a quarter of a mile out at sea. Each of them had a near-drowning experience that session. When the ocean settled down a bit that afternoon, I went out and caught the most enormous closeout I've ever encountered directly on the head. It snapped my biggest board like a toothpick. Luckily, there were a few guys in the lineup on Jet Skis, and I was quickly plucked from danger. I came away feeling I could survive almost anything.

I stayed in Hawaii for a few weeks after Pipeline as I always do, surfing with my friends as the peak-season crowds thin out. A really big swell filled in over the next few days, and on December 23, Waimea Bay was twenty feet (the faces were nearly double that).

It was a year to the day after Mark Foo died surfing Maverick's in northern California. Mark lived by the motto, "If you want to get the ultimate thrill, you've got to be willing to pay the ultimate price."

I was having my best Waimea session ever, trading waves with my friends Ross Williams and Donnie Solomon. A couple of hours into our session, I dropped into a big one. The wave exploded behind me, but out of the whitewater emerged Donnie. I took off late; he must have been beyond late. He made the wave and rode up next to me screaming at the top of his lungs with joy, claiming it was the best ride of his life. He sat up on his board and gave me a hug, and we paddled back out together. Everyone who saw the drop congratulated him on the way out, and you couldn't have pried the smile from his face.

Donnie was from Ventura, California, and spent months each year on the North Shore riding big waves, small waves, everything. He had plenty of experience surfing at Sunset, Haleiwa, and Pipeline. We had competed together as amateurs and stayed together at the Hill House. After catching that wave, he was on top of the world. He was also happy because his personal life was working out better. He hadn't been on the best of terms with his family, but he began to make amends with them while he was in Hawaii. A week earlier at the Johnsons' house, he said, "Kelly, as long as I can remember, I've never told anyone that I loved them. I talked to my grandmother tonight and told her I loved her. It felt great." He was flying home later that day to spend Christmas with his dad for the first time in years. He couldn't have been happier.

After Donnie's amazing ride, we decided it was time for breakfast and agreed to take the next wave in. Ross, Donnie, and I paddled for a wave, but Donnie missed it and paddled back into position for another one. Ross and I rode to the beach and turned around to see the biggest set of the day closing out the bay.

When a set of waves closes out Waimea Bay, pandemonium sets in. Guys bail their boards, Jet Skis are forced into the rocks, and the crowd on dry land holds its breath. We watched some guy paddle straight up the face of a huge wave and try to poke through the lip. He didn't make it and was pulled over the falls backward. "No way," I said to Ross, "that guy in yellow trunks just got killed." It was a figure of speech. You see crazy stuff like that at Waimea all the time, and guys pop back up.

Another friend of ours, Ricky Irons, was watching from the point and said the guy in the yellow trunks didn't come up before the next wave. Ricky lost sight as the waves pushed around the corner but figured he probably surfaced farther inside. There were more waves in the set and people were losing boards everywhere. We were starving and had to go back to our house to get money before meeting Donnie, who had driven to the beach separately, for breakfast.

On our way to the showers, a Hawaiian guy came up to me and said, "The spirits are looking out for you today. I can see it; you're really in tune." I had no idea who the guy was and thought it was kind of odd, but I thanked him as Ross and I drove away.

Half an hour later, we came back around the bay on our way to breakfast and saw a group of people huddled on the beach. When that happens, it means somebody is hurt. Since I knew a lot of the people in the water that day, I pulled over to have a look. I was walking toward the crowd, and when I was about thirty feet away I heard a friend of mine yelling, "Come on, Donnie!" My heart sank. I ran the rest of the way and saw that the person being tended to was Donnie Solomon. The lifeguards were performing CPR on him, and even though Donnie was bloated and pale, I believed he would start coughing up water and come around. Along with the shock of seeing my friend in that position, a wave of guilt came over me as I realized it had been Donnie whom Ross and I saw get smashed by the closeout set from the beach. I had seen it happen and wondered if there was anything I could have done to save him.

There were so many boards floating around, that it had taken thirty minutes for anyone to realize Donnie was attached to one. He apparently got knocked out underwater and drowned. I kept asking the paramedics if he would be okay, because I didn't want to accept that he was dead.

Donnie was staying with a guy named Norm Thompson and his family on the North Shore. That morning, he had gone to grab his board and told Norm he was going to catch one last wave at Waimea before heading home. It ended up being his best and last.

Norm's family was devastated. His kids loved Donnie and were sitting around moping all Christmas morning. After they opened their presents, they noticed a box hidden behind the tree. They pulled it out and realized it was from Donnie. They didn't know he had bought them anything, but inside was a bunch of clothes for the kids. It helped cheer them up.

Only a handful of surfers have died in big waves during recorded history. (It just so happens that I knew the last three of them—Mark Foo in 1994, Donnie in 1995, and Todd Chesser in 1997.) Other than those guys, there hasn't been a big-wave death for years. For my friends and me, losing Donnie was a wake-up call to be more careful, but not something that kept us from riding big waves. Donnie's death, like that of Mark's—who probably got his leash tangled on a submerged rock—seemed to be a freak accident. It appeared Donnie made a fatal mistake by trying to paddle over the wave instead of bailing off his board and diving for the bottom. With caution, the odds of dying in big waves are slim.

Riding big waves is part of the evolution of surfing and of growing up. When you're a baby, nothing is more exciting than learning that you can control your fingers and grab things. Then you learn to crawl, and walk, and within a few months, you want to do something more difficult, and that progression goes on throughout your life.

Surfing is the same way. When you start, you think paddling through the water is the greatest thing in the world. You're like, "Wow, I have enough balance to paddle. I can catch waves by myself." Next thing you know, paddling is a chore, but you did your first bottom turn, got your first barrel, or did your first off-the-lip. It keeps evolving. You don't get as excited about small waves after you catch a twenty-footer. The next time you want to get barreled on it. It's an insatiable desire.

Peer pressure, ego, and a lot of other factors are involved in riding big waves, but basically it's the nature of progress. My development was a steady, calculated process. Each time I went bigger, I was scared, but by the next time, I was ready for more. They say if you're not scared you're lying, but there are some guys—maybe a handful at any given time—who are willing to take off on waves that can kill them. Brock Little has told me, "I didn't care. I took off on waves where I thought I would die and refused to back down and look like a puss."

TOWING IN

Around the time of Donnie's death, a new development in the sport was changing the way we looked at big waves. People were getting towed into them, and the quest to ride the world's biggest wave was on.

There comes a point where manpower alone isn't enough, where a giant wave is moving too fast to catch by conventional means. The bigger the board, the faster it paddles, but even on the old ten-foot elephant guns, as big-wave boards are called, you can paddle only so fast. Getting towed into waves by a personal watercraft so far has been the biggest advancement in surfing during my lifetime. I would regard it as its own sport, but in essence it's still surfing. The idea goes back to the 1930s, when some genius hired a helicopter to pull him into waves. It didn't catch on until the early 1990s, when a crew of guys on Maui started using Jet Skis to tow into waves that were too big to catch by paddling. The biggest change was that since they didn't have to paddle, they could ride a really small board, which meant they could maneuver easily on the wave. The way it works is, a surfer stands on the board holding a towrope, his feet are strapped in, and he is pulled behind a Jet Ski—or other type of personal watercraft—as though he is water-skiing. When the wave starts to take shape, he lets go of the rope and drops into it. Tow-surfing has developed its own equipment, using short, narrow, heavy boards that are easier to maneuver than the bulky guns needed for paddling. Tow-surfers use foot straps to keep from bouncing off their boards when they hit a big hunk of chop in the ocean.

By towing in, you can literally catch as many waves as you want. In the past we were lucky to catch more than a handful on a really big day. Now, you see a wave, and you go. Even if it's almost breaking already, the speed of the Jet Ski can whip you in the perfect position to catch it. You can place yourself anywhere on the wave—the shoulder, deep in the pit, even in the barrel. After years of trying to paddle into big waves, I say to myself, "What have I been doing?"

In theory, you can take someone who has never surfed and pull him into a thirty-foot wave. And that's what tow-surfers are worried about—inexperienced riders bumbling into life-threatening situations. So far, no tow-surfers have drowned, while a number of conventional surfers have lost their lives in the line of duty. Having a partner able to swoop in and rescue you makes surfing safer.

The camaraderie is still there, even more so because you're relying on your driver to snatch you from a bad situation. You grab hold of a sled mounted behind the ski and never experience the misery of getting caught inside and taking your thrashings the old school way.

I had my first tow session in 1998, at a place called Jaws on Maui. By the next year, I was starting to get a feel for it. Like anything, it was awkward at first, but since then I've had a dozen or so sessions in Hawaii, Indonesia, Australia, Tahiti, and Fiji. The bulk of those were in small waves, but I've ridden a few big days along the outer reefs of Oahu. Since it requires a major investment of time and money to purchase a Jet Ski and learn the ins and outs of rescues, there are too many things on my plate right now to pursue tow-surfing as much as I'd like. But there are guys pushing the limits each year, and I'm confident that it's only a matter of time before one of them breaks the hundred-foot barrier.

10

Never Give Up

FINDING MOTIVATION AFTER THE way things ended at Pipeline in 1995 was almost impossible. I had achieved all I wanted from surfing. Since I had taken better care of my money, I had all that I'd ever need. There was no way I could get so much satisfaction from a surf contest again. It almost seemed a waste of time to try. After seeing a good friend like Donnie die and knowing that I was about to bring another life into this world, putting all my focus on surf contests seemed almost inconsequential.

I kept going because I wanted to try to match Mark Richards's record of four world titles. At the same time, I was thinking ahead to a fifth title, because that would tie Mark's record of four in a row. But nobody wants to just tie a record; I'd have to go for six. It wasn't cockiness, but I needed to set high goals to stay focused. If I didn't seize the opportunity while I had it, I might be too old to do it down the road. I didn't want to look back and think "coulda shoulda."

Perhaps I was getting ahead of myself, because after my first place finish in February 1996 at the Coke Classic in Narrabeen, Australia, it was all downhill from there. I finished ninth on Australia's Gold Coast, seventeenth at Bells, and ninth in Japan. Looking over my results from years past, I figured that I needed to average third place points in each event to have a shot at the title. If I won a couple, I could slide on a few others. To me, a ninth place might as well be thirty-third because it meant I didn't do well, but I didn't do too bad either. The middle of the road was not where I wanted to be. On the ASP tour, the organization drops the lowest 25 percent of your results in the final standings. In 1996, there were fourteen events, so they dropped three events from the final tally. After my first four contests, there was no more room for mistakes.

Fortunately, we were headed for Grajagan at the end of May for the second annual Quiksilver Pro. Once again the waves were perfect lefts, and I had high hopes of backing up my 1995 win. In the semifinals, I faced Gary Elkerton for the first time since losing to him at Reunion almost a year earlier. The waves were flawless, and the heat was going my way, right down to Gary's final wave. It's rare that someone scores a ten in competition. In some events there isn't a single one; at the most, perhaps you'll see a handful. He needed a near perfect score to turn the heat. He got a deep barrel, scored the first perfect ten of his career, and beat me.

There was so much media hype around the generation clash that losing to Elkerton brought out the worst emotions in me. I was so flustered after the heat that I sat out in the water screaming and even punched myself in the head. At least this time I was smart enough to release my anger far enough from land so that no one could see me. I got it all out of my system, and afterward went over to Gary's tree house to apologize. We had a good talk and shook hands. In fact, we became good friends after that.

Elkerton went on to face Shane Beschen in the final. Shane won, and having previously won in Japan gave him back-to-back victories. No one had done that since Tom Curren in 1990. Shane jumped out to a huge lead in the ratings. He was a great competitor and a wave magnet, and in 1996 he hit his stride. On the Gold Coast, he got three insane barrels at Kirra and scored a ten for each, with thirty points, and it was the only perfect heat in ASP history. Before that, my 29.7 points against Rob at Pipe was the highest. Even though my third place at Grajagan fit into my overall plan for winning the world title, Shane was pulling away.

Throughout my career, I've had mini rivalries with many surfers, but none bigger than the one with Shane. We traveled together on the U.S. team and were friends, but professionally we were definitely rivals. Since 1985, when I beat him in the Boys' Division at the U.S. Championships at Sebastian Inlet, we were going head-to-head, always meeting in the big contests and battling for first and second. It was beginning to look like I had a fight for the 1996 world title on my hands.

ZITLESS AND FITNESS

During the summer of 1996, I went to the *Surfing* magazine office in San Clemente, California, to look at some photos. There's a big wall in the reception room that people scribbled graffiti all over. They wrote things like "So-and-so was here" or tried to come up with something witty. I was with a girl I was dating from Virginia Beach named Jenny, and when we walked into the office, one of the messages seemed to jump right off the wall. It said, "Kelly Slater has zits." I tried to laugh it off, but inside it was killing me. I was a late bloomer, and from the time I was eighteen years old, I had really bad skin. In fact, the first time a story about me appeared in an Australian surf mag, it detailed in bold print that I had a giant zit on my face and popped it. My dad and Sean had the same skin problems, so I figured I was doomed. Jenny saw how upset it made me and convinced me to see a dermatologist, who gave me a prescription for Accutane. Like any medicine, it has a long list of side effects, but the most problematic one for me was that it made my skin highly sensitive to sunlight. I had to cake sunscreen all over me for the six months I was on the medication. Eventually it worked, and my skin cleared up.

Around the same time, I came across some information that made me think my diet had a lot to do with my overall health. I read an article by Brazilian jujitsu master Rickson Gracie (who happens to be an avid surfer) about food combining. He explained how the body was intended to ingest one food at a time, not a bunch of different things. With conflicting foods, your mouth gets mixed signals and sends out the wrong digestive enzymes. When Rickson eats a carrot, he eats carrots and nothing else. I stumbled upon a book called *Fit for Life,* also on the topic of food combining. It made me aware of the effect of eating everything in sight. The idea is to eat either one form of carbohydrate or one form of protein in a single meal, along with fruits and vegetables. The result is quicker metabolism and more efficient digestion.

I began to realize that I couldn't live on Doritos and Oreos and expect to be healthy. Mixing all sorts of different foods can make a person feel sluggish. After reading the articles, and remembering how unhealthy I was as a kid, I realized that I could have prevented a lot of illnesses if I had just eaten properly. So I changed my diet and noticed that as soon as I did, my skin and my energy level improved.

FATHER KNOWS LITTLE

On June 4, 1996, around the time I was punching myself in the head after losing to Elkerton at Grajagan, my daughter, Taylor, was born. It took me two full days of traveling to get from Indonesia to Florida to see her. I wanted to be there to offer Tamara my support. Taylor was born with a rare and potentially fatal bacterial infection and had to spend ten days in intensive care. I was able to hold her, but I had a hard time knowing how to act as a father. I pretty much got off the plane from Grajagan, dropped my stuff off, and went to the hospital. It was as if the stork dropped a package in my lap and said, "Here's your baby." I felt lost and yearned for support from my own family, but none of them came down to the hospital.

It was awkward being in such close quarters with Tamara. She still wanted us to work on a relationship, but I had moved on and was dating Jenny, who was upset that I hadn't told her about Tamara and the pregnancy sooner. But I didn't know how to tell anyone, let alone my girlfriend. I was slightly ashamed of having a child with someone I wasn't in a relationship with, and as selfish as it sounds, I was worried about how the media would handle the situation. Some of my closest friends didn't know I was a father until I announced it in a *Surfer* magazine interview with Matt Warshaw two years later.

As hard as it is to be a good parent, it's even harder when you're never around. Before I had time to master the art of burping and diaper changing, I was off for the next event.

WIN AT ALL COSTS

The season was nearly half finished, and I was way behind. The stress and expectations of winning another world title were wearing me down. I put so much pressure on myself to narrow the gap on Shane Beschen that I couldn't surf freely. Another ninth place finish would put me so far behind Beschen that I'd lose hope.

The next event took place in June at Reunion Island. When we weren't surfing, my friends and I passed the time by playing a game that was sort of like shuffleboard without a stick. There was a board, and we each took turns sliding discs on it. On the last throw we could knock everybody's pieces off the board and win the game. Each time we played, I was losing bad but ended up winning on my last turn. Playing the game suddenly gave me a new perspective on surfing. I realized focusing on the big picture was holding me back. I had to concentrate on what I was doing every second and keep in mind that as long as there was time on the clock, I still had a chance.

I labored through a few heats before coming to the fourth round. My opponent was the brilliant tactician Barton Lynch. I was still struggling with the mental block I had when competing against Barton, but it was all about to change.

At Reunion, the waves were easily double overhead. My objective was to focus on the moment, but at the moment I was losing. It was a long paddle back to the lineup, and I started paying attention to every stroke I took, every breath, and every movement. The title chase became secondary to the here and now. I broke everything down into baby steps—put one arm in front of the other to paddle and didn't think about anything else.

I caught a wave just before the buzzer, knowing I needed a strong ride. Rather than tightening up, I felt completely free. Riding into the shallow, unpredictable inside section of the wave, I took a chance and snapped my board around under the lip, escaping just before the thing landed on my head. I made the move and beat Barton. It had taken me seven years, but I broke his spell over me. It felt great.

Next came the semifinals and I was up against Sunny Garcia. Sunny's first ride was a ten. The waves were huge, and giant mounds of whitewater were pummeling us. Guys were winning heats with total scores of twelve or thirteen on three scoring rides. There wasn't much chance of finding another ten out there, but I forgot about Sunny's scores and concentrated on myself. I found a nice wave and scored a 9.5, while Sunny got cleaned up by a few sets and barely caught another wave. I went on to win the heat and the contest. It was true: you're never out of it until it's over.

I was feeling unstoppable by July as the tour headed for one of my favorite places in the world: Jeffreys Bay, South Africa. There, in my semifinal heat, Australian Luke Egan only needed a two-point ride to beat me, but the ocean went flat. He couldn't find the wave he needed before time ran out. I got lucky and went on to the final against Taylor Knox.

July is midwinter at Jeffreys, and mornings are miserably cold, even wearing a full wetsuit. (They don't get any waves during their summer, when it's warm.) The sand makes your feet so cold that they burn with pain as you're running into the water—you have to wear booties just for walking across the beach. I was wearing booties during the final, but they made my feet slip all over the wax on my board. I had to nurse my board through a few safe turns and try to get barreled. Luckily, there were plenty of barrels. I got five on my first wave, scored a perfect ten and took the wind out of Taylor's sails. He figured he couldn't catch me and seemed to not really try, which was a good thing, because I was so cold I couldn't put my fingers together.

From there, it was back to Huntington, California, in August for the U.S. Open, where, as fate would have it, Shane Beschen and I ended up in the final. As far as I was concerned, this heat was going to determine the world title, since we each won two of the last four events coming into this one. Winning here would set the tone going into Europe. He was surfing with such strength and confidence that I was nervous.

As soon as the final heat began, Shane and I paddled for the same wave. Nobody had priority, so the surfer who is closest to the curl of the wave has the right of way. It was technically my wave, but he didn't realize I was paddling for it. Winning on an interference is still a win, so I wasn't going to back down. I took off behind him and stood up on my board and kicked out. Shane never knew I was there, but the judges nevertheless scored his ride a zero for interfering and as a penalty would only count his two best rides instead of the typical three. He rode the wave to the beach, oblivious to what had happened. He paddled back out and rode two more waves to the sand. If the contest had been based only on surfing, he would have won. But with the penalty, there was almost no way he could beat me.

Halfway through the twenty-five-minute heat, he finally heard the commentator say, "Shane Beschen, you need a twelve-point ride to catch Kelly." First he was confused, which was soon replaced with anger. He asked me the same thing I've asked people who've pulled similar stunts on me: "What, you can't beat me without giving me an interference?" He claimed I was scared of him, and to be honest, as far as competition went, I was.

All twenty thousand people who were watching were rooting for Shane. It was California against Florida, right against wrong, sportsmanship against being a prick. There was pressure from Shane, pressure from the crowd, and pressure from my conscience. I considered dropping in on Shane to incur a penalty, even the score, and try to win on talent alone. "Nah," I thought. "That would be stupid." It's like playing blackjack. If you have twenty-one, you never ask for another card. I had it in the bag, and if I didn't take the win right there, it might cost me the world title, which was my ultimate goal. I had to suck it up and take the criticism.

As I rode my last few waves, I was being booed on the beach and people were bad-mouthing me. I felt I had burned my bridges in Huntington Beach. Onstage for the awards, the air was tense. Shane almost refused to show up, making me feel even worse, but he reluctantly accepted his second place trophy. He considered it a compliment that I would go to such extremes to beat him, but he was also bummed that I ruined his momentum for the year.

The World Tour isn't a popularity contest, and even though a lot of people weren't happy with my sneaky tactics, I was on a roll. In France, I kept winning. After a fifth in Lacanau, I scored back-to-back first place finishes at Hossegor and Biarritz. For the quarterfinals at Grande Plage in Biarritz, the waves were so small they considered canceling the event and splitting the points and

prize money between the eight remaining competitors. Shane had already lost in the event, so obviously I wanted the opportunity to win and put another couple hundred points between us. Even if I lost, he wouldn't gain any ground on me. We were way ahead of the pack, and no one else had a chance of catching up for the season. I did my part to convince the organizers to go on with the contest and ended up winning. From there, all I had to do was show up at the next event in Figueira da Foz, Portugal, and I would be the world champion.

We had almost the entire month of September off before Portugal, so I went home to Florida. I was tired of traveling and needed some time away; besides, I had a daughter who was waiting to see me.

INSTANT KARMA

Airlines have never rolled out the welcome mat for surfers, and I am definitely included in that. Golfers don't have to pay an excess baggage fee to take their clubs on an airplane, but the fees for surfboards can be outrageous. For some reason, airlines won't give me a card that says, "Kelly Slater, Professional Surfer, Boards Travel Free." The average charge is around $80, but I've paid nearly $300 coming home from Japan after an agent opened my bag and charged for each individual board. Some agents let you slide; others thrive on ripping you off.

After hanging out at home for a few weeks after the French leg of the tour, I drove to Orlando on the last day of September to catch my flight to Portugal. Since the world title race had all but been decided, I didn't bother leaving early to warm up for the event. I only needed to surf a heat, win or lose, to gather enough points for an insurmountable lead, so I planned to show up the morning of the first round. I arrived at Orlando International in plenty of time to check in, but the ticket agent took an hour to decide what to charge me for my boards, a predicament surfers face all too often.

I had already checked in for my flight to Portugal, and the agent was twiddling his thumbs. I said, "Look, charge me whatever you want. I don't care. I have to leave." He wasted more time, ended up charging me $50, and said, "Run to the gate. The plane's about to leave." When I got there, the plane was gone.

I called the ASP to let them know I couldn't make it, but the director, Graham Stapleberg, said, "You've got to make it. You can't miss showing up to win the world title. You can't do that to the ASP." If I took the next flight, which wasn't until the following day, I wouldn't arrive until three P.M., and my heat was starting at eight A.M. Graham promised to hold my heat off until the end of the day, so I made a reservation on the next flight out.

The following day, I was upgraded to first class for my troubles, and I arrived half an hour before my heat against Bruno Charneca, a local wild card no one had ever heard of outside his hometown. Toward the end, I only needed a 5.5 to win, but I let a few waves go. I had completed my job for the year, and it would mean a lot more for him to win than for me. But as the heat wound down, I thought it might look bad if I didn't at least make an effort. My competitive nature got the better of me, and I was scrounging for a wave at the end. Nothing came, and he won. It made him an instant local hero. Someone later told me that he wouldn't have to pay for another meal in that town for the rest of his life because of his new status.

It was announced after the heat that I won my fourth world title. Nevertheless, I still didn't have much leverage when it came to the airlines. On my flight home, the airline refused to put me in first class as promised. I was one row back, staring at an open seat in the front cabin the whole flight. I was making enough money by that time to fly first class, but why spend more money on a plane ticket than I win in a contest? I knew from experience that I couldn't count on money always being there, so I was afraid to spend it. When I rented cars, I always went for the cheapest option. All I needed was a ride from point A to point B, something I could strap the boards to and go. It always ended up being a bright green Geo Metro. No one actually bought one of those little boxcars, and they ended up at low-budget rental car companies.

Still, that open seat in first class haunted me. Suffering

through a horrible meal, all I could think was, "That seat's supposed to be mine." It was like a Seinfeld episode—in fact, I think something similar happened to Elaine. Perhaps it was karma for snaking Shane at Huntington.

After clinching the title, I was homesick. There was no way I was getting back on a plane to go to Brazil for the Rio Pro the following week. Traveling and competing were the last things I wanted to do. By October I went thirty-five days without surfing. I was happy to be in Florida. The ASP tried to fine me five thousand bucks for skipping Rio, which was as much as you would make for third place in the event. I got a doctor's note because I was doing some physical therapy for my old recurring hip injury, so I avoided the fine and got to stay in Florida. The Brazilian media went into a frenzy, claiming it was a slap in the face that the world champ wouldn't compete in the event. They thought I had something personal against the country, which wasn't the case. I had put so much effort into the season that I was just tired of traveling.

With the world title in the bag, I didn't even want to go to Hawaii in November for the start of the winter season. For the first time since 1990, I didn't compete in the Hawaiian Triple Crown. In fact, I didn't compete in any World Qualifying Series events the entire year. I was focused only on competing in and winning man-on-man heats on the World Championship Tour. I had surfed my brains out for so long that I didn't even want to see the water.

I made it to Hawaii just as the Pipe Masters got under way in early December. It was the only Hawaiian event that I wouldn't miss for anything. It was an emotional letdown after the high-pressure event in 1995, but my mom came with me, giving me a good reason to win the contest. She'd never been to Hawaii, so I bought her a ticket and set her up with a place to stay with some friends of mine. Sean and Stephen happened to be in Hawaii that winter as well, but we were all staying in different places along the North Shore. We'd meet up at the beach each day, but there was so much going on around the contest that we didn't spend much time together.

This was the first year the Pipe Masters switched from four-man heats to man-on-man, which takes longer to complete an event. The locals are always making a stink over the amount of time their breaks are tied up with competitions, and they have a good point. They stick it out during the summers when the waves are flat, and as soon as the winter swells hit, the crowds are out of control. Man-on-man heats are better for competitors, but they don't make the locals happy.

I made the final against Hawaiian Sunny Garcia. People who don't know Sunny think he's a bully because he usually walks around with a snarl on his face. He's a couple years older than I am, but he turned pro when he was only fifteen and was already walking up to pros and threatening to kick their ass. He still talks more trash than probably any other pro surfer. When I was fifteen, I was five-feet tall and running around with a squeaky voice, too frightened to even talk to the pros. Sunny and I met in Hawaii at the 1982 U.S. Championships, and we've always had a good friendship. He stayed with my family in Florida a few times and is like another son to my mom. Usually competing against Sunny in Hawaii is intense, but my mom walked up to him before the final and jokingly said, "Don't screw with Kelly, or I'll smack you." Without the world title on the line, it was like we were surfing for fun.

Sunny started the heat with a ten, but I snapped to attention and took over with a few nice little Backdoor barrels. I had the final in the bag toward the end when we both started paddling for the same wave. Sunny looked at me and said, "There's no way I'm letting you have it," and dropped in on me. He knew the judges would penalize him, but there was no way he could catch me anyway. We pulled into the barrel together, and adding insult to injury, I rode up behind him and pushed him off his board.

He fell, and I emerged standing. It was my third straight win at Pipe.

With that, I finished the season with an ASP record $140,400 in prize money, as well as a $50,000 bonus from the ASP for winning the title. I was on a roll. I won half the events that season—seven in all, tying the ASP record.

My family rented a house after the contest and we spent our first Christmas together since 1992. It wasn't like we hung out and opened presents on Christmas morning, though. The waves

were really good, so all the boys went surfing and left my mom to go walking on the beach. She found a glass buoy from a Japanese fishing net that had washed up on the beach. Glass buoys haven't been used in a long time, and it's extremely rare to come across one. They're supposed to bring good luck.

11

One for Cheese

ON FEBRUARY 13, 1997, I was at the surf industry trade show in Long Beach, California, to make an appearance for Quiksilver. I came walking around a corner and saw Hawaiian big-wave surfers Mike Stewart and Shawn Briley hugging and crying in plain view in the middle of the day. When you see big, burly men bawling like babies, they're either blind drunk or something is horribly wrong. A crowd of friends quickly gathered, and Shawn broke the news that a friend from Hawaii had called to say that Todd "Cheese" Chesser had drowned.

Todd was one of my very good friends. He started surfing in Cocoa Beach a few years before me, but his mom, Jeannie, who was a really good surfer, decided to move to Hawaii rather than suffer through Florida surf. My most endearing memory of him is from a night in California after we went out to have a few beers with some friends. When we got back to the house in which we were staying, Todd couldn't wait to use the bathroom, so he peed over the top of our car—not on it, but clear over it. It looked like a rainbow. It was amazing; I didn't know that was possible.

Todd surfed professionally for several years before settling into a role as one of Hawaii's best big-wave riders. He was ultra-fit, pumping out hundreds of sit-ups every morning, and was right behind Brock Little in terms of fearlessness. He was a few years older than my crew, so we tagged along a few strokes behind him. When Todd couldn't talk any of us into surfing with him in giant waves, he'd go alone. The day Donnie Solomon died, Todd surfed waves at a reef a half a mile from the beach that were so big even he said he felt like an ant.

On February 13, Todd was supposed to be in Maui, Hawaii, doing stunt work for a Hollywood surf movie called *In God's Hands,* but he stayed on Oahu to spend Valentine's Day with his fiancée. He was three days shy of his twenty-ninth birthday and a few months away from getting married.

The swell on that day came up fast. Just as the waves on the outside reefs were getting big enough to break, Todd was standing on his truck with a pair of binoculars, checking it out. Civil Defense was riding along the streets warning people that the waves would be building rapidly, but Todd turned to his buddies Cody Graham and Aaron Lambert, who were also pro surfers, and remarked, "Yeah, whatever. Those guys don't know anything about the ocean." The three of them got their boards and headed out to surf.

By the time they got in the water, the waves were huge. Derek Ho, the 1993 world champion from Hawaii, was driving toward the beach and witnessed a massive, seemingly endless, set of waves. Back at the outer reef, the set broke in front of Todd, Cody, and Aaron. When the first wave hit, they all bailed off their boards and dove for the bottom. Cody temporarily blacked out underwater but managed to come up, as did Aaron. Todd didn't. He was under for several waves, and Cody and Aaron eventually reached his board and pulled him above water by his leash. If they had been tow-surfing with a Jet Ski, Todd likely would have been pulled to safety and survived. Instead, they were powerless to go in for help. The waves were too big to try to pull Todd to shore, so Aaron went in to find a lifeguard. By the time he returned, it was too late for Todd to be saved.

At the convention center in California, the news spread quickly and we were in disbelief. Todd was well known in the world of surfing, and the shock quickly spread throughout the entire building. Everyone sat around and cried.

We all flew to Hawaii, where a huge ceremony was held on the beach at Haleiwa, one of Todd's favorite breaks. Hundreds of surfers from around the world came in to say good-bye to Cheese and help spread his ashes in the Pacific.

I couldn't put Todd's death into perspective and cried nonstop for two weeks. It seemed to me like the deaths of Donnie Solomon and Mark Foo were fluky events. Donnie made a bad decision by trying to paddle over the wave at Waimea instead of bailing off his board and diving underwater for safety. Mark had traveled all night from Hawaii to get to Maverick's in northern California and was probably a bit out of sorts in the cold water. Todd simply got taken out by a big wave and drowned, making it harder to understand as he seemed invincible.

Todd was such a huge part of all our lives that, as a permanent reminder, somebody got the idea that we should all get tattoos on the inside of our arms that read, "In loving memory of Todd Chesser." We were sitting around at our friend Ross Williams's house on the North Shore getting inked up by a tattoo artist, when out of the blue someone mentioned that Todd hated tattoos and used to make fun of people who had them. Everyone laughed, and those of us who hadn't gone through with it yet, including me, were spared. I didn't have any tattoos and was thankful to get out of this one.

Wanting to do something to honor his memory, I asked Quiksilver to print some trunks with Todd's picture on them. They made forty-five pairs for me to pass out to his closest friends and family on the North Shore, but it was hard to draw the line. A steady stream of people came to my house saying, "I need a pair of the Chesser trunks." The trunks were really special to me, so I couldn't see giving them out to every person in Hawaii. We didn't make any more than the original forty-five, so they are collectors' items.

LET'S GET THIS OVER WITH

I flew back to Florida a few days after Todd's ceremony and thought about the year ahead. Fueled by grief, I pledged to win the world title for Todd. And I wasn't going to wait until the end of the season. I wanted to get it over with as quickly as possible.

According to plan, I went to Australia in March, and won the first two events in Sydney and the Gold Coast. I finished ninth at Bells, then went to Japan in May and won the next two events. It was pretty much a done deal, and we weren't even halfway through the season. In some cases, I had a feeling ahead of time I was going to win, having already seen it play out in my head.

My closest challenger that year was Mark Occhilupo, who was on his first full season back on the WCT after qualifying through the WQS and looked stronger and leaner than ever. He was so focused that I knew I had to be at the top of my game.

In the first of the Japanese events, the Tokushima Pro, I faced Occy in the final. Tokushima has some of the best surf in the world, but unfortunately the contest took place at the wrong time of year for good waves. It appeared Occy and I would be battling for the world title, so it was important for me to establish the upper hand. I went out in the final thinking it was going to be a really tough heat, but I started with a few strong waves, while Occy couldn't get in rhythm with the conditions. I won without feeling like I really had to work for it.

The next event was the Marui Pro in Torami Beach, Japan. Torami has a very small window for good surf. Most swells pass right by it, but this time we got lucky. I reached the final against Shane Beschen, whom I hadn't met in a heat since our run-in at Huntington in 1996. Before the event at Torami Beach, Shane's sponsor O'Neill ran a two-page ad of him in all the major surf magazines with the quote, "Next time I get him in a heat, it's on." He tried to talk them out of using the ad, but Shaun Tomson, the 1978 world champion and marketing director for O'Neill at the time, figured it would spark some interest and that Shane could back up his words. Most everyone who follows pro surfing knew the quote was directed at me and that it would fan the fire between us, which I welcomed. Anything to get me motivated was all right with me. The pressure was on for Shane to live up to his words.

I didn't say anything to anyone about the ad before the heat. Shane had been the high scorer in every round leading to the final, which freaked out a lot of guys. I had learned to pace myself. In the final, it's okay to try to blow away your opponent because you won't get another chance. And that's exactly what I did. I was on every good wave and didn't give Shane an inch. At one point, the announcer said, "Shane Beschen, you need an eighteen-point ride to gain the lead." Since it was Shane's comment that got me fired up for the heat, I thought it was funny. Shane wasn't laughing.

On the plane the next day, I was sitting two rows behind him. He turned to me and said, "I just want to know one thing. Did you see that ad in the magazine?" I told him I had, and he went into a tirade against Shaun Tomson for running it. Having competed against me for so many years, Shane knew what effect it would have on me.

THE MISSING LINK

Competitively, I was having my best run ever, and I can say with confidence that it was because I started golfing. Mitch Varnes, a stockbroker from Florida who I hired to help me manage my money in 1995, asked me to play golf so we could discuss some business when we first started working together. From the first nine holes, I was hooked. I went back to play the very next day. Golf is one area that I don't mind splurging in a little. I have friends that work for Titleist and Taylor Made, so I get clubs for free. But when I'm playing a lot, the greens fees can add up to the cost of another mortgage payment each month. When I go to a golf tournament, it's like being at a pro surfing contest as a kid. I study all the players and check out their gear like I used to, and I'm still just as amazed.

I'll be the first to admit that surfing and golfing, on the surface, don't have much in common. The country club lifestyle, the tedium of chasing a tiny ball around all day, and the silly pants—they're completely the opposite of surfing. The key element I took from golfing was that the guys with the best technique were the most consistent. Golf seems like an easy sport, but actually it's extremely difficult to get good at it. So many little things can go wrong with your swing, and that got me thinking about my technique on a surfboard. I began obsessing over pictures and trying to figure out where my weight was distributed on my board, how that applied to the curve of the wave, and whether I came out of turns with more speed or less, and if that was intentional or not. I reasoned that if I had to recover from a move, I'd performed it slightly wrong.

Instead of ever being fully satisfied with my surfing, I constantly search for ways to do it better. There's always room for micro-improvements. I can do a turn that feels as good as it gets, but on video I realize my weight's off or there's a different way I could have approached it that could have led me into the rest of the wave a little better. There's a perfect form for every place on a wave, and the trick is finding it. When it's found, a surfer should be able to get as radical as he or she wants and never be out of control. Ideally he or she can change direction anywhere on a wave without losing speed.

Considering that waves are an ever changing surface, it's a complex process of predicting what the wave's going to do and adjusting accordingly. I called my theory "the Surf Lesson" and am making notes on it in hopes of one day turning it into a book. It would apply to anyone who wanted to improve his surfing, from a complete novice to Mark Occhilupo and anyone in between, if they're willing to adhere to the rules.

I focused on my technique whenever I surfed and still do today. I don't think it was a coincidence that when I began applying my theory, my results drastically improved.

After Japan, I had won ten of my last thirteen events, by far the most successful stretch of my career. With such a fast start to the 1997 season, I had the luxury of easing up for the second half. At Grajagan in early June, the waves were again flawless, and Australian Luke Egan earned his first win after twelve frustrating years as the most underrated surfer on tour. It was the kind of surf surfers dream about, possibly the most flawless waves on earth. I lost to Luke in a great heat in round four, where we were both scoring nines and tens across the board. It never feels good to lose, but it's a great feeling to be a part of such an exciting heat.

To clinch the title, there wasn't much I needed to do during the European leg that went from August through September, so I wasn't too focused on winning. After earning a second place finish at the Lacanau Pro in France, I fell into a string of bad results, including a ninth and two seventeenths. At the Figueira Pro in Portugal, I needed to finish at least ninth to accumulate enough points to seal the ASP title. Unfortunately, I fell one heat short, but I still had a chance. Occy was the only surfer who could catch me in the ratings, so I sat around and watched him surf against another Australian, Shane Powell. Shane was oblivious to the fact that he was eliminating his fellow countryman for me, but he beat Occy and gave me my fifth title.

Although the race was over, I felt a sense of obligation to go to Brazil for the Kaiser Summer Surf Pro in Rio since I skipped that leg of the tour the year before. In the end, it was a good decision. I had a memorable heat against my friend from Hawaii, Ross Williams. While Ross was getting pounded by waves for fifteen minutes, I caught a perfect wave, got a great barrel, and did the longest floater of my life—I was riding weightlessly atop the folding lip of the wave for what seemed like forever (although it was probably just a couple seconds). The crowd went absolutely ballistic. Everyone on the beach stood and screamed. For that moment, I understood how it must feel to hit a game-winning home run in the World Series. It was the first time in my career that I felt like a superstar rather than just a surfer. I went on to once again face Occy in the final, and I beat him.

Surfing was great, but by the time the tour reached Hawaii for the Pipe Masters, all I wanted to do was golf. If the waves weren't perfect, and sometimes even when they were, I was off to Turtle Bay Golf Course, which is the only course on the North Shore, for my daily fix of fairways and greens. A lot of my friends were taking up golf as well, so I always had someone to play with. In the morning, I'd call Rob Machado and say, "Let's go play a really quick round." The quick games turned into all-day events. People would say, "I didn't see you out. Where'd you surf today?" It all went in one ear and out the other; I had a serious case of the golf bug.

Prior to the main event of the Pipe Masters, a trials event is held for the top local surfers. Since Pipe is such a demanding wave, the Hawaiians usually surf it better than the traveling pros, making the trials event almost more difficult than the main event. I felt I could command a solid performance at will and didn't bother warming up for the event. Only a couple surfers advance through the trials, and since I was the number one seed for the event, I faced the lowest seed, a local trialist named Johnny Boy Gomes. In my three-man round one heat (with the top two advancing), I finished second to Johnny. We were scheduled to meet again in a man-on-man heat later that day. With time to kill, Rob and I grabbed our clubs and went to play golf. The whole time I was stressing about making it back for my heat, but not enough to let it cut my game short. I showed up just in time to surf and fell several times on waves for no apparent reason. I knew I wasn't mentally focused to contend with Johnny and ended up in seventeenth, my worst showing ever at Pipe.

Nevertheless, that December I finished well ahead of Occy for my fifth world title, giving me the all-time lead and tying Mark Richards's record of four in a row. I earned $208,200 for the season, topping my 1996 record by 50 percent. And since Todd Chesser had been such a big part of my inspiration that season, I gave my trophy to Todd's mom, Jeannie.

February 13, 1998, a year to the day after Todd's death, was the coldest day of the year in Cocoa Beach, Florida. I was the only soul on the beach. In Todd's honor, I had just shaved my head and was wearing the trunks with his photo on them. I was freezing my balls off, but surfing a cold day in trunks was just the sort of thing Todd loved to do. I wanted to run for cover back inside my warm condo, but the memory of Todd kept me honest. The only option was to ignore the pain and paddle out. It's what he would've done.

"This isn't so bad," I thought as I made it out to the surf. But once I stopped paddling, I realized how cold it really was. A tiny wave popped up in front of me, and I took it, careful not to fall and prolong the pain.

I hit the sand running straight back to my condo. So much for tributes.

the surfers are:

peter king, rob machado, and kelly slater

the debut album songs from the pipe

in stores july 21

produced by t bone burnett

www.epicrecords.com   www.thesurfers.com

12

Winning Isn't Everything

THE 1998 ASP WORLD TOUR was due to start on the Gold Coast of Australia in the middle of March. There was so much pressure—from sponsors, the media, the public, and mostly from myself—that my hair was falling out. Maybe it was hereditary, but either way, I wasn't about to resort to a comb-over at twenty-six years old. I decided to continue shaving my head, not only as a tribute to Todd but also to serve my own vanity.

I had no motivation to compete. Frankly, I was sick and tired of the World Tour. For the past seven years, my life had been a nonstop barrage of airport layovers, autograph signings, and contest jerseys. The only thing that got me going in a competition was the thought of losing.

I never intentionally waited until the end of a heat to turn on my competitive drive, but there were times that it only worked in the last minutes. It shouldn't have come as much of a surprise, I have been late all my life. I was stubborn about leaving the womb, the last teenager to reach puberty, and the last one in his seat before the tardy bell rang at school. I'm late for heats, weddings, plane flights—you name it. But in a heat, when somebody pulled ahead of me, it infuriated me and I did all I could to catch up. If I had lost all the heats I won in the final minute, I might now have only one or two world titles.

Winning so much in 1996 and 1997 gave me a ton of confidence, but it also made me feel guilty. I wasn't having fun. I was fueled by anger—I felt I needed to get mad at my opponent to win. I was so driven that I alienated the people who helped me get where I was. It was impossible for me to differentiate my "contest mode" from real life, and I failed to recognize what was happening to my friendships.

I went on a three-week boat trip to Indonesia in 1997 with Ross Williams, Taylor Knox, Pat O'Connell, and Chris Malloy, all of whom were my close friends. I didn't realize it at the time, but I barely had a conversation with any of them the entire trip. No one said anything about it directly, so it took me a while to get the message. Chris says the oddest thing was that on the plane ride home, I had a five-hour conversation with a complete stranger, an older man sitting next to me. The guy had no idea who I was and that anonymity was what I was craving.

I'M WITH THE BAND

I guess I always wanted to be a singer. When I was younger, my dad played guitar around the house and my mom played banjo and sang. It was like *Hee-Haw*. When I was four, I memorized the lyrics to Melissa Manchester's "Midnight Blue" and would perform it for my family in the car while standing on the backseat. During my shy teen years, I ignored the urge to sing, but when I was eighteen my friend Peter King, a former pro surfer from San Diego, showed me a few chords on the guitar. After that, I spent most of the downtime on the World Tour playing with Peter, Rob Machado, Jack Johnson, Donavan Frankenreiter, and sometimes Tom Curren. Those guys were all way better than I was on guitar, so I ended up singing. We sat around writing songs and jamming for fun.

Peter stopped by my house in 1994 with a friend who worked for Sony Music named Roger Klein. We were messing around with a few songs and Roger asked us what we were doing with our music. Other than making a few tapes to send as Christmas presents, the answer was "nothing." Peter jokingly suggested he sign us, and Roger said, "I will." Just like that, I was in a band. We made a demo on a four-track recorder that I bought after winning my first Pipe Masters and through a connection Roger had made, we were soon signed by Epic Records. Rob agreed to join us, and we started recording in 1996.

We didn't have a name when our recording sessions began. Peter's idea of "Fear of Hair" was a little too goofy for me. I was thinking of something a little deeper, such as "Thoughtspace" or "Tomorrow in Review." Everyone at the studio referred to us as "the Surfers." They'd say, "The surfers are recording today." All of a sudden everything was out of our hands and the record label was calling all the shots. I got a call one day from Peter, and he said, "That's it; we're the Surfers." I thought it was stupid. I didn't want the band to have anything to do with surfing. But what did I know? I was just the singer. Thus, we became a novelty act. He told me it wasn't as bad as it sounded, and I said, "I know; it's going to be worse." It meant that our music would be misunderstood from the beginning.

Whenever we were in California, we were recording—two weeks here, a month there—and we worked some strange hours. The band was cutting into our lives. Each day we'd record from around noon until midnight or beyond. We were turning into vampires, hardly seeing the sun, much less surfing. By the time I woke up, no restaurants were serving breakfast. I started to think, "What am I doing?" But before I completely came to my senses, it was off to another surf contest somewhere around the world.

I gave our management the benefit of the doubt and sort of bit the bullet to get through it, but we had become so far removed from what we had set out to do that it wasn't fun anymore. We'd record a song for two days and come in and play it for our producer, T-Bone Burnett. T-Bone is one of the most prolific producers in music. He has worked with musicians such as Los Lobos, Elvis Costello, and Counting Crows, and we were starstruck when we were around him. We'd hang out at his house, and Elvis Costello would come over. He'd open letters from Puff Daddy and talk on the phone with U2.

T-Bone is a perfectionist, and he'd tell us to totally change and rerecord our songs. It was frustrating, but he taught me so much about song structure, production, and performing—things I couldn't learn any other way. As a whole, our vision didn't come across in the album. *Songs from the Pipe* sold around seventy thousand copies, mainly in Japan. By then, the people who were responsible for signing us to Epic Records, Vice President Richard Griffiths and Peter's friend Roger Klein, were no longer with the company. Our album became a low priority and didn't get the attention it needed.

It seemed like the mainstream media hadn't taken time to listen to the music and just wanted to ask us why we were called the Surfers. We got a little play on college radio, where every once in a while we were interviewed and actually had a chance to talk about the music, which was nice.

Our manager, Justine Chiara, scraped together funding for a little tour of the East Coast, which for me was a learning experience. I was clueless about playing in a band, being onstage, and dealing with music fans. Being on the road as a musician—sleeping all day and being up all night—was much more difficult than being on the road as a surfer. On a surfing tour, I get to be in the water all day and stay in one place for a week or so. On the band's tour, I was constantly moving, got little sleep, and as a result, I got really sick. I was laid out for almost a week and had to drink a bunch of tea and try to sing.

Because of my "rock star" status, I had a chance to go to the Grammy Awards party in 1996. I only knew two people but recognized almost everyone. It was a who's who of popular music. At one table were Boyz 2 Men, Stevie Wonder, Mariah Carey, and Brandy. At another table was Eddie Vedder from Pearl Jam. Pearl Jam was *the* band when I was in high school, because almost every angst-ridden teenager could relate to their lyrics. Since Eddie Vedder and I had mutual friends, I walked in his direction to introduce myself. Before I made it all the way over to him, he looked over at me and said—almost sang—in a sort of drunken slur, "I been watching yooouuu." We talked a little and Eddie told me he grew up surfing. As it turned out, Rob Machado and Al Merrick went to the same high school he did. Our interests in the ocean and music gave us an instant bond.

Two years later in 1998, Rob and Eddie had become pretty good friends, so Rob asked him if we could open for Pearl Jam sometime. Eddie was pretty impressed with our record. He said, "I thought it was going to be a punk rock thing, but it sounds like a good Neil Young record." And he worked it out so that we had a chance to open for them. We got to play in front of eighteen thousand people in a venue near West Palm Beach, Florida. We were on a side stage, but everyone could hear us. When Pearl Jam came on we ran like little kids backstage to watch the show. Sometime after that, Eddie and I became good friends. He loves to surf, and we sometimes meet up in Hawaii or other parts of the world to go surfing.

The next night we went from West Palm Beach to Miami for

our own tour. A hurricane was bearing down on the coast, so Miami was deserted. The area was evacuated, and the storm was supposed to hit that night.

The wind was howling, it was raining, and when we pulled into the parking lot to do a sound check, there were only two cars in the whole place. Just before we went onstage that night, I counted twenty-seven people in the audience, and that included guys from the band who played before us. Our manager, Justine, huddled us together for a pep talk. We all took a shot of tequila and decided not to worry about the crowd, to just have fun. It was actually our best show because there was no pressure. Afterward, we disco danced for most of the night and around four in the morning, Rob, Peter, and I decided to get out of town and drive back to my house in Cocoa Beach. The rest of the band stayed at a hotel and got so drunk they ended up sleeping on the balcony. They woke up getting pelted by eighty-mile-per-hour rain. I heard the waves in South Beach were six feet and perfect the next day.

Between 1998 and 1999, the Surfers toured around California and in Germany. Music was my pastime, so it was impossible for me to devote enough time and energy to the process to make it work. I wasn't willing to sacrifice my surfing career, and the Surfers eventually went their separate ways. In May 2000, we played our farewell tour in Japan. The crowds in Japan stared in amazement, like thousands of deer in headlights. I tried stage-diving into the audience, but the crowd wasn't hip to that concept. Everyone backed away and fell like dominoes. Next thing you know, I'm sandwiched between clumps of people, squishing these poor little Japanese girls with my knees. Nobody got hurt, but it was an interesting way to end my career as a rock star.

I still love to play, write, sing, and listen to music daily. I've written a lot of songs that I'd like to record someday, but I'll probably just give them away as Christmas presents.

A KINDER, GENTLER ME

I decided things would be different in 1998. I wanted to stay positive and feel connected to the people around me. Because I used surfing to escape my emotions, I had built up a wall that separated me from my family and friends. For years I had been so focused on winning that I shut everyone out. I wasn't close to my family, friends, daughter, and romantic relationships were strained because I kept my girlfriends at a distance. I wanted to achieve my ultimate mission of six world titles, but not by sacrificing everything else. Win or lose, I wanted to enjoy the ride.

Because of my resolution, I felt unusually free in Australia at the year's first event, the Kirra Pro. The finals were held on a beautiful March day with perfect little waves, and my opponent was my friend Pat O'Connell. Sitting in the lineup, waiting for the heat to begin, I turned to Pat, and said, "Look at this. All those years surfing Salt Creek (Pat's home break in San Juan Capistrano, California), with guys dropping in on us, and now all these people are watching us. Isn't this great?" It was all part of the new me. I surfed for the fun of it, but that didn't mean I was giving the heat away. I didn't blow Pat out of the water, but I won.

I earned a seventeenth at Bells in April, followed by a fifth at the Coke Classic at Manly Beach in Sydney. Even though I lost in the quarterfinals, my result at the Coke Classic was strangely satisfying. In the previous round, I had caught a wave in the last five seconds and beat Australian Richie Lovett. I was so close to finishing ninth, but something let me have that wave. I regarded it as a gift, and had a notion that winning the heat would be significant at the end of the year.

In May at the Tokushima and Marui Pro in Japan, Australian Danny Wills came out of nowhere to win back-to-back events, a feat that hadn't been performed since Shane Beschen and I did it two years earlier. Winning two in a row makes a surfer more likely to win the world title. Danny was a young guy who had no major results up until then, so we hadn't taken him seriously. All of a sudden, he was leading the tour. My shiny, happy approach was barely keeping me in the game.

Through the summer in South Africa and Europe, it was much of the same. I finished near the top, but my ratings suffered. Danny faltered as well, and his best friend, Mick Campbell, had leapfrogged us both. I dropped to fifth after Jeffreys Bay, which was my lowest position since 1993. I was beginning to lose focus. The stress of possibly not winning the world title was starting to get to me. I knew the bigger purpose for my life was to feel good—and my emotional state was more important than contest results—but I was in danger of slipping back into "contest mode" and ruining all the progress I had made.

As the tour returned to America for the U.S. Open at Huntington Beach, California, my philosophy was put to the test in a big way. I made it to the last day of the event, the quarterfinals, and I faced my good friend Shane Dorian. Shane was beating me, but about halfway through the heat I had wave priority and had a chance to get him on an interference. He was paddling for a wave and not paying attention to me. I couldn't have made the wave, but when you have priority it doesn't matter.

It would have been blatant, and a lot of thoughts ran through my head. Mostly I thought about two years ago and what had happened with Shane Beschen at this same place. A lot of people on the beach felt they were cheated out of a fair contest. On a deeper level, I knew it was all part of competition, but I didn't want to be tagged as someone who wins heats that way.

Shane Dorian had never beaten me in a man-on-man heat, and it sort of felt like it was going to happen there no matter what. So I didn't take the wave that would have penalized Shane. I thought maybe I could surf my way back into contention, and if so I would feel a lot more confident about winning. As it turned out, I was too far behind. Losing was hard to take. It was early in the morning of the last day of the event, and I had to sit around and watch from the sidelines.

Losing at Huntington Beach was good for my well-being, but it didn't do much for my ratings. By the time I got to Brazil for the next-to-last event, the two sides of my personality were fighting. Mick Campbell and Danny Wills were pretty far ahead and there wasn't much time for me to catch up. I came up against Mick in the semifinals, and he didn't back down. Still, I refused to let it get to me.

He destroyed me in the heat. I watched the final from the competitors' area and checked the ASP ratings. I started figuring out the possibilities going into Pipeline. If Mick won in Rio, I would have no margin for error at Pipe. To win the title, I would have to win the event, and he and Danny would have to lose early. If he lost, I'd have a little more room to breath.

Mick was up against a Brazilian named Peterson Rosa. There weren't many good waves coming in, and Mick was winning the heat. It came down to Rosa's last ride, and he needed a 7.5, a nearly impossible score considering the surf. Rosa did a couple big moves and pulled out all the stops with a totally uncharacteristic aerial in the shore break. He got the score he needed and won the heat. He made my chances of coming from behind to win the title at Pipe a whole lot easier.

SHOWDOWN

The 1998 ASP tour shaped up to be the ultimate Australia-America rivalry. My back was against the wall going into Pipeline in December, but among Danny, Mick, and me, I felt I had the home field advantage. Neither Mick nor Danny had much experience at Pipe. There were no other Americans in the race, and that was a new experience for me. It felt good, for once, to have Hawaii on my side.

I was stressed. If I didn't win, I'd never have another chance at five straight. I had to find something to keep me from thinking about that, so in between heats, I took up guitar making.

Earlier that year, I had traveled to the events in Europe with my friend Jack Johnson as he was making a surf film called *Thicker Than Water*, which was sort of a documentary about our group of friends. Jack and I were reading *The Ultimate Guitar Handbook*, which included a section on how to build a guitar. That's what got the whole thing started.

When we got to Hawaii, we turned it into a challenge. The rules were simple: We could only use things we found in Jack's dad's garage. He completed his first guitar in two days, and his second guitar while I was still busy with my first. I knew if I finished, my attention would wander back to the contest, and I had to keep my head in a clear space.

The waves at Pipe were really big, which made it tougher on my rivals since they didn't have that much experience in Hawaii. Mick's first heat was a doozy. He advanced, but ran straight into a young Hawaiian named Bruce Irons in round two. Although Bruce was only eighteen, he was already considered one of the best surfers at Pipe. As it turned out, Mick failed to make a single takeoff and only scored a total of 1.9 points on three rides. It was the all-time lowest three-wave total on the ASP tour.

I made it through the first round and came up against another talented Hawaiian and one of the toughest draws in the contest, Braden Dias. He knows the place as well as anyone, especially when it's big. The waves were around triple overhead, but I started with a good one at Backdoor. It gave me a big lead, and Braden never caught up.

Danny Wills beat another Pipe specialist, Pancho Sullivan, and advanced to the round before the quarterfinals. If he won two more heats, it wouldn't matter what I did, Danny would be the world champ. His confidence was huge as he faced Ross Williams. I was in the following heat against Rob Machado, and we both sat in the Johnson's backyard looking out at Pipe and getting ready to go out. Ross broke a fin on his first ride and spent the next ten minutes of the twenty-five-minute heat waiting for a caddie to bring a backup board.

I could feel the tension rising up my spine. The heat between Danny and Ross was close. Danny needed an average ride in the closing minutes. He took off on a decent left, got to the bottom, and spun out like a top. There wasn't time for him to get another ride, so he lost and was eliminated from the contest.

Holy crap! Here was my chance. My season, my career, and my legacy would all be decided in a twenty-five-minute session with Rob Machado. I could seize the opportunity or buckle under the pressure, and I felt myself buckling.

Utterly frazzled, I disappeared into the Johnson's house to find my wits. Fortunately, Tom Carroll saw what was happening. He had been there for me when I won my first title in 1992 and help me deal with pressure situations throughout my career. He could tell I was stressed and led me through some relaxing yoga poses to get back in the moment.

The yoga helped, and at the last minute, I emerged in my Todd Chesser trunks ready to go. Some of our friends were asking Rob if he was going to throw the heat, but Rob knew that I wouldn't want him to give me anything. We prepared our equipment on opposite sides of the yard, making certain to avoid eye contact. He was split between wanting me to win and refusing to concede the heat. Heading into the water, Rob said, "I hope you get some good waves," implying he wasn't about to roll over. We did rock-paper-scissors for the first wave, and I won.

On December 19, 1998, the waves were eerily similar to 1995—six to eight feet with perfect rights and lefts. The only difference was that all our friends were united in their support. They wanted to see me defeat the Australians.

Rob surfed really well and pushed me to perform outside myself. I stuck to riding the slightly longer waves at Backdoor while Rob caught mostly lefts at Pipe. It was a great heat, but I won. It was hard to imagine that fourteen years earlier, I had seen Backdoor for the first time and wondered, "What is that guy thinking, going right at Pipeline?" Now it had become the cornerstone of my career, earning me yet another title.

As soon as the horn ended the heat, I rode to the beach with my hands in the air. The pressure was over. My friends picked up Rob and me by carrying us up the beach. I soaked it all in and hoped the moment would never end. The semifinals lay ahead of me, but they were meaningless. I had won my sixth world title and had nothing left to prove.

I broke Mark Richards's record of straight world titles, something he and many others thought would never happen. Mark told me he was convinced that no one would be able to win more than four in a row. When I did it, he was complimentary, saying, "If I had to see it fall, I'm stoked to see it be to a guy who has changed our perception of what high-performance competitive surfing is. I'd hate to see it go to someone who managed to win a billion contests by riding four waves to the beach rather than a guy who pushed the boundaries." It was the ultimate praise.

It would have been easy to have a big head. Just a few days earlier, winning the title seemed impossible. Now at twenty-six, I was the most accomplished surfer in history. I was getting mobbed by friends, fans, and reporters, and my thoughts were somewhere in the clouds. Out of the commotion, I spotted my daughter, Taylor, on the beach. Tamara surprised me by bringing her to Hawaii a couple days earlier. I thought Taylor would be impressed by what I had done, but during the definitive moment of my career, she had her back turned to the ocean, building castles in the sand.

As I led the mob of people to where she was playing, she looked up at me and said, "Daddy, help me build castles." To her, we were the only two humans on earth.

My bubble burst, and I realized my head wasn't in the clouds. It was buried in the sand.

The hoopla meant nothing to Taylor. She wanted to spend time with her dad, doing things that mattered, like building sand castles and family bonds. According to my resolution, I hadn't been a total contest drone like before, but I was still missing out on life's simpler pleasures.

At the Association of Surfing Professionals awards banquet

the next night, I made the announcement that I was retiring. I had informed Quiksilver, my sponsor, earlier so we could plan the year ahead, but other than that I hadn't told anyone. I knew during the Pipe Masters that it would be my final event on tour. Not my last contest ever, but possibly my final appearance as a full-time competitor.

13

Retiree

FOR MOST OF MY LIFE, I derived my self-worth from how well I rode my surfboard. Even though I wasn't aware of it, from the time I was eleven and my family split up, nothing came before surfing. In my mind, winning contests, getting pictures in magazines, and making money determined my worth. I thought that the better I did, the more people would like me. Obviously, that wasn't the case. I had lots of fans, but that's superficial.

Would I change the way I spent my years on tour if I could? No, I wouldn't. I don't know if I would have accomplished the things I did otherwise, and I'm really proud of that. Even so, I had missed out on a lot. My family barely knew me, and I didn't really know myself. In the blink of an eye, I climbed from Cocoa Beach to the top of the world. Taking some time away from the tour allowed me to get to know my family, my friends, and myself. There had to be more to life than trying to adhere to others' criteria of how they think I should ride a wave.

I realize how extremely fortunate I am. If I had come along earlier, I wouldn't have been able to retire from surfing without having to step into another job. In my lifetime, surfing has evolved from a hippie pastime into a booming industry and legitimate career path.

When I stepped down from full-time competition at the end of 1998, rather than building my beer gut and reducing my golf handicap, I had a greater desire to surf than I'd had in years. And thanks to Quiksilver, I basically had a hall pass to do as I pleased. If the waves were good somewhere in the world, and I felt like surfing, the company sent me there. I would still compete in a few select events and appear in promotions, but I was more or less free. Thanks to Quiksilver's support, I maintained my high standard of living without having to worry about world titles.

STAYING IN THE GAME

I would be lying if I said I no longer cared about winning contests during my retirement. I set a goal of winning one WCT event each year. It wasn't the most important thing, but it served as a reminder to myself that I still knew how to surf. I planned to compete in any World Tour event sponsored by Quiksilver, and any others that occurred in places I enjoyed to give myself a fair shot at reaching my goal.

Try as I might, I couldn't get Pamela Anderson out of my system. In 1998, we started an off-and-on relationship that didn't really end until 2000. After three years of marriage, two kids, and more time in the public eye than the president, Pam decided she was after the true-to-my-roots sort of life I was leading. Her husband, Tommy Lee, had pushed her around and was serving time for felony spousal abuse, and while he was in prison, she divorced him. Her popularity had become so extreme that keeping our relationship a secret was impossible. All of a sudden, I became more famous for dating her than for anything I had achieved in surfing. I was in gossip magazines every week. One gossip show on the E! Channel went as far as saying I was going bald and Pam was going to cut her hair and donate it to me for a weave. We looked at each other, like, "What the heck is that?" Then it wasn't true, but if she's interested now, my hair is getting pretty thin and I might take her up on it.

During most of our relationship, Pam and I kept to ourselves. When I was in California, we'd hang around at her house in Los Angeles. We took her kids to the beach or the playground, went out to dinner, and I sometimes met her at work when she was shooting *V.I.P.* She stayed at my condo in Florida a couple times and met all my old friends. Even though we spent a lot of time with her kids, I didn't feel comfortable introducing her to Taylor. Since I didn't see Taylor much myself, I thought it would just confuse her to see me with a girlfriend.

Because of Pam's sex symbol status, she was practically a regular on *The Howard Stern Show*—she still is. She loves to try to shock Howard, so to him she's a goddess. He loves to put down whomever Pam is with at the time, partly out of jealousy and partly for the fun of the show. He wanted to know how a surfer punk could be sleeping with Pamela Anderson. I don't think he even knew my name. He had no idea of our previous friendship, and to him it didn't matter. During one show, Howard called and said, "Oh man, I got my hands all over her. It feels great. What do you think about that?" I said, "That's wonderful. Can you put Pam back on the phone now? I'll talk to her while you feel her up." According to Howard, every one of Pamela's relationships is a joke. In our case, I have to respect the guy for being able to foresee the future.

In March 1999, I surfed in the Billabong Pro in Australia at one of my favorite waves, Kirra. Since I had retired only three months earlier, I didn't have much desire to compete. Quiksilver wanted me in Australia to do some promos, so I figured why not surf some perfect waves and make some money in the contest. The Gold Coast was in the middle of its worst flat spell in years, so the waves offered no incentive. On top of that, my relationship with Pam was on the rocks. Rather than stick around in Australia, I left before my third-round heat and flew back to California.

After serving sixteen weeks in prison, Tommy was released in September 1998. He would drop by Pam's house to pick up their kids, and his visits gradually became more personal. She and Tommy got back together in April 1999. I'd never met Tommy and didn't have anything personal against him, but I thought he had a lot of issues with insecurity. Because of this, Pam didn't even want to talk to me. Rather than fight it, I just went away to deal with it on my own.

At the end of May, I went to the Quiksilver Pro, which was moved from Grajagan because of political instability in Indonesia, to Tavarua, Fiji. The waves on Tavarua are just as good as Grajagan, but there wasn't much swell for the event. I made it to the semifinals against a Brazilian named Victor Ribas. I only needed an average wave in the last few minutes to beat him, but he followed me everywhere I paddled and kept me from catching anything.

Later that summer, I went to France and South Africa for promos before heading to a trade show in Brazil. I didn't have a travel visa, but somehow I was allowed on the plane in South Africa. When I got to São Paulo, Brazil, the customs officials told me I couldn't enter the country and would have to fly to Miami on the next flight. I called a friend who works for Quiksilver in Brazil and told him what happened. He spread the word around the trade show, and pretty soon people were calling the airport on my behalf, including the governor of São Paulo, who was a surfer. Right before the flight to Miami left, the customs agent said, "I don't know who you are, but somebody really wants you in this country. This has never been done before, but you're free to go in."

After the trade show, I returned to Huntington Beach, California, for the latest incarnation of the Op Pro—it was called the Gotcha Pro. Gotcha, a clothing company, wanted to be the only sponsor for the event, but the following year it went back to being the U.S. Open. The waves at Huntington were so bad that it didn't bother me to lose in the quarterfinals. I couldn't get motivated and was relieved I wasn't on tour. For once, I was happy to lose.

I was still moping around because of my breakup with Pam, but by Halloween I was ready to laugh at it all. I was in Cocoa Beach pondering what to wear to a costume party when I got a call from my old friend and modeling agent, Stephanie Gibbs. She said, "I've got the perfect outfit for you. Come over and we'll dress you up as Tommy Lee." It was somewhat therapeutic, just the thing I needed. She drew temporary tattoos all over me and tied my hair into little beads. I put dark circles around my eyes, ripped up some jeans and a T-shirt, and I *was* Tommy Lee. I was the hit of the party.

Nevertheless, my goal of winning was slipping away, but there was still Pipeline. It had been twenty-one months since I won the Billabong Pro on Australia's Gold Coast in March 1998, and I'd forgotten how it felt to stand in the winner's circle.

Luckily, the waves at Backdoor were great. I faced Occy in the semifinals. He had already clinched the world title that year and was desperate to validate his win by beating me. He killed me for most of the heat, but with three minutes left I pulled within range, still needing an 8.5. Occy starved me for waves, but I pretended to be interested in a crumbly little right and baited him into going, giving me priority. I thought I saw a wave on the horizon, but when I looked again there was nothing. Staring out to sea, I laughed and thought, "Yeah, right. No waves are coming in the last minute. My luck has run out." Sure enough, a beautiful peak popped up, and I barely made the drop, pulled into the barrel and came out to score a perfect ten. The Australian contingent on the beach was shocked, going, "Aww, not again." Occy was the world champ, but for my confidence, I needed to show him I could still win. My momentum carried through to the final against another Aussie, Shane Wehner, and my goal was met. I had my one win for the year.

RODEO CLOWN

Something about being on the World Tour had inhibited my imagination—the structure can take the fun out of competing, since judges traditionally reward consistency and wave selection more than creativity. Without having to worry about the politics of competition, I was free to experiment for the first time in my life. I wanted to see if the moves I imagined as a kid were possible.

It used to be that skaters mimicked surfing. When the ocean was flat, they grabbed their skateboards and surfed on land. Now, more than thirty years later, we are starting to mimic skating tricks. We're way behind skateboarders (and even bodyboarders) as far as pulling off big spins in the air. The main reason is the size of our boards. It's a lot harder to control and land a six-foot surfboard than a two-and-a-half-foot skateboard. Plus, the wave is a moving target as opposed to a ramp or sidewalk. Bodyboarders face the same problem, but they are on their stomachs and holding onto the rails on the sides of their boards the entire time. With all the focus on getting air, surfboards are getting more and more specialized, so it's just a matter of time before we catch up.

Every surfer mind-surfs by staring at waves and envisioning what is possible. I sit on the beach at Pipeline, and wonder how deep I could take off and if there is room to do an aerial. I visualize doing barrel rolls and riding out of them cleanly. This way, when I'm not in the ocean my body tries to copy what my mind envisioned. It's helped improve my surfing because it trains my mind to think the move is possible. I've been doing it since I was a kid.

When I started doing 360 reverses in 1989, it was an extension of what I saw the older guys—Matt Kechele, John Holeman,

and the other guys at Sebastian Inlet—doing. In my mind I pictured doing their tricks, and then taking it one step further. The one move that really stuck with me though was that time at the Surfside Playhouse when I thought I saw Buttons pull off a full flip in a movie. Ever since, it had been in the back of my mind. So when I retired I got serious about pulling it off. I'm a long way from mastering the move, but I've managed to pull off a few while landing on the back of the wave. It's a lot harder to stick a landing on a moving target.

Retired or not, the Pipe Masters was one event I wouldn't ever miss. In the 1999 Pipe Masters, I tried a flip in a heat with Rob Machado and nearly made it. I twisted 540 degrees and just missed the landing. I came in from the heat and walked up to the Johnsons' house. Jack Johnson was there and asked me what I was going to call the move, and I said, "Rodeo Clown" after a song he had written for G. Love and Special Sauce, a band I was into at the time. There's also a move that snowboarders do in the half-pipe that's called a "Rodeo Flip" that's similar. Since then I've made a few Rodeo Clowns using foot straps attached to my board. A couple kids—Jamie O'Brien from Hawaii and Aaron Cormican from Florida—have pulled off variations of the flip a bunch of times. I think within five years, surfers will be consistently making them.

THE SLATERS TAKE TAHITI

In February 2000, I was at the surfing industry trade show in Long Beach, California, to sign some posters at the Quiksilver booth. Bruce Raymond, one of my bosses at Quiksilver, told me that the waves in Tahiti were going to be really good in a few days and asked if I wanted to go. Quiksilver had put together an ongoing boat trip called "the Crossing". The company took a seventy-five-foot diving-and-survey vessel called *Indies Trader,* decked it with a fancy paint job, and set off to discover new surf breaks and document the state of our world's coral reefs for a United Nations–supported environmental program called "Reef Check." Each segment of the journey lasts two weeks, and there's room aboard the boat for four surfers, one photographer, a cinematographer, a marine biologist, a captain, a cook, and three Indonesian crew members.

I was allowed to pick the other three surfers for the trip, and I chose Shane Dorian and my brothers. Since Sean and I had been at each other's throats for a couple months, I thought the trip would be a good opportunity to work things out.

A few months earlier, I had been in Hawaii when I heard from a friend at home that Sean was living in my condo in Florida and driving my car, each without my consent. I called Sean from Hawaii and told him I was pissed off about it. He never came out and said it, but I could tell he felt left out of my life. It was obvious we needed some time to work things out.

Stephen, Sean, and I had never been on a surf trip together. As we each travel the world, I'd sometimes meet up and surf with Stephen, who is also sponsored by Quiksilver. No matter where I am, somehow he always manages to find me. If I went down to Chile tomorrow, he'd most likely be there too. So to get him to go on the trip was easy. He threw some trunks in his board bag and was ready to leave within minutes. With Sean it wasn't so easy. He actually has responsibility beyond surfing these days. After he left Quiksilver he went to a company called Volcom to manage its surf team on the East Coast and the Spy Sunglasses team. In addition, he occasionally writes articles for *Transworld Surf* and shapes Slater Surfboards, a company he started in the mid-1990s. He was stressing over some obligations and didn't think he'd be able to go on the trip. If there's one thing that gets Sean motivated it's fishing, so I told him the fishing in Tahiti is phenomenal. He was sold and all prior commitments were swept under the rug. Sean, Stephen, Shane, and I met up in California and flew together to Tahiti to get on the boat.

Before our trip, I had time to put myself in his position and think about how he must have felt as a teenager when we were both surfing. Even though we didn't compete against each other too often, it must have been hard for him so see me get so much attention. And although on our trip to Tahiti we never had the heart-to-heart conversation that you see on TV—there was no crying, hugging, or any other kind of *Oprah* moment—the trip brought us closer together. Tahiti was like old times. Anytime we weren't surfing, we were fishing. The time we spent together strengthened our relationship.

That's not to say we aren't still competitive. He's always telling me he's the better fisherman, and he brings out pictures to prove it—even though he always seems to catch a lot of fish when I'm not around.

MAVERICK'S

Most people equate California surfing with fun and sun rather than serious danger. But about an hour's drive south of San Francisco, there is a wave that can kill you. It breaks a quarter of a mile from land, and there are lots of big sharks and bigger rocks to go along with 50 degree water. A local guy named Jeff Clark rode it alone and named it after his dog, Maverick. The surfing world had only found out about Maverick's in the early 1990s, and it quickly became a cold water alternative to the North Shore.

Quiksilver began sponsoring an event at Maverick's in 1999 called Men Who Ride Mountains. The name alone should tell you it's no ordinary event. Jeff Clark handpicked twenty surfers each year to compete, and in 2000 I made the list. I had never surfed Maverick's, and a prerequisite was that you had to surf it at least one time before actually competing in the contest. I kept an eye on the weather, and in January when I saw there was a little swell, I took the red-eye from Hawaii and barely slept on the way over. After two cups of coffee (and I never drink coffee), I was pumped up and ready to go.

It was a small day for Maverick's, maybe twenty feet on the face of the waves, and after a few hours I was cold and tired. Just then, the biggest set of the day rolled through. I was caught off guard and was a little bit out of position for the wave, but I had to go, just so I could tell Jeff I caught one. I made it to the bottom of the wave but was too far back to get around the whitewater. I had no choice but to jump off my board before getting steamrolled by the wave. When I came up a few seconds later, another wave was bearing down on me. Like I said, it wasn't that big of a day, so I wasn't concerned about diving under it. I'd dealt with far bigger waves, but this thing picked me up and body-slammed me like some superhuman wrestler. I was pulled underwater and whipped around like a rag doll. I was out of oxygen and started to panic. It finally released me, but I still had to swim up to the surface and arrived just in time to deal with another of those monsters. After taking a second beating, I was in no shape to handle a third. Fortunately, a guy zoomed in on a Jet Ski and pulled me out of harm's way. I realized why Maverick's is the scariest wave in the world. I was lucky I started on a small day.

On March 1, 2000, I came down with the flu in southern California and couldn't get out of bed. Wouldn't you know it, I got a call that day that the Maverick's event would likely be held on the third, so I dragged myself to the airport the following day to fly up to San Francisco with my shaper, Al Merrick. I didn't get much sleep and showed up the next morning at Maverick's feeling lethargic. The wind was howling, the water was 53 degrees, and the waves were a solid twenty-five feet (forty feet on the face). It was as big as anything I'd ever surfed. I couldn't take a deep breath without coughing, and I was debating whether or not to go out for my heat. I suited up but told the first alternate for the event to be ready in case I chickened out. I would have been hesitant to surf that day if I had been healthy, so doing it in my condition was sketchy. From the lineup, I decided the waves looked manageable and decided to give it a go.

My first wave was the biggest I rode all day. I made it to the bottom and thought I was in the clear. All of a sudden the white-water blasted me from behind. It was a repeat of my first Maverick's experience on a grander scale. The wave picked me up and drove me what must have been twenty feet underwater. Fortunately, the water patrol was there when I came up, so I didn't have to deal with the rest of the set. I played it safe the rest of the day but still managed to make the final and finish second behind Flea Virotsko from nearby Santa Cruz. He surfs Maverick's all the time and was free-falling into huge waves that the rest of us wanted no part of. We were paddling for our lives, but to him it was fun. I have a huge amount of respect for the guys who charge at Maverick's. Finishing second was a pleasant surprise for me, considering earlier that morning I doubted I'd even be surfing, let alone making the finals.

PAMELA, TAKE THREE

In early 2000, Tommy and Pam split up, and again she started calling me. Against my better judgment, we made another stab at a relationship. This time it seemed like she was truly finished with Tommy, and we were getting along great. There were rumors flying around the tabloids that we were engaged, but they were false. I heard that she said I was trying to marry her, when she was the one who wanted us to get a house together. I guess after all that she had been through, the idea of marriage had begun to lose meaning and she tossed it around easily.

The bottom line was that our lives were too different.

In May 2000, I left for a three-week trip to Japan, Tahiti, and Fiji. While I was gone, Pam wouldn't return my calls and was nowhere to be found. I had called her from all over the world, and she was usually easy to reach. I knew something was wrong but tried to convince myself everything was normal. When I went to the airport in Fiji to fly home, I stopped at a newsstand, and there, on the cover of a gossip magazine, was a picture of Pam with her arm around some hunk. The headline read, "Pamela's New Guy." I came to find out it wasn't her new guy, just someone she was dancing with, but she did have a new boyfriend, a super-model named Marcus Schenkenberg.

I was devastated, mostly because she couldn't tell me herself. Only in Hollywood does someone find out he's been dumped through a tabloid. The relationship taught me a lot about myself and about how to make better decisions—this time, it was over for good.

Shortly after I got back from trip, I did an interview with *ESPN* magazine. I was excited. I'm a freak about sports, and to finally be recognized as a real athlete was an honor. The magazine flew a reporter out from New York, and we spent some time together in Hawaii. I couldn't wait to see the story, but attached to my copy the reporter sent me was an apology. It read, "Kelly, I'm so sorry about this. I had no control over it. My editors over-ruled me and changed it at the last second. There was nothing I could do." I thought, "How bad can it be?"

Then I saw the contents page: "Dumped by Pamela Anderson Lee, Kelly Slater Gets Back Up on the Wave." It was an article about Pamela that had almost nothing to do with me. It mentioned my surfing credentials, but I was just an avenue to get Pamela's name in there to sell magazines.

That wasn't the only case. I was a guest on *The Craig Kilborn Show*—the late, late, late, late, late show. It was right after Pam and I split up, which is probably the only reason the show wanted me. Every time he asked about Pam, I changed the subject, so he resorted to making fun of the fact that surfing was my job. I had it, and felt like I needed to retaliate. I had one thing on him, which was that he was trying to date a friend of mine who had been denying him. As the tape was rolling, I said, "We have a mutual friend. She told me to say hi." He pretended not to know what I was talking about, looked at the camera, and said, "And this is where we cut. We come back in three, two, one . . . so, Kelly . . ." and went on with the interview and totally cut my retaliation from it. When the interview was over, he leaned over and said, "Hey, tell her I said hi." I was pretty pissed, but there wasn't much I could do to him on the set of his show. I left thinking, "You prick."

ASP 2000

Maverick's wasn't a WCT rated event, so my first opportunity to keep my goal of winning one event each season came in May at another frightening wave, a place in Tahiti called Teahupoo. (This was during the whole Pamela fiasco.) Like Maverick's, Teahupoo was a relatively recent phenomenon. People considered the wave unridable until the mid-1990s when my friend Vetea David from Tahiti surfed it along with a few other locals and the occasional demented visitor. The wave isn't nearly as big as places like Waimea or Maverick's, but it packs just as much power and is even more difficult to ride. For a few years, I had seen video and magazine coverage of Teahupoo and was bummed I wasn't there to meet the challenge. The wave is more powerful than Pipeline and has become the place where one's tuberiding skills in danger-ous surf are judged. Since I wasn't on tour full-time, I had to compete in the trials, from which three surfers made it to the main event. The level of surfing in the trials was mind-boggling, so I considered myself lucky to finish second behind Hawaiian Andy Irons, who put on one of the most amazing tuberiding displays ever.

I surfed against Mark Occhilupo in the semifinals and won, remaining unbeaten against him. Afterward I told him, "Don't worry. There's always next week," which turned out to be prophetic. For the final against Shane Dorian, a sideshore wind had turned the waves into crap, at least by Teahupoo standards. If the wave isn't a perfect barrel, people usually won't even surf it. Still, at most any other spot, people would kill for that kind of surf. It seemed like every good wave came to me, and I accomplished my goal of winning my one event for 2000.

By the time we got to Tavarua, Fiji, the next week for the Quiksilver Pro, my motivation was gone. Since Quiksilver sponsored the event, I had to compete. It took place at Cloudbreak. In the third round, I surfed against Occy, who was still really pissed about losing to me in Tahiti. He had been trying to beat me for years, so my comment after that heat probably made him try even harder at Tavarua. I was completely out of rhythm, and Occy absolutely smoked me. It was a huge win for him, and for me, my loss was no big deal.

The Billabong Pro at Trestles in southern California that September, on the other hand, was an event I was psyched to win. Since it was the site of my first win as a pro, at the Body Glove Surfbout in 1990, winning it again in front of my bosses at Quiksilver and the rest of the surf industry would be huge. Without competing full-time, I felt pressured to make my appearances count. I was feeling a little nostalgic, so I asked Al Merrick to build a replica of my board from the 1990 event, decorated with the same distinctive blue, orange, and yellow airbrushing. Quiksilver had reissued the trunks covered with stars that I wore back then, so my ensemble was a blast from the past.

My board sure looked neat, but it was made thin and narrow

for good waves that never arrived. Stephen was flying out to California, and I asked him to bring my small-wave board with him from Florida. It's amazing that airlines can find a way to lose a surfboard in transit, but it happens periodically. And it happened this time. I had to ride the wrong board and lost in the first round, which isn't the end of the world. Instead of going straight to round three, I had to compete in round two against Shane Dorian. The waves didn't improve, and neither did my perform-

ance. I lost a nail-biter heat to Shane and finished thirty-third—dead last—for only the second time since 1993. Shane had some extra motivation to win because I had just started dating his ex-girlfriend, a model from Los Angeles named Lisa Ann. It was a difficult situation, but I felt a deep connection with her and Shane told me he was all right with it.

I didn't feel that losing to Shane was the end of the world. He was on tour, so winning meant a lot more to him than to me. And while the rest of the tour was heading to Brazil to compete in crummy beach breaks I went straight to Europe for a month of perfect surf.

GOING MAINSTREAM

In July 2000 I filmed an episode of *The Jersey*, a kids' show on HBO, and I had no idea what it was about. I didn't have the time to read the script beforehand, so I literally showed up and had ten minutes to memorize my part for each scene, so I spent the whole day with no clue what I was shooting. Since a lot of high-profile athletes had been on the show, I trusted their judgment and figured it couldn't be too bad. I later found out that the show was about a kid who puts on the jersey of a professional athlete and assumes the power of that person, while the athlete turns into the kid. Unfortunately, I still haven't seen the show, so I don't know what to think of my performance. Everyone who saw the episode said it turned out great. And so started take two of my Hollywood career.

Other offers came my way and I took them, such as a cameo in the movie *One Night at McCool's* and a small part in an episode of the HBO series *Arli$$*. I've also turned down a few offers, including the lead role in *In God's Hands*. Matt George, a surfer who also acted in the movie, wrote the screenplay. It was a big-budget film, but another horrible depiction of surfing by Hollywood, just slightly more tolerable than *Point Break* or *North Shore*. My manager, Bryan, read the script and called to tell me about it—even he thought it was bad, and if Bryan thought it was bad, it was really bad. The dialogue was corny and the plot wasn't developed, but the basic idea of a bunch of guys traveling around the world surfing was pretty cool. I passed, and the role went to Shane Dorian. At least the surfing in the movie was great.

Surf writer Matt Warshaw once said in an article about surf

films, "The only Hollywood movie to get it right was *Apocalypse Now*." He was right. It touched on surfing just enough to show it was something people were passionate about and willing to risk their lives for, but it didn't make surfing, or surfers, look stupid. *Big Wednesday* was another good one. It came out in 1978 and starred Jan-Michael Vincent, Gary Busey, and William Katt as three friends dealing with the responsibilities of growing up while surfing in California. But *Point Break* got it wrong. There are too many inaccuracies in it. For instance, the fifty-year swell? What's that? And anyone who surfs knows that when Bells Beach is twenty feet, two hours away the swell is forty feet. So why would Patrick Swayze go to Bells?

I'd like to see a surf movie come out that's about a surfer, such as Duke Kahanamoku, Miki Dora, or Jeff Hakman. They are the legends of the sport and have had lives that movies are made of. They've all been through major personal struggles. Duke introduced surfing to the world but dealt with racism for being Hawaiian, Miki rebelled against society, and Jeff threw away a lucrative career in the surf industry because he got hooked on drugs. He eventually cleaned up his act and got his career back. If anyone ever does those movies, sign me up.

WHAT NEXT? KELLY SLATER UNDEROOS?

If you ever visit Universal City Walk in Hollywood, you'll find the Kelly Slater Quiksilver Boardriders Club, wedged between the Vans shoe store and Hollywood Harley-Davidson. You won't find me working behind the counter, but there is a big glass case filled with a bunch of my old stuff. As a perk in my contract with Quiksilver, the company offered me a percentage of a new surf shop. Quiksilver has Boardriders Clubs all over the world, where they carry only products from Quiksilver and their girls' line, Roxy. It would have been nice if it could have opened up in Disney World—since it is so close to my hometown—but it didn't work out. I had to settle for Los Angeles. For months, I gathered memorabilia—trophies, pictures, news clippings, old surfboards, everything except my stinky, mildewed wetsuit. The second board I owned, the one I was riding in my first published photo, hangs alongside the board I rode to victory in the 1999 Pipe Masters. I also helped design the look of the store and approved the layout inside. The store opened in April 2000 and started out great. We had a huge grand opening party featuring my friend Jack Johnson playing guitar at the BB King Club around the corner. There were hundreds of people and paparazzi from *Access Hollywood, E!,* and a bunch of others. I don't own the store, but I get royalties from it.

In 2000, I also began working on my video game. In December 1999, I got a call from an agent named Peter Hess, who had helped Tony Hawk put together a deal to create "Tony Hawk's ProSkater." Because of the success of Tony's game, the video game industry was looking toward the action-sports market for future titles. Peter wondered if I'd be interested in having my name attached to a similar game for surfing.

I'm no video game junky, so I didn't know much about the industry going into it. As a kid, I played pinball, Asteroids, and Pac-Man back at the Islander Hut and the Starlite Roller Rink, but not much since then. I had offers from six different companies to produce "Kelly Slater's ProSurfer," but I got a good feeling from meeting with the people at Activision and Tony's involvement with the company reassured me that Activision was the way to go.

Several games have tried to replicate the surfing experience, but none have been successful for one reason: creating a realistic wave is a nightmare. You want a wave that is interesting, lifelike, and always changing. Otherwise, the game gets boring after a couple times of playing it.

Activision hired a company in California called Treyarch to create my game. Basically, an animator named Craig Dregeset worked twelve hours a day for more than a year and did almost everything by himself. The moves on "Tony Hawk ProSkater" were created using a bunch of cameras in a motion-capture session, where Tony skated in a black Spandex jumpsuit covered with white Ping-Pong balls. Since the cameras had to capture three different angles, the same process couldn't be used for surfing because it doesn't take place in a controlled environment. The animator had to look at millions of surfing photos of me and the other people in my game and plug every position of every part of our bodies into a computer. The program Craig Dregeset used had a stick figure on a surfboard, and he moved the body parts to replicate each of our styles. Thanks to technological advancements, the game looks frighteningly real.

Activision and I recruited an awesome list of surfers—Tom Curren, Tom Carroll, Rob Machado, Bruce Irons, Lisa Anderson, Kalani Robb, Donavan Frankenreiter, and Nathan Fletcher—and incorporated all styles and approaches to waveriding, from power carvers, to guys who are into tricks, to style masters. The only problem I have with the game is that my character surfs better than me.

LESSONS IN PARENTHOOD

It seems the hardest things in life are the ones that bring the most joy and healing. Throughout my life, I had never been that close to my dad. After he and my mom split up, I didn't see or hear much from him. In October 2000 when I was in France competing in a few events, my mom called me to say that my dad had been diagnosed with throat cancer. Close or not, he was my dad, and so I flew home to be with him and offer my help.

Mark "Doc" Renneker is a friend of mine. He is a well-respected big-wave surfer from San Francisco, California, who also happens to be a doctor who treats cancer patients. When I found out my dad was sick, I called him because I valued his advice. I wanted to know who Doc would see if he had cancer. He gave me the names of two doctors, one of whom was also a surfer who lived in Chicago named Keith Block. Keith is known for his alternative cancer treatments. He focuses a lot on the patient's diet so that the body has the nutrients it needs to create healthy cells and the energy to fight off the bad ones. He prescribes lots of vitamin supplements and minimal radiation and chemotherapy.

When Keith explained his program to my dad and me, I knew this was the doctor for us. He understood my dad's lifestyle and the aggressive treatment he prescribed seemed better than the standard medical procedure. Keith wrote the total cost of the treatments down on a piece of paper—around $80,000—and handed it to me. Some of the drugs involved are extremely expensive, and since his approach is considered alternative, most of it isn't covered through insurance. My dad saw the figure and said, "I'm going home. You're not spending that kind of money on me." But I insisted. With all money I had made throughout the years, my dad never asked me for a dime. He didn't even want to ask when his life depended on it. He was more worried about me using up all my money and possibly screwing up my future. His selflessness showed me a lot about his character. I was prepared to pay whatever it took to get my dad healthy. Because Keith was based in Chicago, he wanted my dad to move there for treatment, but my dad refused to go. He had spent his whole life in Florida and wanted to be close to his friends and family. As a favor, Keith agreed to oversee my dad's treatment from afar.

First, my dad underwent surgery to remove the cancer. They had to cut out his internal jugular vein, remove muscles in his neck and lymph nodes in his chest and neck. He could no longer raise one of his arm's after the surgery, so there was a lot that he couldn't do. He couldn't surf. He couldn't really fish because he couldn't cast the pole more than a few feet. He couldn't smoke cigarettes or drink beer. He was on a strict diet and lost thirty pounds. Basically, everything he loved in life was taken away from him.

My dad and I grew closer because of his illness. Confronting mortality helped him admit a lot of his mistakes, and we were finally able to move on with our lives. We spent a few weeks together in Hawaii in 2001, and he got to watch me compete in the Pipe Masters for the first time. I made it to the final and finished second to Hawaiian Bruce Irons. As always, I used the Johnsons' house as my base at Pipe, so my dad watched my heats from their backyard. I couldn't figure out why every time I came

in from another heat, my dad was standing down on the beach instead of in the yard with my friends. A year later, when he was in the hospital, I asked him why. He said that he was so proud of me that he started crying during every one of my heats. He didn't want anyone to see him, so he had to walk away.

Being a parent myself helped me see how difficult of a job it can be. Even though I'm not around as much as I would like to be to help with Taylor, I've spent a lot of time in Florida between competitions trying to get to know her. Her mother does a good job explaining why I'm rarely around, and I collect shells for Taylor from every beach I visit. She prizes her collection and remembers the day I gave her each one, just as she remembers everything we've ever done together and is always saying, "Daddy, remember the time we did this?"

Taylor is crazy about the water. Just after her second birthday, I took her surfing on one of Stephen's longboards in Cocoa Beach. The waves were tiny and, while carrying her, I pushed the board and jumped on for a short ride. Her mom took a picture of it. I'm holding Taylor in my arms and we're both looking down at the board.

I gave her a necklace for Christmas in 1999, and she pulled a ring from her jewelry box and told me to put it on. I haven't worn jewelry since my pooka shell necklace was retired in 1985, but I haven't taken the ring off my pinky since she gave it to me. It was green, but all the color has worn off.

THIS IS RETIREMENT?

Between working on my video game, filming television shows, and doing promos around the world for Quiksilver, 2001 was the busiest year of my life. I had become pretty serious with my girlfriend Lisa Ann and was spending as much time as possible with her in Los Angeles. Fortunately, most of the things I was working on were in southern California, so it was a convenient place to set up camp. I surfed around Malibu and went to so many Laker games that I was starting to feel like a Californian. For the first time in twenty years, competition fell way down on my list of priorities.

It had been more than two years since I competed full-time, and I wondered how much longer I could stay away before I was too old. In my absence, Occy became the oldest world champion in history in 1999 at age thirty-three, and Sunny Garcia won it in 2000 when he was thirty. I was only twenty-nine years old and felt like I still had time.

I went to Australia in February 2001 for the Quiksilver Pro. There was a press conference before the contest, and I spoke along with a few other Quiksilver athletes. Most of the Australian media showed up. They asked questions concerning the event and then asked me when and if I would return to full-time competition. I slipped and said, "There's a good chance I *might* be back." Those were my exact words. The surfing media jumped on it, and everywhere you looked, the headlines screamed, "He's Coming Back!" It was a year away, and people were already starting to hound me about it. With all the hype, I seriously considered scrapping the whole idea.

My string of winning an event each year was snapped that year at nine, one short of the record shared by the two Toms, Curren and Carroll. At Bells Beach in April, I was beat twice by my old nemesis Sunny Garcia, who was then the reigning world champion. I didn't compete in Tahiti or Brazil. The ASP season was shortened to four events due to travel uncertainty caused by the September 11 disaster, and I only competed in two of the four. At Sunset Beach for the final event, I failed to advance through the trials and lost to a sixteen-year-old Hawaiian and an unknown guy from Brazil. At the Pipe Masters, which wasn't a rated event because no sponsor came through with the money in time, I finished second to Bruce Irons. Despite that positive finish, it was the worst competitive year of my life. I felt I was surfing better than ever, but the distractions in my life kept me from winning. My competitive nature was taking a beating, and it was time to do something about it.

14

Back in Action

I COULD TAKE MYSELF OUT of competition, but I couldn't completely get the competitiveness out of me. Don't get me wrong—while away from the tour I made huge strides in improving my personal relationships. I've become a better person in many regards, but I still feel I have a long way to go. I've started to become aware of things I couldn't see when I was only worried about winning. But what can I say, I like to compete, and I missed being on tour. So by 2001, returning was on my mind.

When Occy came back, the ASP told him that he would have to prove himself on the World Qualifying Series because he hadn't competed at all for several years. If I had had to rough it around the world to qualify for the World Championship Tour, I would have stayed retired. After all I'd accomplished, I couldn't see going back to square one. It wasn't as if I was sitting on the sofa eating potato chips when I was off the tour. I was surfing and competing in events here and there. When I retired, I asked Rabbit Bartholomew, 1978 world champion and the director of the ASP, if I'd be able to return whenever I wished. He made it clear that there would be a spot waiting for me.

I've always felt that athletes who have achieved a high status within their careers should be compensated with eligibility to perform at top-level competitions even after retirement. It's absurd that Tom Curren wouldn't be allowed to surf any contest he wants. If a surfer wins an event, he should be able to surf that event forever, and if he wins a world title, he should be welcomed at any event for the next five years. It works that way in golf. If a golfer wins one of the big events, he is exempt from having to qualify for the tour for several years or can compete in that event forever. Long after Tiger Woods retires, he will most likely still be making appearances on the PGA Tour. We need that sort of tradition in surfing. It would raise the public's attention of the event as well as give the young pros something to aspire to.

On October 23, 2001, I issued a press release stating I was set to return to the tour full-time at the start of the next year. The ASP had granted me a wild card for the entire 2002 season.

THE EDDIE

Eddie Aikau is a true Hawaiian legend. One of six siblings, he grew up poor, quit school, and was working a dead-end job at the Dole pineapple factory on Oahu when he discovered his life's mission. During a humongous swell that hit the North Shore in the winter of 1967, Eddie—an unknown—paddled out at Waimea Bay, the most notorious big wave along the entire stretch. He outshone the best big-wave surfers around and earned a reputation for riding the biggest waves the North Shore could produce. At the time, there were no lifeguards patrolling the beaches, so Eddie petitioned the city of Honolulu to appoint him

to that position. Guards were soon posted at each major beach, and Eddie was allowed to focus on his beloved Waimea Bay, where not a single life was lost under his watch. He was fascinated by his Hawaiian heritage, and in 1978 he joined a crew that was traveling 2,400 miles from Oahu to Tahiti aboard a replica of an ancient Hawaiian voyaging canoe. The boat ran into trouble immediately and capsized in a storm. Eddie set out to paddle twelve miles to the nearest island to get help while the rest of the crew clung to the wreckage. The crew was rescued the following day, but Eddie was never found.

In death, Eddie had become a mythical figure. Starting in 1987, an invitational big-wave event has been held at Waimea in his honor. For the Quiksilver in Memory of Eddie Aikau to take place, the minimum requirement for surf is twenty feet according to Hawaiian measurements, which can be as much as double that on the face. Only thirty of the best big-wave riders are chosen each year by a panel of the most influential and experienced watermen around, making "the Eddie" the most prestigious event in the world. Just to be invited means you are among the greatest watermen in the world. The event is about charging big waves. Most of the invitees aren't even full-time competitors. They are just guys who love to ride big waves and who carry on the spirit of Eddie Aikau.

The format is different from that of other surf contests. The thirty surfers are split into three groups of ten, and each group has two hours in the water, one in the morning and one later in the afternoon. Of all the rides, the top four of the entire day for each competitor are tallied for his final score. There is no final; the surfer with the highest point total is the winner and receives the $50,000 first-prize check.

Since the inaugural contest in 1987, Waimea has only reached the required size on a handful of occasions. Many years, the entire three-month waiting period comes and goes without the event director, legendary Hawaiian surfer and shaper George Downing, even putting the competitors on call. But when the waves are big enough and the event does happen, traffic comes to a standstill along the entire North Shore. People crowd along the cliff for a view of the action.

I finally got the courage to paddle out at Waimea when I was seventeen. My friends had already been surfing it for several years, so I was playing catch up. In 1993, after I won the world title, I was invited to attend as an alternate. (It was also because Quiksilver sponsored the event.) I had been surfing Waimea Bay for a couple years but not in anything over twenty feet. I was scared and felt I didn't deserve an invitation over other guys who surfed Waimea on a regular basis. I didn't want people thinking, "What is this guy doing in the contest?" I was ready to give up my alternate slot to the next person on the list.

One night I was playing cards with Brock Little, and he asked what I would do if I got in the contest. I said, "With my luck, I'll win the thing." What I meant was, I would probably go and get a few waves and make them, and all the big guys would be charging so hard they would eat it and not get any scores. Brock laughed and said, "That's Slater luck. You probably *would* win the stupid thing."

Fortunately, the waves didn't get big enough to run the event all winter, so I didn't need to worry about it. In fact, after the event ran in 1990, the elements didn't come together again until 1999. And by then, I was dying to surf the contest. Every time my friends Ross Williams, Shane Dorian, Keoni Watson, and I heard about the possibility of a big swell, we called one another and cackled like a bunch of teenage girls.

When the perfect day finally occurred in 1999, twenty-four-year-old Noah Johnson won the event. I finished ninth, but having someone from my generation win made me feel like a part of the contest. With the exception of Brock, who had been a fixture at Waimea for a decade, I always expected the older, more experienced crew to dominate out there. In 2000, I was actually leading on two waves, the event halfway through, when the waves stopped breaking and the competition was called off. The next year, 2001, Australian Ross-Clarke Jones won and I came in fifth.

When the call was made to run the event in January 2002, I was surfing on Maui with Lisa Ann and some friends. On just a few hours' sleep, we caught an early flight to Oahu. I normally like to watch a few heats to get a feel for how to approach it, but I didn't have time to really check out the conditions since I was in the first heat of the contest. I was the first to reach the lineup. The water patrol had cleared all the noncompetitors out of the area and the rest of the surfers were around fifty yards behind me paddling out. For the first time in my life, I was the only person out at Waimea. In normal waves, that's a blessing, but here you need other surfers in the lineup to use as landmarks. I had to trust my instincts.

At a lot of big-wave spots, sea turtles sit right at the edge of the reef where it meets deep water. I saw a big turtle floating next to me and figured I was just on the "ledge" though no waves had broken in a few minutes and I wasn't positive. I also check my lineup on the hill. When everyone on the beach and in the channel started hooting, I knew there was a set coming, and I was still alone. This one was too good to pass up, and whether the contest had started or not I wanted to get my sea legs. It was a nice, easy wave and ended up being one of my four scoring waves for the day. From there, I could be patient and wait for a few more good ones. My scores were pretty good, but I didn't dwell on it.

When I knew the contest would be on at Waimea, I called Eddie Vedder and invited him. He said he couldn't make it but would be thinking about me. After I came in from my first heat, I was walking to the bathrooms, and there was Eddie. He hadn't wanted to stress me out with helping him get from the airport to the beach, so he flew over from an outer island without telling me. We sat around with more of my friends, and when it was my turn, I went back out and caught a couple more good ones. There was a big leaderboard on the beach, and according to the scores, I was in third place behind two Australians, Tony Ray and Paul Paterson. I was only two points from winning and was kicking myself for not going that extra yard to finish on top. To be so close in such a prestigious contest and not win was frustrating. I thought back to a few waves I hadn't taken and wished I had. My friends called to congratulate me on my third place finish, which was my best yet at the Eddie.

As the awards presentation was getting under way on the beach, I looked at the leaderboard and realized they had added the wrong score for one of my waves. They were already calling out fifth place, and I told Brock, "They wrote my scores wrong. I have three more points. I win the Eddie Aikau." When I told the event directors about the mistake, they stopped the presentation for five minutes to check my math. One of the organizers went to the scoreboard—in front of the giant crowd that had gathered for the awards—and changed my scores. Out of the crowd, a bunch of Aussies started grumbling, "Aww, what're they doin'? This is a setup." They thought it was a conspiracy because it was a Quiksilver event, and I rode for them. I started feeling guilty for finding the mistake. It certainly looked suspect when they put my name atop the leaderboard—but I had won.

Wearing my Todd Chesser trunks, I accepted the check (which read "Quiksilver" and was made for $55,000, five grand more than it was supposed to be) and dedicated the win to Todd, Donnie Solomon, and Mark Foo. I had never thought of myself as a big-wave rider. On the average day, I felt I could hold my own with anyone out there, but when it came to getting serious about the contest, I still idolized the older generation of Waimea surfers. I hadn't reached that level in my mind. Winning the Eddie was sort of the culmination of my career, having evolved from tiny Florida dribblers to the most important big-wave contest in the world.

A HARD LESSON

At the beginning of March, I set out for Australia for the start of the 2002 World Tour. The first event of the season, the Quiksilver Pro on the Gold Coast, was held in perfect righthand point surf. I lost to Joel Parkinson and finished ninth. He won the contest. There was almost a month before the next event, Bells Beach, and I was looking forward to hanging out in the meantime with my brother Stephen and my best friend since childhood, Johnny Ross, in Australia.

We drove up the coast to a friend's house, and I got a call from Lisa Ann saying I needed to call my mom quick, because my dad wasn't doing very well. I got my mom on the phone and she said, "If you want to see your dad alive again you better come home now."

In January, my dad had slipped and fallen down the stairs in my condo in Florida. He bruised his hip, and he was on the couch for a few weeks. He wasn't the kind of person who could sit around the house, and after the fall, he realized how bad his condition had become. The cancer had spread to his lungs, and he began withering away to nothing.

My dad's throat hurt so bad he couldn't eat. When Stephen and I flew back from Australia, he weighed 109 pounds. It was horrible to see what cancer does to a person. Both of his parents had died of throat cancer, and you could tell he dreaded going down the same path. He got a feeding tube, which was working all right, but he wasn't getting any better.

It was a tough time for us, but we came together. My parents told each other they loved each other for the first time in almost twenty years. Through the whole ordeal, he never complained or felt sorry for himself. He would still sit up in bed and tell a joke or tell me how he was going to get stronger and come on another trip with me. He was so pumped the whole time.

He told me all kinds of stories about when he was a kid, like when he won the first surf contest he ever entered. He made a hundred dollars and wanted to use the money to fly to California, but it wasn't enough to get there. My dad asked me to praise God every moment of my life and appreciate things every day. He had fun all the time, which may not have been a good thing in a family sense.

At one point while I was home, my dad realized I was missing the Bells contest. I didn't want him to know, but he overheard someone mention it. He was incoherent a lot of the time I was home, so I hoped it would go right by him. He sat up and said, "What, the Bells Beach contest is on? What the hell are you doing here?" I told him I wanted to spend time with him and he said, "That's not doing either of us any good. Get out there and do what you do. Get out there and win." He kept saying, "You can't do that, Kel." I just kept laughing at how he was only concerned about me, considering the shape he was in.

It got really stressful being cooped up in the house for days on end, and finally I called Dr. Block to see if there was anything else we could do for my dad. He said we had done everything possible. Hearing that gave me permission I needed to relax and enjoy the final days with my dad. I was able to let go without wishing I could change anything. There was never a time in my life that I grew so much in such a short time. It was as if every day I gained a year's worth of maturity. I stopped thinking the world revolved around me and started becoming more of a man and a person.

After three weeks at home, I left for a photo trip and figured

it might be the last time I saw my father alive. Fortunately, he went quickly from that point, and didn't have to suffer long. I returned ten days later, when he passed away, to spread some of his ashes in the ocean in front of the end of Minuteman Causeway where he played pinball and hung out with his friends. So many of my dad's friends came to say good-bye and tell us stories about him. At that point, I saw how many people he touched and how everyone enjoyed being around him. Since then, my brothers and I have also spread some of his ashes in Tahiti, South Africa, Australia, and Nicaragua. We literally take a small part of him wherever we go.

NEXT GENERATION

In every generation, in every sport, there are people who erase the feats of earlier generations. For forty years people who followed baseball said that the home run record couldn't be broken, until Mark McGuire broke it in 1998. Then, three years later, Barry Bonds came along and broke McGuire's record, making it look easy. Someday, when another surfer figures out the correct combination of surfing ability and competitive knowledge, my record of six world titles will be broken. I welcome that and hope I'm around to witness it.

I'm human. I know I can't keep excelling at surfing forever. I wouldn't say I've hit a plateau, but guys like Bruce and Andy Irons are getting better and better. I have a lot of respect for those guys and love to see them trying huge moves on big waves. As I get older, I've changed my approach a bit. When it's big out there, I see waves that humble me. Someday when I get married, surfing will become secondary to my family. I can see myself still pushing the limits in giant surf, but I'm sure I'll have other priorities pulling at me. I hope I'm still competitive many years from now. I'd love to be competing at Pipe long enough to surf against

kids like Jon Jon Florence, the preteen heir to the North Shore throne. Jon Jon's only ten years old, but he's already charging at Pipe. When he's twenty, I'll be forty, and hopefully I'll have a chance to surf against him.

Right now, the young Australian surfers like Joel Parkinson, Taj Burrow, and Mick Fanning are making a huge impact on the World Tour. More than half the WCT is from Australia. It's always been the dominant country in pro surfing, but when I started to win a bunch of world titles for America, it was their wake-up call. In response, a bunch of Australians, including Rabbit Bartholomew, started a program from the ground up. It included surf camps for beginners and a Junior Pro Tour for intermediates, which gave aspiring pros a clear path to follow. By the time this newest crop of surfers hit the ASP, they already had heaps of competitive experience. That sort of grassroots involvement has been lacking in the United States for a long time.

Americans, as a whole, have been spoiled, and our surfers are no exception. The surf industry and the economy here are so much stronger than anywhere else. America can handle losing for only so long before we get our act together. We need a national program similar to that of Australia's to nurture talent. Competition is a fundamental part of our sport because through it we keep pushing ourselves, and the limits of surfing.

As for my own comeback season, it never really got going. I missed a few events, made just one final (placing third in the Pipe Masters), and was never a threat to win the world title. In the year-end ratings, I finished ninth. Hawaiian Andy Irons jumped out to a lead in Australia and went unchallenged throughout the year. I figured going into the season that it would take me a few events to get back in the swing, but I didn't think it would take as long as it had. I went back on tour for 2003 and wanted another world title.

MAKING THE WORLD (TOUR) A BETTER PLACE

I came back to the World Tour because I wanted to win another world title—I wouldn't have done it if that weren't my objective. But a funny thing happened upon coming back: I decided contests couldn't make or break me. My dad's death gave me some more perspective on life. So much had happened in my life, and I had so much to be thankful for that I couldn't ask for much more. But in some ways it has caused me to hole up in my world again.

I realized that I wanted to help improve surfing more than I wanted a world title. Instead of being vocal, I've been in a subtle pissing match with the ASP to change some things. All pro surfers are frustrated with the lack of money and exposure. They dream of being viewed as legitimate athletes and of being seen on TV like basketball players or even skateboarders are. I wanted to help us. Before I left competition all I thought about was fitting into the system and winning. Now I want to help make the system better for competitors and spectators.

I've been brainstorming about a new and very different format for professional surfing. I feel we need a leaderboard for each event so we're competing against everyone. As it is now, the two best surfers in an event face off in the third round, and the loser is finished. I want to develop a system in which surfers can bomb out one day and still compete and have a shot at winning on the final day. I feel surfing shouldn't just be about going into a heat and beating a guy. It should be geared toward performance. When I'm finished competing, hopefully the tour will be more professional, more exciting, and the competitors won't be going, "Damn, I have to go on tour again."

THE NEXT CHALLENGE

In the ocean, swells only last so long, and they're unpredictable. Any one of a number of elements—tide, wind, sand buildup, and shark frenzies—can ruin an otherwise perfect day. The likelihood of everything coming together at the same time is slim. Plus, more and more natural waves are being destroyed by what many people call "progress." Lots of great surf spots around the world have vanished thanks to marinas, roads, and housing developments (although we have gained a few too). This has led to surfing population increases because there are fewer and fewer places that can handle the crowds. Because of all this, surfers have dreamed of creating the ultimate wave machine. The perfect setup would take surfing to every town in America and make the sport as mainstream as soccer. People who've never seen the ocean could become avid and able surfers. All my friends would be able to quit their jobs and become resident pros. But short of wave machines popping up around the country like Wal-Marts, surfing will remain a small-time sport and stuck as a cultural and fashion influence.

Wave pools have so far been the great, unfulfilled surfing prophecy. In 1969, the world's first wave pool—the horribly misnamed "Big Surf"—was introduced in Tempe, Arizona, and the surf was anything but big. In 1985, the ASP Tour decided to stop for a contest in Allentown, Pennsylvania—a hundred miles from the nearest ocean—drawing the sort of odd stares you'd find at a genuine UFO sighting. The competition was held in a wave pool, and the waves were so bad that most of the guys couldn't get going. Professional surfing sank to an all-time low. If wave pools were indeed the future of the sport, the future looked grim.

Not much has happened since then, but people are still trying to create a perfect man-made wave. The closest we've come so far has been with the development of standing waves. The inventor of the Flow Rider, Tom Lochtefeld, created a machine that mimics water flowing along a river that is interrupted by an abrupt change in bottom contour, which vertically shoots the water upward. Even though the rider stays in one place, the flowing water gives the sensation of riding a wave. Snowboarders, skateboarders, and wakeboarders—who all use a double-ended board like that used in the Flow Rider—pick it up with ease, but for surfers—whose board's nose and tail differ—the transition is as hard as the concrete lurking inches below the surface.

Lochtefeld is working on other kinds of artificial waves, including the Water Wing, which is a large device shaped like an airplane wing that runs horizontally on a track along the bottom of the ocean to create a wave. It has huge potential because there's no need to build a giant pool. Using different size wings and approaching the beach from different directions can tailor the wave to various shapes and sizes.

SOMEDAY I WILL RETIRE—REALLY

Even though I've decided to give the World Tour another go,

I'm planning ahead to when I retire for good. Hawaii represents the ultimate in surfing and is my favorite place to be, so that's where I'm going to live. It's always nice to go back to Florida, where it's familiar, but Hawaii has always felt like home with the Johnsons', and Benji's, and the Hill House, and all of our friends being such a tight unit.

As nice as it is on Oahu's North Shore, the other islands in Hawaii are even better. The difference between the two is as drastic as that between Los Angeles and Oahu. The average person would come to the North Shore and think, "Gosh, this is so nice and relaxing." But with the life that I lead, the North Shore is like work. I have to deal with crowds and being recognized.

I purchased a piece of land in Hawaii, and I'm getting it ready to build a house and grow old there. My lot is in the mountains outside of town, so if I want to go and be around people or go out at night, I can, but for the most part it's about getting away from everybody and being on my own. It is the perfect retirement spot for me. I've always wanted to grow my own food, and now I have enough land in the right sort of climate to do that. It has pretty much everything I could possibly want. There are plenty of places to surf with only your friends, it's nice and cool in the evenings, and I can fish, golf, and swim to stay healthy.

As I get older, more of my time will be taken up by golf. I may want to be a pro golfer on the Senior Tour when I'm fifty. Most of the guys on that tour probably won't have much motivation after playing their whole lives, but I'll be approaching it with the excitement of a grommet. If I apply myself, the potential is there. I don't see myself competing against Tiger Woods, but maybe.

Financially, I need to get my investments in order before retiring. For the most part, I live a pretty simple life. My biggest expenses are going out to eat, phone bills, and playing golf—I'm not into buying cars and having planes and things like that. My land will be full of avocado trees, so I guess if I get really desperate, I can sell avocados along the side of the road.

But my biggest goal is to have a happy, healthy home, and I look forward to it with excitement. It's really important to me to one day be married and have a family (my dad told me when he was eight, he decided the same thing). My relationship with Lisa Ann did not work out as she and I had hoped and we split at the end of 2002. I guess there are still a lot of lessons I am in the process of understanding and when I finally do, I know that part of my life will be fulfilled.

It's funny, as a kid, I thought there would be a point where I'd say, "Yeah, I made it." But as I get older, I don't think that's the case. There's still further to go. A friend of mine, John Swift, once told me, "It's really easy to learn everything everybody knows, but from there you have to work from theories so the process slows down. You have to discover new things."

Life is a constant process of discovery, like moving farther from the Islander Hut into bigger and bigger waves. In my career, I've made it out to the lineup. Now, coming back on tour and looking ahead to the rest of my life, it's like I've returned to the beach and have to make it back out again.

Appendix A

Kelly's Top 10 Lists

FAVORITE WAVES

1. Pipeline (Oahu, Hawaii): The place I dreamed of surfing as a kid. It has brought me my most special moments in competition and still gets me excited every day.
2. Kirra/Snapper Rocks/Greenmount (Gold Coast, Australia): The greatest sand bottom pointbreak barrel that exists. With new dredge developments, the wave has reached 2.5 km long.
3. Sebastian Inlet (Florida): My home break and original training/proving ground. Strong local crew and really fun, playful, short rides off a jetty.
4. Soup Bowls (Bathsheba, Barbados): Surf and hang on the beach all day and eat breadfruit and sugarcane with Rastas. Amazingly fun wave on its day.
5. Cloudbreak/Restaurants (Tavarua, Fiji): Two distinct waves and one great island. My introduction to confronting big waves in front of the cameras happened here. One wave (Cloudbreak) has huge character, the other is perfection.
6. Lance's Rights (Mentawai Islands, Indonesia): The empty rights (in 1994) that I always dreamed of surfing one day in the Mentawai Islands, Sumatra.
7. Sandspit (Santa Barbara, California): Fell in love with it in photos but still have yet to catch it on a classic day.
8. G-land (Java, Indonesia): Probably rode the best left of my life here. I was scared at the thought of going there as a kid. Flawless perfection.
9. North Point (Cowaramup, Western Australia): Never surfed it, but I know I will love it. A big, distinct, and unique barreling wave.
10. Three's (Big Island, Hawaii): Our little secret spot.

BIGGEST INFLUENCES

1. My family: They made me who I am. I owe them all my love and appreciation.
2. Al Merrick: The best man I know. My second father and board shaper.
3. Tom Curren, three-time world champ: I grew up wanting to be him. Thank you, Tom, for your beautiful surfing.
4. Tom Carroll, two-time world champ: For his friendship and friendly, competitive spirit. He showed me the ropes, and I would not be here without him.
5. Trevor Hendy, four-time Ironman champion: A new friend and an old friend. He is helping me to have the life I have always dreamed of and to be the person I have the potential to be.
6. Matt Kechele: He taught me about the world I wanted to be a part of and was a big brother to Sean and me. Thanks for the videos and the surfboards.
7. Bruce Raymond: He's guided me through so many personal and professional troubles that I can't begin to thank him enough. He's the greatest boss I could have. (President of Quiksilver International marketing and former top-rated pro surfer.)
8. Jeff Johnson and Peff Eick (and families): I have never spent a day with them that I didn't absolutely love and talk about with the guys for days.
9. Mark Cunningham: One of my favorite humans. Thanks for the bodysurfing lessons and simple happiness you live.
10. Buttons Kaluhiokalani: Who freed my mind to go anywhere on a wave. Thanks.
11. Nikola Tesla: Opened my mind to the infinite possibilities of science, energy, and invention, and gave me the permission to dream.

FAVORITE SURF TRIPS

1. Oahu, Hawaii (every winter)
2. Cabo San Lucas, Mexico (1986)
3. Mentawai Islands, Indonesia (1994)
4. Barbados (1985)
5. Gold Coast, Australia (1987)
6. Tavarua, Fiji (November 1990)

7. Biarritz/Hossegor, France (August 1989)
8. Mainland Mexico (June 1990)
9. Tavarua, Fiji (May/June 2002)
10. Southern California, Oceanside to Santa Barbara (Summer 1984)

BEST CONTEST MOMENTS

1. Semifinal, Pipe Masters, 1995, against Rob Machado: All the purest feelings of competition and friendship came alive for me during this half hour of my life, and I went on to win my third world title on that day. Thank you for the memory, Robbie Todd.
2. Pipe Masters, 1998: I could never dream of a better scenario for myself than this one: the United States versus Australia, two against one, coming from behind. I won my sixth title that day.
3. East Coast Championships, 1982, first place Menehunes: My first *big* win. I was ten years old. I had no idea this would kick start the rest of my life.
4. U.S. titles, 1984, Makaha, Oahu, Hawaii, first place Menehunes: My first of four U.S. title wins. I met most of my good surfing friends at this event, and it was my first Hawaiian experience.
5. Rip Curl Pro, Hossegor, France, 1992: First win on tour. It put me in the ratings lead for the first time and gave me permission to belong at the top.
6. First Annual Quiksilver Pro, G-Land, 1995, first place: Best waves I've ever had in competition. Quicksilver's first adventure surf contest. Got five barrels on my first wave in the finals.
7. Hart's Birthday Bash, 1984, first place: First win against older competitors in an open field. I won my first ticket to Hawaii at this contest, and I never looked back.
8. Excalibur Cup, Sebastian Inlet, 1986, first place Open Men: I was fourteen years old. I won the pro contest, pulled the sword from a stone, and got the girl.
9. Sundeck Pro, Melbourne Beach, Florida, 1984: I made the main event in my first pro event and won my first man-on-man heat ever against an Aussie pro.
10. Pipe Master's, 1999, semifinal vs. Occy: Occy had me on the ropes to beat me for the first time after I won the world title that year. I

found a ten-point ride at the buzzer to hold him off for a few more months and went on to win the event.

QUESTIONS MOST OFTEN ASKED OF SEAN

1. Do you surf too?
2. Why don't you surf?
3. Are you a good longboarder?
4. Is Evan Slater (editor of *Surfing* magazine, no relation) your older or younger brother?
5. Why aren't you a six-time world champion?
6. Did you teach Kelly to surf?
7. Did you used to be better than Kelly?
8. Aren't you in a band?
9. Can you get Kelly to sign this for me?
10. Where's Kelly?

FAN REQUESTS

1. Will you sign this?
2. Will you take a picture?
3. Can I have one of your surfboards?
4. Will you leave my outgoing voice message?
5. Got any free stuff?
6. Can you get me Jack Johnson tickets (even my friends ask me this one)?
7. Wanna switch jobs?
8. What's Pamela (Anderson) like?
9. Will you talk to my friend on the phone?
10. Can I have your socks or underwear?

NONSURF ACTIVITIES

1. Golfing
2. Playing guitar
3. Listening to music
4. Following world politics
5. Fishing

6. Messing with my Mac computer
7. Buying/playing with gadgets
8. Listening to talk radio
9. Writing
10. Drawing

FAVORITE GOLF COURSES

1. TPC Sawgrass, Stadium Course, Jacksonville, Florida
2. Cypress Point, Monterrey Peninsula, California
3. Riviera, Pacific Palisades, California
4. Hualalai, Kona, Hawaii
5. Links Course, Turtle Bay, Oahu, Hawaii
6. Bushwood Country Club, Boca Raton, Florida
7. Sherwood Country Club, Westlake, California
8. Cocoa Beach Country Club, Cocoa Beach, Florida
9. Seignosse Golf Course, Hossegor, France
10. Ko'Olau Golf Course, Kailua, Oahu, Hawaii

THINGS TO DO IN COCOA BEACH

1. Fish
2. Party
3. Golf
4. Steal the street sign to Slater Way
5. Learn to surf
6. Camp on the islands in the river
7. Pet a manatee
8. Go to the Inner Room
9. Watch the Coconuts Bikini Contest on Sunday
10. Wakeboard

ESSENTIAL ROAD ELEMENTS

1. Girlfriend/wife
2. Friends/family
3. Toiletries
4. Vitamin supplements
5. Phonecard
6. Computer
7. Camera
8. Books/magazines
9. Sleeping pills/malatonin
10. Dramamine

WORST INJURIES

1. Torn labrum in left hip
2. Ripped ligaments in ankle and knee
3. Torn achilles
4. Whiplash
5. Broken collar bone
6. Concussion/amnesia
7. Four stiches in knee, 1982 (missed the only week of waves that summer)
8. Chronic lower back pain
9. Born with two black eyes

WAYS TO IMPROVE THE WORLD

1. Listen to all people but stand up for yourself
2. Calm your mind
3. Figure out how to split water and create fuel from the hydrogen molecules efficiently
4. Understand yourself and your impact on others
5. Plant a garden and eat all your meals from it
6. Accept all things good and bad in the world as if they are part of us and we them
7. Create electricity from alternative sources (thermal, solar, hydro, etc.)
8. Surf
9. Exercise
10. Die happy

MY GOALS AT AGE EIGHTEEN . . . IN NO PARTICULAR ORDER

1. Write a book ✓
2. Skydive ✓
3. Bowl a perfect game
4. Bungee jump ✓
5. Fly a plane ✓
6. Graduate from high school ✓
7. Win an ASP world surfing title ✓
8. Live to be at least 118
9. Earn a million dollars ✓
10. Climb a mountain (metaphorically not actually)
11. Surf twenty-foot waves ✓

Appendix B

Contest Results

1980

Melbourne Kidney Center Benefit, Cocoa Beach, Florida	1st 8 and under

1981

Seventeenth Annual Canaveral Easter Surfing Festival	1st Menehune
ESA Central Florida District, November	3rd Menehune
ESA Championships, Cape Hatteras, North Carolina	7th Menehune

1982

Eighteenth Annual Canaveral Easter Surfing Festival	1st Menehune
APS Miller Time Florida Pro	1st Menehune
ESA Central Florida District, April	1st Menehune
ESA Central Florida District, June	1st Menehune
Roosevelt Surf Club	2nd Boys'
Patrick's Air Force Base Open Surf Contest	2nd Menehune
Third Annual Smyrna Safari Open, New Smyrna, Florida	3rd Boys'
ESA Championships, Cape Hatteras, North Carolina	1st Menehune

1983

ESA Central Florida District, February	1st Menehune
Turkey Trot Surf Festival	1st Boys'
ESA Central Florida District, April	1st Menehune
APS Cocoa Beach Coors Open	1st Menehune
Satellite Surf Festival	1st Menehune
ESA Central Florida District, May	1st Menehune
ESA Central Florida District, July	1st Menehune
Playalinda Pro-Am Team Challenge	2nd Menehune
First Annual ESA Florida Championships	1st Menehune
ESA Championships, Cape Hatteras, North Carolina	1st Menehune
ESA Central Florida District, October	1st Menehune
Hart's Birthday Bash, Jacksonville, Florida	1st Menehune, 3rd superheat
NSSA Florida Championships	1st Boys'

1984

ESA Central Florida District	1st Menehune
ESA Central Florida District	1st Menehune
Twentieth Annual Lite Beer Easter Surfing Festival	1st Menehune
Wave Masters Surf Festival	1st Menehune
Ponce Inlet Surf Classic	1st Boys', 3rd superheat
Sundek Classic, Melbourne Beach, Florida	3rd Open Am, 17th pro-am
NSSA Florida Contest #3	1st Boys'
ESA Central Florida District #7	2nd Menehune
Second Annual ESA Florida Championships	1st Menehune
ESA Championships, Cape Hatteras, North Carolina	1st Menehune
Hart's Birthday Bash, Jacksonville, Florida	1st Menehune, 1st superheat
ESA Central Florida District #1	1st Boys', 1st superheat

ESA Central Florida District #2	1st Boys',
	3rd superheat
U.S. Amateur Championships, Makaha, Hawaii	1st Menehune

1985

Turkey Trot Surf Festival	1st Boys'
Caribbean Cup, Puerto Rico	1st Juniors',
	1st superheat
NSSA Ormond Beach Open	1st Juniors'
Twenty-first Annual Cape Canaveral Surfing Championships	1st Boys'
NSSA Jacksonville Open	1st Boys'
ESA Central Florida District	1st Boys',
	1st superheat
Sundek Classic	5th Open
ESA Southeast Surf-Off	1st Boys'
U.S. Amateur Championships, Sebastian Inlet, Florida	1st Boys', 3rd superheat
NSSA National Championships, Huntington, California	1st Boys', 2nd superheat
ESA Championships	1st Boys'
Third Annual Hart's Birthday Bash	1st Boys',
	1st superheat
ESA Central Florida District	1st Boys',
	2nd superheat
ESA Central Florida District	1st Boys',
	2nd superheat
ESA Central Florida District	1st Boys',
	1st superheat

1986

ESA Central Florida District	1st Boys'
ESA Central Florida District	1st Boys',
	3rd superheat
ESA Central Florida District	1st Boys',
	3rd superheat
U.S. Amateur Championships	1st Boys'

ESA Championships, Cape Hatteras, North Carolina	1st Boys'
World Amateur Championships, Newquay, England	3rd Juniors'
NSSA Nationals, Huntington Beach, California	1st Boys'
Easter Classic, Cape Canaveral, Florida	1st pro-am, 1st Boys'
Excalibur Cup, Sebastian Inlet, Florida	1st pro-am
Caribbean Cup—Sebastian Inlet, Florida, Bruce Walker	1st Mens and Juniors'
U.S. team trials, Ventura, California	1st Open
Sundek Classic, Ventura, California	1st Open

1987

ESA Championships	1st Juniors'
Pacific Cup, Australia	1st Juniors', Open
PSAA Wild Rivers Waterpark	1st Pro
U.S. Amateur Championships	1st Juniors'
U.S. team trials	10th Open

1988

ESA Championships, Cape Hatteras, North Carolina	3rd Juniors'
ASP East Platt's Spring Surfari, New Smyrna Beach, Florida	10th Pro
ASP East Gotcha Fall Surfari, New Smyrna Beach, Florida	1st Pro
U.S. Amateur Championships, Sandy Beach, Hawaii	Did not place

1989

ASP Aloe Up Cup, New Smyrna Beach, Florida	17th Pro
ESA Central Florida District	2nd Juniors'
U.S. Amateur Championships, Oceanside, California	7th Juniors'

PSAA Body Glove Surfbout, Trestles, California	Did not place
ASP East Natural Art/Carib Pro, Barbados	2nd Pro;
	1st Open Am
ASP East Platt's Spring Surfari,	33rd Pro
New Smyrna Beach, Florida	
U.S. team trials, Oceanside, California	1st Open
ASP East Gotcha Fall Surfari,	13th Pro
New Smyrna Beach, Florida	

1990

ESA Central Florida District	1st Juniors'
World Amateur Championships, Japan	5th Open

Turned professional, July 1990

ASP Life's a Beach Pro, Oceanside, California	17th
ASP Op Pro, Huntington Beach, California	57th
ASP Quiksilver Lacanau Pro, France	3rd
ASP Rip Curl Pro, Landes, Hossegor, France	17th
Bud Tour, San Clemente, California	5th
Bud Tour, Body Glove Surfbout,	1st
Trestles, California	
Fletcher Cabo Classic	1st

1991

ASP Op Pro, Huntington Beach, California	5th
ASP Alder Surf Pro, Fistral Beach,	9th
Newquay, England	
ASP Quiksilver Lacanau Pro, France	5th
ASP Rip Curl Pro, Landes, Hossegor, France	17th
ASP Arena Surfmasters, Biarritz, France	5th
ASP Marui Pro, Chiba, Japan	65th
ASP Miyazaki Pro, Miyazaki, Japan	33rd
ASP XCEL Pro, Sunset Beach, Hawaii	5th
ASP Wyland Hawaiian Pro, Haleiwa, Hawaii	41st
ASP Marui Masters, Pipeline, Hawaii	5th

ASP Hard Rock Café World Cup, Sunset Beach, Hawaii	57th
ASP Final Ranking	43rd

1992

ASP WCT Coca-Cola/Rip Curl Classic, Bells Beach, Australia	30th
ASP WCT Coco-Cola Bottlers Classic, North Narrabeen, Australia	2nd
ASP WCT Gunston 500, Durban, South Africa	17th
ASP WCT Yoplait Reunion Pro, Saint Leu, Reunion Island	3rd
ASP WCT Lacanau Pro, Lacanau, France	2nd
ASP WCT Rip Curl Pro, Landes, Hossegor, France	1st
ASP WCT Quiksilver Surfmasters, Biarritz, France	5th
ASP WCT Marui Pro, Chiba, Japan	5th
ASP WCT Miyazaki Pro, Miyazaki, Japan	2nd
ASP WCT Alternativa Surf International, Rio de Janeiro, Brazil	9th
ASP WCT Marui Masters, Pipeline, Hawaii	1st
ASP WQS Margaret River Masters, West Australia	3rd
ASP WQS Newcastle City Pro, Newcastle, Australia	2nd
ASP WQS Manly Classic, Manly Beach, Australia	9th
ASP WQS Wyland Galleries Hawaiian Pro, Haleiwa, Hawaii	17th
ASP WQS Hard Rock Café World Cup, Sunset Beach, Hawaii	17th
ASP World Championship Tour Final Ranking	1st

1993

ASP WCT Rip Curl Pro, Bells Beach, Australia	5th

ASP WCT Coke Classic, North Narrabeen, Australia	33rd
ASP WCT Gunston 500, Durban, South Africa	9th
ASP WCT Lacanau Pro, Lacanau, France	5th
ASP WCT Rip Curl Pro, Landes, Hossegor, France	17th
ASP WCT Quiksilver Surfmasters, Biarritz, France	33rd
ASP WCT Miyazaki Pro, Miyazaki, Japan	9th
ASP WCT Marui Pro, Chiba, Japan	1st
ASP WCT Alternativa Pro, Rio de Janeiro, Brazil	5th
ASP WCT Chiemsee Pipe Masters, Pipeline, Hawaii	2nd
ASP WQS Surfmasters, Margaret River, West Australia	33rd
ASP WQS Op Pro, Huntington Beach, California	25th
ASP WQS Billabong Country Feeling Classic, Jeffreys Bay, South Africa	2nd
ASP WQS Wyland Galleries Hawaiian Pro, Haleiwa, Hawaii	2nd
ASP WQS World Cup of Surfing, Sunset Beach, Hawaii	49th
ASP World Championship Tour Final Ranking	7th

1994

ASP WCT Rip Curl Pro, Bells Beach, Australia	1st
ASP WCT Marui Pro, Chiba, Japan	3rd
ASP WCT Reunion Pro, St. Leu, Reunion Island	9th
ASP WCT U.S. Open, Huntington Beach, California	2nd
ASP WCT Gotcha Lacanau Pro, Lacanau, France	1st
ASP WCT Rip Curl Pro, Hossegor, France	2nd
ASP WCT Quiksilver Surfmasters, Biarritz, France	17th
ASP Sud Oueste Trophee, France	1st
ASP WCT Alternativa Surf, Rio de Janeiro, Brazil	5th

ASP WCT Chiemsee Pipe Masters, Pipeline, Hawaii	1st
ASP WCT Coke Classic, North Narrabeen, Australia	9th
ASP WQS Billabong, Santa Cruz, California	9th
ASP WQS Bud Surf Tour, Seaside Reef, California	1st
ASP WQS Billabong Kirra Pro, Kirra, Australia	9th
ASP WQS Bud Surf Tour, Pismo Beach, California	13th
ASP WQS Bud Surf Tour, Huntington Beach, California	1st
ASP WQS Gunston 500, Durban, South Africa	2nd
ASP WQS Op Pro, Huntington Beach, California	2nd
ASP WQS XCEL Pro, Sunset Beach, Hawaii	2nd
ASP WQS Wyland Galleries Pro, Haleiwa, Hawaii	49th
ASP WQS Hapuna World Cup of Surfing, Sunset Beach, Hawaii	9th
ASP World Championship Tour Final Ranking	1st
ASP World Qualifying Series Final Ranking	1st

1995

ASP WCT Rip Curl Pro, Bells Beach, Australia   9th
ASP WCT Marui Pro, Chiba, Japan   3rd
ASP WCT Quiksilver Pro, G-Land, Java,   1st
   Indonesia
ASP WCT Oxbow Reunion Pro, St. Leu,   9th
   Reunion Island
ASP WCT U.S. Open,   2nd
   Huntington Beach, California
ASP WCT Gotcha Lacanau Pro, Lacanau, France   9th
ASP WCT Rip Curl Pro, Hossegor, France   3rd
ASP WCT Quiksilver Surfmasters,   5th
   Biarritz, France
ASP WCT Rio International Surf Pro,   5th
   Rio de Janeiro, Brazil
ASP WCT Chiemsee Pipe Masters,   1st
   Pipeline, Hawaii
ASP WQS Mark Richards Newcastle City Pro,   13th
   Australia

ASP WQS Gunston 500, Durban, South Africa	2nd
ASP WQS Billabong Country Feeling Classic	65th
ASP WQS Wyland Galleries Hawaiian Pro, Haleiwa, Hawaii	5th
ASP WQS World Cup of Surfing, Sunset Beach, Hawaii	49th
Hawaiian Triple Crown	1st
Quiksilver King of the Peak, Sebastian Inlet, Florida	1st
ASP World Championship Tour Final Ranking	1st

1996

ASP WCT Coke Surf Classic, Australia	1st
ASP WCT Billabong Pro, Kirra, Australia	9th
ASP WCT Rip Curl Pro, Bells Beach, Australia	17th
ASP WCT Marui Pro, Chiba, Japan	9th
ASP WCT Quiksilver Pro, G-Land, Java, Indonesia	3rd
ASP WCT Rip Curl Pro, St. Leu, Reunion Island	1st
ASP WCT CSI Billabong Pro, Jeffreys Bay, South Africa	1st
ASP WCT U.S. Open, Huntington Beach, California	1st
ASP WCT Gotcha Lacanau Pro, Lacanau, France	5th
ASP WCT Rip Curl Pro, Hossegor, France	1st
ASP WCT Quiksilver Surfmasters, Biarritz, France	1st
ASP WCT Coca-Cola, Figueira, Figueira da Foz, Portugal	33rd
ASP Sud Ouest Trophee, France	1st
ASP WCT Chiemsee Pipe Masters, Pipeline, Hawaii	1st
Da Hui Backdoor Shootout, Oahu, Hawaii	1st
ASP World Championship Tour Final Ranking	1st

1997

ASP WCT Coke Surf Classic, North Narrabeen, Australia	1st
ASP WCT Billabong Pro, Gold Coast, Australia	1st
ASP WCT Rip Curl Pro, Bells Beach, Australia	9th
ASP Australian Grand Slam	1st
ASP WCT Tokushima Pro, Tokushima, Japan	1st
ASP WCT Marui Pro, Chiba, Japan	1st
ASP WCT Quiksilver Pro, G-Land, Java, Indonesia	9th
ASP WCT Kana Beach Lacanau Pro, Lacanau, France	2nd
ASP WCT Rip Curl Pro, Hossegor, France	9th
ASP WCT Buondi Sintra Pro, Sintra, Portugal	17th
ASP WCT Expo '98 and Figueira '97, Figueira da Foz, Portugal	17th
ASP WCT Kaiser Summer Surf, Rio de Janeiro, Brazil	1st
ASP WCT Chiemsee Pipe Masters, Pipeline, Hawaii	17th
ASP WQS G-Shock U.S. Open, Huntington Beach, California	2nd
ASP WQS Hawaiian OP Pro, Haleiwa, Hawaii	17th
ASP WQS Rip Curl World Cup of Surfing, Sunset Beach, Hawaii	33rd
ASP Typhoon Lagoon Surf Challenge, Orlando, Florida	1st
ASP World Championship Tour Final Ranking	1st

1998

ASP WCT Billabong Pro, Gold Coast, Australia	1st
ASP WCT Rip Curl Pro, Bells Beach, Australia	17th
ASP WCT Coke Surf Classic, Manly Beach, Australia	5th
ASP WCT Tokushima Pro, Tokushima, Japan	5th

ASP WCT Marui Pro, Chiba, Japan	17th
ASP WCT Billabong/MSF Pro, Jeffreys Bay, South Africa	5th
ASP WCT Op Pro, Huntington Beach, California	5th
ASP WCT Rip Curl Pro, Hossegor, France	3rd
ASP WCT Kana Beach Lacanau Pro, Lacanau, France	9th
ASP WCT Rio Marathon Surf International, Rio de Janeiro, Brazil	3rd
ASP WCT Mountain Dew Pipe Masters, Pipeline, Hawaii	3rd
ASP WQS Gunston 500, Durban, South Africa	5th
ASP WQS G-Shock Hawaiian Pro, Haleiwa, Hawaii	7th
ASP WQS Rip Curl World Cup, Sunset Beach, Hawaii	3rd
G-Shock Hawaiian Triple Crown	1st
ASP World Championship Tour Final Ranking	1st

1999

ASP WCT Billabong Pro, Gold Coast, Australia	17th
ASP WCT Quiksilver Pro Fiji, Tavarua, Fiji	3rd
ASP WCT Gotcha Pro, Huntington Beach, California	5th
ASP WCT Mountain Dew Pipe Masters, Pipeline, Hawaii	1st
ASP WQS G-Shock Hawaiian Pro, Haleiwa, Hawaii	25th
ASP WQS Rip Curl Cup, Sunset Beach, Hawaii	33rd
ASP Quiksilver Eddie Aikau Memorial, Waimea Bay, Hawaii	9th

2000

ASP WCT Gotcha Pro Tahiti, Teahupoo, Tahiti	1st
ASP WCT Quiksilver Pro Fiji, Tavarua, Fiji	17th

ASP WCT Billabong Pro, Trestles, California	33rd
ASP WCT Mountain Dew Pipe Masters, Pipeline, Hawaii	9th
Quiksilver Men Who Ride Mountains, Maverick's, California	2nd

2001

ASP WCT Rip Curl Pro, Bells Beach, Australia	17th
ASP WCT Rip Curl World Cup, Sunset Beach, Hawaii	49th
Quiksilver King of the Peak, Sebastian Inlet, Florida	1st
ASP WQS Quiksilver Pro, Gold Coast, Australia	49th
ASP Quiksilver Eddie Aikau Memorial, Waimea Bay, Hawaii	5th

2002

ASP Quiksilver in Memory of Eddie Aikau, Waimea Bay, Hawaii	1st
Pipeline Bodysurfing Classic, Pipeline, Hawaii	7th
ASP Quiksilver Pro, Gold Coast, Australia	9th
ASP Billabong Pro, Teahupoo, Tahiti	17th
ASP Quiksilver Pro, Tavarua, Fiji	9th
ASP Billabong Pro, Jeffreys Bay, South Africa	17th
ASP Billabong Boost Mobile, Trestles, California	3rd
ASP Quiksilver Pro, Hossegor, France	3rd
ASP Billabong Pro, Mundaka, Spain	9th
ASP Rip Curl Cup, Sunset Beach, Hawaii	17th
ASP XBOX Pipeline Masters, Pipeline, Hawaii	3rd
ASP World Championship Tour Final Ranking	9th

2003

ASP WCT Quiksilver Pro, Gold Coast, Australia	9th
ASP WCT Rip Curl Pro, Bells Beach, Australia	9th
ASP WCT Billabong Pro, Teahupoo, Tahiti	1st
ASP WCT Niijima Quiksilver Pro, Niijima Island, Japan	5th
ASP WCT Billabong Pro, Jeffreys Bay, South Africa	1st
ASP WCT Boost Mobile Pro, Trestles, California	5th
ASP WCT Quiksilver Pro, Southwest Coast, France	3rd
ASP WCT Billabong Pro, Mundaka, Spain	1st
ASP WCT Nova Schin Festival, Santa Catarina, Brazil	1st
ASP WQS Vans Hawaiian Pro, Haleiwa, Hawaii	7th
ASP WCT Rip Curl Cup, Sunset Beach, Hawaii	17th
ASP WCT X-Box Pipeline Masters, Pipeline, Hawaii	4th
ASP World Championship Tour Final Ranking	2nd

2004

ASP WQS WRV Open, Sunset Beach, Hawaii	2nd
ASP WCT Quiksilver Pro, Gold Coast, Australia	5th
ASP WQS Snickers Australian Open, Sydney, Australia	1st
ASP WQS Energy Australia Open, Newcastle, Australia	1st
ASP WCT Rip Curl Pro, Bells Beach, Australia	5th

Acknowledgments

First, to my mom and dad who let me do my own thing without any pressure to have to succeed and supported my brothers and me in something they probably never dreamed would do much more than bring us some happiness.

To Sean, for giving me my fighting spirit, teaching me to surf, fish, play football and pool, catch a baseball with my face, eat Oreos, give frogs and charley horses and crispy/fuji's, lose my hair, dress for Halloween, beat up kids who called Mom a lesbian, and not make dumb mistakes. You're a "minded."

To Stephen, for being our family's rock, for showing Sean and I how to be unaffected, noncompetitive, and nice to people, how to camp, ride longboards, eat stingrays, put out hot coals with our feet, catch a 175-pound tuna, drive a bulldozer, be good to Mom, take care of ourselves, and not make a contest the most important thing. I learned a lot from you. Dude, you're "the Dude," man. Blithna-Klithna. Oh, and for teaching Sean to sail.

To my many families around the world who gave me food, shelter, and love. I think of you often and can't wait to return soon. The short list: Merricks, Hills, Johnsons, Raymonds, Hendys, Munros, Greens, Hawkins, Machados, Kays, Rosses, Fischers, Dorians, Morrises, Malloys, Farias, Thornes, Fillibens, Kings, Roys, Suttons, Drollets, Hodges, Coxs, etc. If I missed you, you know who you are.

To Johnny, Rhett, and Drew for keeping me honest and always being my three best friends, and for the handshaka's. I think you guys owe me some rent and clothes.

To Mark Codgen (Young MC), my other brother, for your friendship, goodness, and rap lyrics. You always understand me. Peace to Dave.

To Peggy Rullo, my other mother, who I think of all the time. I miss you, Peggy.

To Bryan Taylor, for seeing my potential at a young age and believing in me. We haven't always seen things the same way, but thank you for "knowing what's good for me." You've been a good friend.

To Shane and Giselle, my South African friends, who bring me a great joy for life, and who I feel like I've known for many lifetimes. Happy Birthday Gigi!

To Donnie Solomon and Todd Chesser, who made a huge impression on all of our lives and whom I miss everyday. You won't go!

To Al Merrick, for guiding me by living it, and for being my second dad. I love you and Terry dearly. (The boards aren't bad either.)

To Bill Yerkes (of Sundek), Pat O'Neill (of O'Neill wetsuits), and Quiet Flight, for the support in my early years. You had tremendous faith in Sean and me.

To Doc Couture, I miss your faithful dedication to amateur surfing and me. You were a good man.

To Bruce Walker, a big "happy circle" to you and Stephanie.

To Dick Catri, I learned how to do fades and always keep my eyes open in the barrel now. Thank you, my man.

To Sunny Garcia, you've pushed me endless times and I've pushed back. Thanks for never hitting me and for teaching me how to do curls.

To Randy Caldwell and Tom Walsh, for running the ESA all those years and dealing with it. It is much appreciated.

To Quiksilver, for the partnership and friendship. I owe each and every person in the company a giant thank you for their help and an incredible job. Congratulations!

To everyone at Channel Islands Surfboards, who work painstakingly to accommodate my crazy life and keep me riding. Can I buy you guys a big dinner, please?

To Bill McCausland and FCS for letting my creative juices flow into something tangible. Good on ya, Bill!

To Kurt Wilson and company, who keep me attached to my board and send me last second goodies around the world. Thank you, Mr. Scientist.

To the Salick Brothers, for my first board and that sick airbrush. I need another 'cause I can't find the first one. Support the National Kidney Foundation! Where's my "team" sticker?

To Anna-lia gift shop in Cocoa Beach and Tony Sasso, for selling me those Styrofoam boards back in 1977. I don't know how I actually rode them.

To Todd Holland, Sean O'Hare, Randy Sanders, Bryan Stamper, Troy Propper, and Sean, for being my first teammates. Now, if only I could get past the shore break at Boardwalk!

To Chris Brown and family, for the beds and wood to make "ice plant boards" for the mesa. Let's shape another board, Chris. Dave, thanks for taking us surfing all over the world and keeping us warm in England. I'm coming over for dinner.

To Rob Machado and Shane Dorian, my eternal travel partners and friends who have pushed me to reach deep and go for it when the time comes.

To Trevor Hardy, for telling me things no one has ever told me, and having more understanding than most everyone I know put together. You have changed my life. I love you, my friend.

To Jason Borte, who worked many long hours to create this book and thus helped me to achieve one of my goals in life. I don't think I yet understand the gift you have given me with this endeavor, and I already cannot express my debt of gratitude.

To Slam Management and Rebel Waltz.

To all my photographer friends who decided to take shots of me, and especially to those who have helped me with this book. Your photos have given me what I have in my life in many ways. I have the greatest scrapbook in the world because of you.

To Shayne Allen, Stretch, and Colbern, I have the greatest memories of you (like the time Colin stole the cow, and he and his friends tried to make it with the cow) and look forward to more. 4-Bolt forever, lawn services rule, surfing for furniture.

To The Moonshine Conspiracy, for helping bring the soul of surfing back to the screen and including me in your projects.

To Taylor Steele, for bringing us all together under one roof (Pat and Betty's) in the beginning. I think either you or Joe Curren owe me $1,500 for that time in Vegas, baby! Keep videoin'.

To all the surfers who have influenced me as a kid, for planting the seeds and visions I have used to find my talents. I wouldn't be here if the Old School didn't pave the way. You showed me how to carve and led me into the air.

To Tom Carroll and Matt Kechele, I am hugely grateful for the guidance and surfboards. Grommie grind sammie!

To Kliney for making me laugh, Emmerson for driving, C-Had for spending the night (month), Matty, Brock, Grinch, Vinnie, Pat O, Ross, Ronald, Jack, Mitz, Frazier, Turbo, Mags, Akila,

Benji, Conan, Jun, Bags (paper or plastic?), Cerny, oh I can't remember you all. I love you guys. You're all in my wedding one day.

To Moe Lerner, for the card games. Come back you big goof. We miss you man.

To PK and T-Bone Burnett, thank you for helping me believe in me and my music. Oh, and the golf lessons. Hi Bunker. Where's our 4-track, PK?

To Sandy and Tommy Armour, for teaching me golf, designer watches, women, and clothing. I'll catch you one day.

To Dr. Keith Block for helping, not only my father, but my whole family deal with cancer. You will never be without a surfboard. Check out www.blockmedical.com. Tell 'em Kelly sent you.

To my brother Matt Mates and family, we've really missed you. Where were you? Welcome to our family.

To Mr. Nuuhiwa and family, for the years of friendship and wise words. You are an inspiration to my family and me.

To the city of Cocoa Beach and Tony Sasso, for recognizing my achievements and blessing my family with "our" street. We love it.

To Al Hunt and the ASP, Matt Warshaw, Steve Hawk, Slater family and friends, Evan Slater (no relation), *Surfer*, *Surfing*, ESA, Scott the Lifeguard, Smitty, Ant Niggi, and Renee Iwaszkiewicz for her editing and help with research.

To my beloved high school and teachers, for doing your job and allowing me to do mine. I'm still not buying some of that history you taught me, though. Does anyone really believe that crap about Columbus being a hero? I mean he discovered a land full of people he enslaved and stole from, and I'm supposed to waste my time reading about him and being tested on it? Let's buy some new books; I'll pay.

To Lisa Ann, for taking a journey with me and a chance on us, for always filling my belly with delicious meals, and challenging me to stay healthy on all levels. Thank you, Leemer. Good night, sweet girl.

To Bree, for being my first love (after surfing). I learned much from our time together, and I wish you happiness and fulfillment. Make a funny face for me!

To Jenny, for teaching me to take care of myself and someone else, and to stick up for myself. I am proud of you and happy for the knowledge you've gained. You be good now, okay?

To Pamela, you hold many gifts people do not see and you may not even realize. Thank you for your sense of humor and your smile, the endless conversations, and speaking a "new language" with me. Please remember to breathe. "You're the tear that hangs inside my soul forever." Hi Brando and Dilly. Oh, and don't take all those vitamins at one time.

To Tamara and Taylor, First, to Tamara for blessing me with the chance to be a father. I have not done the job I dream of doing, but I am thankful for the miracle of a child. Thank you for being a wonderful parent to her and not judging my space and absence too harshly. I have much catching up to do! Thanks, "Rocker!" Taylor, I think of you every day and dream of showing you the world I know one day soon. I miss you and love you.

To Ross Williams for being there with good advice, avocados, and a bed for me. Now practice up that Scrabble game, B-yatch.

Thanks to Keoni Watson for being the best human I know and talking to me (on big waves).

I would also like to thank . . . Andrew Murphy, Jay Moriarity, Jeff Hornbaker, Ken Bradshaw, Manuel Labor, Adriana, Jesse Faen, Taylor Knox, Sarge, Jessie Billauer, Brian Bleak, Andrea Dalessio, Woolly, John Freeman, DK, Jacque, Maritxu, Peyo, Belly, Greg Arnet, Marie Pascal, Dougie-Boy, Taylor Whisenand,

Vinnie de la Pena, Ronnie Meistrell, Bill Mcmillen, Sulli, The Champions, The Woozleys, The Moriaritys, George Downing and family, Glen Moncata, Perry Dane and family, the Aikaus, The Keaulanas, Shane Beschen, Marvin and Mickey, The Littles, Chris Mauro, Kozo, Sonny Miller, Dave Homcy, Scott Soens, Martha Cabasa, Wire, Chris Jensen, John Roberts, Scott Greenstein, John Freitas, Sam Ainsley, Dozerdave, Mitch Varnes, Taylor Easley, Greville Mitchell, Conan, Jeni Hing and family, Kent Ewing, Tim Brown, Warren Kramer, Maurice Cole, Sean Collins, Peter Brouillet, Donna Gluyas, Will Lewis, Pottz, Gary Freeman, Sherman, Sherry Gannaway, Errol Amerasekera, Poto, Laird, Kalama and co., David Glasser, Jenny Vannes, Kalani Robb, Bobby Martinez, The McKinneys, James Blair, Pat O'Connell and family, The Watsons, Peter and Jaye Adderton, Boost Mobile, Hawaiian, Bernie Baker, Randy Rarick, everyone at Activision and Treyarch, Regan Books, Justine Chiara (21), The Surfers (Alex, Mike, Evan, and Gary), Sunset Sound, Sony Music, The First Peak crew, David Speir, my god daughters Kaila and Kalea, Greg Solomon, Pete Mel, Skinny, Jeff Clarke.

I could go on and on like Jack Johnson, and I know I missed many, but thanks go out to you too.

Photographic Credits and Captions

First, let me say this book would not be as great if it weren't for all of the photos inside. I thank all the photographers for their contributions. If I mix you guys up, or forget to thank you, I'm sorry. Give me a call and let me know.

All photographs courtesy of Kelly Slater and the Slater Family Wall of Shame unless otherwise credited.

8. Call me Bobby. (Back row center.)

10. (Left) Sean and I competing for superstardom, Halloween 1975. (Right) Enjoying our new above-ground swimming *boat* with Sean.

13. Sean, Mom, Stephen, and me.

15. The swinging Slaters.

16. My earliest role model, Hondo.

18. Beware of gators.

19. My best friend, Johnny, and I hung out in this tree for hours at a time.

20. My first board that wasn't disposable, Cocoa Beach 1980.

23. Mom and me.

25. If I stretched my Styrofoam board the way I'm stretching my face, it would snap in two.

27. Skateboarding at the Cocoa Beach Christmas Parade.

30. A brief moment of rest during a Catri Team workout in Indialantic.

31. Me, Sean, and Stephen.

33. 1982 East Coast Champion.

36. Prized memento from the 1984 Surf Expo.

38. (Left) Sean, David Speir, and I upon discovering that there are good waves in Florida. *Courtesy of Matt Kechele.* (Right) My first published surfing photo, 1983. © *Tom Dugan*

41. If I look excited (back row, second from left), it's probably because I ate a half pound of sugar for breakfast.

44. ESA Menehune Champ, Cape Hatteras Lighthouse, North Carolina.

49. Leave it to Kelly, Cocoa Beach All-Star.

53. With trophies and shotguns for the *Sun News*, 1982.

57. Honing my small wave skills.

58. Not many kids get trained in public speaking at age twelve.

60. Clowning around on the beach with Ken Bradshaw, Dick Catri, and friends. © *Roger Scruggs Films*

67. A typical Florida kid from the 1980s—bleached blonde hair, dark skin, and a Sundek Hawaiian print shirt.

68. At Rocky Point on the North Shore with Charlie Kuhn, Matt Kechele, and Alex Cox. © *Tom Dugan*

74. Another embarrassing moment in the spotlight. © *Roger Scruggs Films*

79. This is Sean and I with (from left to right) Walter Cerny, Todd Holland, Jay Bennett, and Chuck Graham. This was our team in Puerto Rico for the Caribbean Cup in 1987. I was so small.

291. 2002 Quiksilver in Memory of Eddie Aikau, Waimea Bay, Oahu. © *HankFoto*

297. This is the last photo we took with my dad a couple of weeks before he passed away. Dad enjoying his last beer at the Cape Canaveral Seafood Festival with me, Sean, Stephen, and our half-brother Matt.

299. Waikiki, where modern surfing was born.

304. Star trunks. © *Todd Messick*

306. Flipping out. © *Jeff Hornbaker*

320-321. Backside tube sequence, Tavarua, Fiji. © *Jeff Hornbaker*

326. Not winning, but still smiling.

Insert Credits

1. © *Jeff Hornbaker*

4. © *Gary L. Prettyman* (top)

5. © *Jeff Hornbaker*

6-7. © *Pierre Tostee*

9. © *Jeff Hornbaker* (bottom)

10. © *Tom Servais* (top)

10. © *Jeff Hornbaker* (bottom)

11. © *Jeff Hornbaker*

12. © *Todd Mesick* (top and bottom)

13. © *Tom Servais*

14-15. © *Jeff Hornbaker* (all)

16. © *Tom Servais*